S0-BHR-631

From Apocalypse to Genesis

By the same author (with Jennifer Henderson)

OUR GOD HAS NO FAVOURITES
A Liberation Theology of the Eucharist

FROM
APOCALYPSE
to
GENESIS

Ecology, Feminism and Christianity

Anne Primavesi

HQ
1233
.P75
1991

BURNS & OATES

Burns & Oates Limited
Wellwood, North Farm Road,
Tunbridge Wells, Kent TN2 3DR

First published 1991

Copyright © Anne Primavesi 1991

All rights reserved. No part of this book
may be reproduced in any form, by print,
photoprint, microfilm, michrofiche,
mechanical recording, photocopying,
translation, or any other means, known or
as yet unknown, or stored in an
information retrieval system, without
written permission obtained beforehand
from Burns & Oates Limited.

ISBN: 0 86012 174 7

Typeset by Scribe Design Limited, Gillingham, Kent,
from computer disk supplied by Mark Primavesi.
Printed and bound in Great Britain by Biddles Ltd, Guildford.

CONTENTS

PART FOUR

GENESIS NOW

In loving memory of our son
John Mark

Preface

During the writing of this book I have had the help of many friends who read drafts and re-drafts, made comments and suggestions, criticized and praised. I have taken note of everything as far as I can, and know that both the book and myself have benefited enormously.

Before I go on to the pleasant task of naming some of these friends, I have to say that in one respect I may appear not to have dealt satisfactorily with a problem they raised: my use of the term "ecofeminism". This arises directly from the juxtaposition of ecology, feminism and Christianity indicated in the subtitle. For some readers, like the artist John Lane, the word "ecofeminism" led him to ask me to broaden the argument for it to include all who subscribe to the tradition it espouses. That I have tried to do. He is fearful, as I am, of a new "ism" becoming, and seen to be becoming, a new exclusivity. From an ecofeminist perspective we need to celebrate not only women and Nature but men, women and Nature (in any order). This chimed in with a comment from a theologian, Joseph Laishley, who said that he would like ecofeminism placed emphatically in a holistic perspective in which Nature is not an adversative concept but an inclusive one.

The problem remains, however, at a level which no amount of statement, special pleading or emphasis can reach. It was summed up very well by another theologian, Brian Marshall, who said that I would lose some Christian readers in agreement with my ecological stance because of my feminist one, and vice versa. This was based on his discernment of ecofeminism as an argument in which the two positions I believe integrally related are not generally so perceived. A further problem with the word itself was pointed out by the scientist James Lovelock, who warned me that in science, double-barrelled words like biotechnology or microbiology are biassed towards the second term.

Discussing the book and this problem with a doctor friend, Nikki Williams, she agreed that this was true in her own reading and in medical practice. She followed this up by asking people what immediately came to mind if they heard the words ecofeminist, geopolitician or medico-legal. On the basis of immediate response to the last one, she tried the word "femino-ecologist" and the reaction seemed right.

Modern technology being what it is, it would be possible for me even now to substitute this neologism for "ecofeminist" without too much trouble. But on reflection, I shall not do so, for apart from its clumsy nature, to abandon the word "ecofeminism" because it has feminist connotations is to concede victory to the kind of excluding consciousness the ecological paradigm of this book seeks to heal. If a word or an argument is seen by either an ecologist, a feminist or a Christian as necessarily one to be ignored or rejected on ideological grounds, then that preconception must be acknowledged by the individual concerned and examined in the context of our total relationship with all the interactive systems of thought, language and behaviour which create modern culture. So the onus rests on those readers unhappy with the term to explain satisfactorily why this is so.

It has already become clear how indebted I am to my friends for their help, encouragement and advice throughout the process of creating this book, and that it is no fault of theirs if it contains errors of fact or judgment. As well as those already mentioned, I would like to thank especially Jennifer Henderson, not only for her comments on the text but above all for helping Mark to compile the index. Grace Jantzen focussed my attention on some of the religious and philosophical implications of what I was saying, and furnished not only suggestions for further reading but often the books themselves. Asphodel Long gave me enormous encouragement, and many insights from a Jewish feminist perspective. I am sorry that I did not have time to take up her suggestion that I read and incorporate Genesis Rabbah into my interpretation. Patricia Herriott Ing inspired me by her understanding and living out of the principles I was trying to articulate. Our mutual friend, Sue Kruger, contributed very practically by sending me books from the United States unobtainable in Britain. Barbara Poteat, also in the States, made detailed comments on the first part of the book which saved me from misusing psychological terms and directed my attention to allied areas of interest. Joe Mulrooney opened up the community aspect of apocalyptic vision and of the canon and so transformed Chapters 4 and 9. Rowan Williams drew my attention to the positive qualities of hierarchy in the vision of Denys the

Areopagite, to the social redemption envisaged by Augustine, and to the problem of conflicting views of the world inherent in Christian doctrines of creation. Elizabeth Nathaniels, the only person I have met so far to have written on ecofeminism, gave me the benefit not only of her advice but of her enthusiasm for the subject. Edmund Power, after a meticulous reading of the whole text, challenged some of my philosophical assumptions and asked me for an ecological understanding of baptism, something I could only indicate at this stage. Paul Burns, my editor, has cheered me on by his enthusiasm and has helped to make the book what it is by his painstaking attention to detail.

The one who has made the book possible, in every way, is Mark, my husband. The endless hours spent programming computers, discussing updates, printing copies, correcting drafts, compiling the index and bibliography are not easily tallied. What can only be hinted at is the way in which the vision expressed in this book belongs to, and is set securely within, the loving interaction of our marriage. Without Mark, in this instance as in so many others, the possible would never have become the actual. And lastly, I must acknowledge the interest and contribution of the two cats who show continuing commitment to our *oikos*.

If I am not for myself, who will be?
And if I am only for myself, what am I?
And if not now, when?

Hillel

Introduction

I live on the mountain, so I first saw them coming;
Grim Death, Disease, and the river of blood.
I pulled on my boots and started down, running;
down to the valley, the acres of mud.

I called at the pub where the men were all drinking,
and talking of money and second-hand cars.
I called at the church, where the women were kneeling,
and thinking of money, and men, and their stars.

I knocked on the doors, threw stones at high windows;
there slowly assembled a crowd in the square;
and stumbling with words, all clumsy with language,
I described what I'd seen through the clear mountain air.

Their faces were puzzled. At first they were laughing,
and then they were angry at being disturbed.
They asked me for proof, which I could not give them,
and then they dismissed me for being absurd.

Up on the mountain, I gave them a welcome;
Grim Death, Disease and the River of blood.
"You've been a long time" I said, then I showed them
the path to the valley, the acres of mud.

This poem was written by Adrian Farey, a friend of mine who
went a few years ago to live according to ecological principles
in a Welsh valley with like-minded friends. All had had a
Christian education, which they considered at best irrelevant
and at worst a hindrance to their vision of living in harmony
with Nature. The imagery in the poem is apocalyptic in that it
describes what he sees as the coming Day of Judgment on those
who evade responsibility for the present ecological crisis. Part
of the anger evident in the poem is directed against the Christian
establishment for its failure to teach or show moral concern for
the environment.

There is a growing realization among theologians that this
anger is justified. More and more they are becoming aware of
the connection between traditional Christian doctrines with their
over-emphasis on human salvation from sin and the destructive
effects of Western culture on the natural world. There is also an
increasing awareness that while churches continue to sanctify

the subordination of women as God's will for them, feminist thinkers are focussing attention on the relationship between this subordination and male domination of Nature.

Taken together, these factors determine the positive and negative tasks for this book. Its first positive task is to give the outline of an ecological paradigm, a contemporary model for Christian thinking about the interrelatedness and interdependence of creation. Its negative task is to provide a systematic critique of the dominant hierarchical paradigm of Christianity and Western society.

The final positive task is a radical re-reading of Genesis chapters 1-3 in the light of an ecological paradigm. This will be contrasted with the prevailing hierarchical view of woman and Nature. It will be argued that a paradigmatic shift towards an ecological perspective on the Genesis narrative would enable Christians to contribute to and share in the spiritual vision of Nature called for by those committed to ecological reconstruction at the practical level.

This means in effect that the argument of the book will move "from Apocalypse to Genesis". Christianity generally looks back to the Day of Creation and forward to the Day of Judgment. Ecology, in its practical approach, faces the present Day of Judgment, Apocalypse now, with faith in a new creation and commitment to the regeneration of life. For ecologists, apocalypse is not postponed until the end of time, but is a vision of *how things really are* at this moment. They see the grim inevitability of death, disease and bloodshed as present judgment on heedless humanity. They do not, however, see this judgment imposed on us by God's vengeance, but by the fact that we now appear capable of destroying life on earth through the consequences of our collective actions.

The things we do to the planet are not offensive nor do they pose a geophysiological threat, unless we do them on a large enough scale. If there were only 500 million people on Earth, almost nothing that we are now doing to the environment would perturb Gaia. Unfortunately for our freedom of action, we are moving towards eight billion people with more than ten billion sheep and cattle, and six billion poultry. We use much of the productive soil to grow a very limited range of crop plants, and process far too much of this food inefficiently through cattle. Moreover, our capacity to modify the environment is greatly increased by the use of fertilizers, ecocidal chemicals, and earth-moving and tree-cutting machinery. When all this is taken into account we are indeed in danger of changing the Earth away from the comfortable state it was once in. It is not just a matter of population; dense population in the northern temperate regions may be less a perturbation than in the humid tropics . . . Bad farming is probably the greatest threat to Gaia's health. We use 75% of the fertile land of the temperate and tropical regions for agriculture. To my mind this is the largest and most irreversible geophysiological change that we have made.[1]

Poised as we are on this apocalyptic threshold, this book is a theological act of faith in the future, faith that the world and Christianity can be regenerated through the power of the Spirit working from within living matter. The world we share with all sentient being is inhabited, indwelt, by countless natural species. But not only by them. In the opening verses of Genesis we are told that the "breath of God" hovered over the waters. It is this which makes us, like all created being, into living beings. This indwelling power of the Spirit of God continuously regenerates life: whether through the root of a tree, the stirring of the ocean bed or the quickening of life in the womb. We theologians separate this life at our peril into one sort of power within Nature and a different sort within the human spirit. For where would the spirit be without the body, and where would the body be unless sustained by the lifegiving properties of earth?

The mystics and poets have kept faith with this unitary vision of being alive in the one Spirit. So Hildegard of Bingen wrote in the twelfth century:

> The Spirit of God
> is a life that bestows life
> root of the world-tree
> and wind in its boughs.
>
> She is glistening life
> alluring all praise
> all-awakening
> all-resurrecting.[2]

PART ONE
An Ecological Paradigm

Chapter 1

Ecological Foundations

Ecology as a practical discipline is generally defined as the study of organisms in their environments, their "homes". The root word *eco* means, in fact, house or home. Traditionally one organism and its "home" environment have been studied together as an ecosystem, on the implicit understanding that any one such ecosystem is not in fact isolated from those surrounding it but that they interconnect within a greater whole. The ecological paradigm being developed here presupposes that ultimately all the ecosystems of the planet interconnect in the living whole we call Earth, and that this interconnectedness must be made explicit whenever possible.

Reflection on this interconnectedness is the basis for ecology as a philosophy, as a way of thinking about the world in its complexity and totality. This attitude of mind recognizes that isolating the parts out into separate systems distorts both them and the whole. Nor does it allow us, the thinkers and observers, to isolate ourselves from the information-gathering process. We are part of it and affect it, not least by the questions we pose and the answers we expect.

Growth in Ecological Awareness

A recent poll in Britain asked, not the usual questions about the standing of political parties, but what people fear most nowadays. People feared nuclear disaster, then pollution of rivers and water, then poverty; but heading the list was the fear of what is happening to the ozone layer.

There are some striking things about the results that emerged, not least that the Soviet Union under Gorbachev is no longer commonly perceived here as a threat. Nor is nuclear disaster feared as a consequence of war between the super-powers, but in a more generalized way as "fall-out" from human inability to cope with the forces it has unleashed. The use of nuclear power for energy, with the resulting problems of decommissioning reactors and disposing of nuclear waste, is an increasingly large item on the ecological agenda at the very time that the reduction of nuclear weapons called for by the Brundtland Report in 1987 is being negotiated by Eastern and Western diplomats.[1]

Two of the other things most feared today also come directly under the human environmental umbrella: pollution and the destruction of the ozone layer. There are those who would place poverty in their company. For as destruction of natural resources causes poverty (African farmers made destitute by drought are a tragic example), then the progressive impoverishment of air, earth, and water threatens us all. Someone gloomily remarked to me recently that fire seems to be the only element the human race has not yet managed to destroy. We have, however, turned it into a means of destruction on a global scale by burning the rain-forests.

In spite of the global implications of the poll results, when people are asked about their fears, by pollsters or anyone else, they usually name something which they are experiencing as a threat at that moment and in that particular place. One's own ecosystem naturally takes priority. Those who live off the land will have different priorities from those who live by the sea or in the city. For instance the women of Khirakot, a rural community in Northern India, campaigned for two and a half years against the danger to their villages posed by a businessman with government backing who had started a soapstone quarry in the vicinity. This spoiled their village forest, their cultivated fields, their drinking water and their footpaths.

In Southern Britain people are more likely, as in my home town, to be fighting battles against property developers and planning officers over "town cramming". Those who live further North try to save some of the open spaces left in the Lake District or the Highlands of Scotland from either tourist over-use or commercial tree-farming. Others again may be campaigning anywhere in the country against nuclear refuse dumping, gravel extraction, battery farming or other manifestations of our technologically miraculous but naturally lethal society. Wherever or whatever the cause, our personal and partial perspectives shape our responses.

This concentration on particular needs and immediate dangers to the environment can obviously be effective: the Khirakot women saved their land. Less obvious, but of equal importance wherever one is situated, is the continuing exercise of making connections between single issues and other larger ones. The women of Khirakot would not have been threatened by a quarry unless Western companies had sold technology to the business-man and promised him a market for what he produced. The Indian government would not have supported him except for the post-colonial assumption that the improved well-being of their people depends upon the adoption of Western economic categories of productivity and of growth.

One's immediate awareness of any issue is always partial. This comes from the fact that the field of awareness must be divided into relatively simple units which can be taken easily into account. The simplified units of attention thus selected are but a small part of the whole truth about the matter under review. The recognition of this partiality is the first step on the road towards acquiring some sense of the whole, towards an attitude of mind which takes account of the larger interactive systems within which we live. Ecology as a way of thinking about the world monitors our tendency to take the part for the whole. In an ecological analysis of the Khirakot campaign the interdepend-ence of maldevelopment and Western economic forces in Third World countries must be set within the larger context of differing assumptions about the world and society. This is being done by scientists and writers like Vandana Shiva and Radha Bhatt. A similar exploration of the wider context is required whenever a local or seemingly isolated problem is being tackled.[2]

Their approach to any particular environmental crisis uses an ecological paradigm for writing about it, for discussing it, for suggesting its solution or better still, its prevention. Whether they start with an agricultural system, as in Khirakot, or I start with an urban system, we must go on from there to consider the cultural and societal systems to which the particular system is related. In Khirakot one can presume that the villagers work near home and travel on foot, so the footpath systems are important. But here, where most workers commute and there are 1.5 motor-cars per household, the road systems assume importance. Linked with these again, in both cases, are the support systems of food production, health care and religious ritual. In Khirakot these are necessarily much closer to the village centres because they do not have our high degree of mobility.

These over-simplified examples may help us understand how an ecosystems theory is valuable in approaching ecological problems. Whatever basic system one starts with, it is necessary to build up a model of it (visual or mental) in relation to those others linked with it. As this becomes more complex it helps expand consciousness to take account of factors outside an individual's experience. An inspired teacher got her pupils to walk along their town High Street writing down the names of the shops, banks, travel agents, estate agents, building societies, etc. Then she told them to take each one and trace its links with other towns, countries and continents. This simple exercise in constructing an ecosystems model is one they will be able to build on all their lives.

Making Connections

However obvious or simple it may seem, an inability to employ such models at different levels of organization lies at the heart of many ecological predicaments today. This is true whether local planning officers consider schemes for housing develop-ment in isolation from highway policy (because that is determi-ned by central authorities); or agribusiness directors refuse to cut back nitrate use because their concern is only with improving crop yields (whereas the responsibility for providing nitrate-free drinking water falls on others). Determining relations between larger and smaller systems is not easily absorbed into hierarchical organization.

There are many reasons why this is so. At the purely organizational level, hierarchical systems of government prevent different contexts being taken into account. A hierarchy is a sequential system in which face-to-face relationships do not or cannot occur between members, as they are separated by intervening members: the only communication between A and C passes through B. This means that those who make central policies (A) are neither those who implement them (B) nor those most directly affected by them (C). The system of command and obedience separates them one from another. So any decisions taken at central level are perceived at local level as "theirs", not "ours". Inevitably, local people react by giving up on the whole process.

The difficulty of open exchange between bodies within a hierarchical system of government is part of and is perpetuated by a lack of interrelatedness at the deeper level of personal and communal relationships within our society. This again is symptomatic of the worldview which has shaped modern

Western consciousness. This supposes that we relate to the world as detached observers who separate that world into discrete objects in isolation from their larger contexts and the observer's context also.[3] Such a view encourages the making of hypotheses and their testing through ever more sophisticated techniques. This apparently promises rational mastery over passive, isolated objects to be experimented on by an observer separated from them. Nature is regarded as a world to be conquered and re-ordered, to be made subject to the technology of the masculine intellect which has somehow shaken off its roots in the very organism it is working on. Technology here entails far more than its individual material components. It involves organization, procedures, symbols, new words, equations, and most of all, a mind set.

This mind set Newton bequeathed not only to Western scientific method but also to all its teaching. The presuppositions upon which the teaching are based are that mind is separate from matter and that phenomena can and shall be studied and evaluated in quantitative terms.[4] The resulting philosophy of nature was one based on mechanical analysis and division of matter into atomic parts separated by void space. A mechanistic model of the world was built on the notion of passive, inert matter acted upon by external forces. Mechanical models of the self, society and the cosmos became accepted and are still used in spite of evidence from modern science that organisms influence their own destiny in interesting, complex and interconnected ways.[5]

In Newtonian systems, a phenomenon is studied at a distance from the observer through techniques ranging from a book to a simple microscope or a robotic arm, and the only relationship acknowledged is that of passive object manipulated by active subject. The hierarchical distancing of bodies, particles or whatever, through technical or bureaucratic means, makes it possible for them to be observed, measured and evaluated for their potential use. Not "why", but "how", and then "how much", becomes the important question. So the pursuit of truth in education becomes identified with the pursuit of utility, and this in turn is measured by the creation of wealth. The usual training in science and practical technologies today is part of this continuum. The phenomena studied are not assumed to have intrinsic value or worth in their own right.

By contrast, modern communications and systems theories such as are basic to the kind of ecological thinking advocated here work within a complex network of "metarelations", by crossing between contexts and setting up context markers. This kind of discipline is essential for dealing with the kinds of environmental problems we face now. Yet agribusiness, for instance, still restricts its thinking to a context exclusive of that of water authorities, not to mention the contexts of the human and non-human end-users of both their products. In Nebraska, expensive bore holes have been installed for corn irrigation with the vegetation crowded round the holes. But corn grows best when generously spaced so that air can circulate freely, and if it is crowded around bore holes requires pesticides to counter diseases. Biotechnicians hope to develop a pesticide-tolerant corn which will flourish in tropical growing conditions and tolerate chemicals which "will harm the pests but not the plants".[6] What about all the other users of the contaminated water in the bore holes, as it seeps into the ground and the water table?

The kind of blinkered policy which isolates one goal (higher production) or one problem (a particular pest) from its attendant systems continues to get backing, financial and otherwise. However, the results are becoming only too evident, and we are now seeing a change in policy, or more realistically, change advocated. The energy policies outlined in the Brundtland Report take a global view of the problems faced and the strategies required. There is also an admission that energy efficiency can only buy time for us to develop "low-energy paths" based on renewable sources. These should form the basis of the global energy structure during the 21st century.[7] Such proposals for global policies come from the growing realization that Nature cannot wisely be exploited or controlled in the same way in which it has been studied – piecemeal. Nature is through and through relational, and interference at one point has interminable and unforeseen effects.

There are many kinds of interactive systemic modelling to help us understand our own bond with relational Nature: cultural, biological, physiological, familial, psychological, political or meteorological, to name but a few. Where such models are used, they can serve to counteract the effects of previous bad solutions to immediate problems: bad precisely because they acted destructively upon the larger patterns within which the problem is contained. A bad solution has a single purpose or goal, such as increased production. It is typical of such solutions that they achieve such increases at exorbitant biological and social costs. A good solution, however, is good because it is in harmony with those larger patterns. It acts within them the way a healthy organ acts within the body. But it must at once be understood that a healthy organ does not – as the mechanistic approach would have us believe – "give" health to the body. It is not exploited for the body's health, but is a *part* of its health. The health of organ and organism is the same, just as the health of organism and ecosystem is the same.[8]

The Planet as Ecosystem

The particular challenge posed by ecology today, which is also its most exciting opportunity, is that we adopt a systemic approach to life through accepting the systemic nature of the individual human being, the systemic nature of the culture in which we live, and the systemic nature of the biological and industrial systems which surround us. Then we may go on to the recognition of and guidance by a knowledge of the total systemic creature, the world.

James Lovelock has named this creature Gaia: this living planet on which the living things, the air, the oceans and the rocks all combine in one. We have no trouble, he says, with the idea that noble entities such as people are made up from an intricate interconnected set of cell communities. We don't find it too difficult to consider a nation or a tribe as an entity made up of its people and the territory they occupy. But what of large entities, like ecosystems and Gaia? It took the view of Earth from space to give us the personal sense of a real live planet.[9] It also gave us, on our television screens, a marvellous picture of this creature. The astonishing thing about it is its aliveness as it floats free in a dark void. We see swirling drifts of cloud cover and uncover the half-hidden masses of land, and if we could look at these for a very long geologic time, we would see the continents in motion, held aloft by the molten rock beneath.

This moon's eye view of the world has been made possible for us by space technology. We can never go back to flat earth thinking now that we have made this leap in perception, in our detailed knowledge of the planet's life and motion. The price we pay is that the image of a freefloating world, viewed by us from a point *outside* it, can reinforce a Newtonian viewpoint so that we perceive the world as totally discrete from us and treat it accordingly. Our very ability to visualize the larger entity of which we are a part can make it more difficult for us to perceive ourselves as inseparable from it.

The two approaches have to be kept in balance. Our partiality has to be complemented by a conscious decision to keep the whole in view, and vice versa. When there is a bulldozer wreaking havoc outside my front door, I have to do something about it then and there, even though I may be aware that the amount of earth it moves is insignificant in relation to the total land-mass on the earth's surface. Or is it? My awareness of the relationship between this shovelful of earth and my ecosystem must be complemented rather than superseded by my awareness of its relationship with the whole Earth.[10]

Detachment or Commitment?

Until the air and space travel of this century made it a reality, the view of ourselves in isolation from the world, detached observers of it, was only a mental construct. It first came to expression in the visual arts, in the science of perspective developed in the first flowering of the Renaissance. This science perfected a method of conveying an impression of spatial extension in depth. Such an interest was, according to John Lane, only one of a number of radical new elements which were aspects of a changing worldview. Brunelleschi, Alberti, Uccello and Piero della Francesca replaced traditional attitudes with a method predicated on a point of view at once unique and rational – that of a single observer, a human being who no longer inhabits eternity, but time; no longer inhabits infinity, but space. By the adoption of perspective the primal vision of unity was shattered beyond restoration; the hypothetical perceiving subject of the painting ceased to be God and became man. Pride in human reason took the place of the paradigmatic universe created and inhabited by God and animated by God's spirit. "Pride in man sets us apart from the world. Knowledge demands this detachment because certainty cannot be had without it. A small enough change, it might be thought, but one colossal in its implications."[11]

In the three centuries between the death of Piero and the birth of William Blake in 1757 some of those implications became plain. The years following the publication in 1637 of Descartes' *Discourse on Method* saw a profound change in attitude among intellectuals, law-makers, scientists and mechanists which ushered in and consolidated what is now known as the Scientific Revolution. What did this mean for the way human beings viewed themselves and the world?

> It meant a feeling of total reification. It meant that humans lived in an indifferent, mechanical universe, subject to "laws of Nature" operating autonomously, outside mind and thought. It meant that the cloak of unconsciousness descended over the "inferior orders" – Nature, animals, women and, of course, the "coloured" races. It meant that the natural beauty of the human mind and the natural dignity of life at its normal, natural, ancient, slower pace had been destroyed.[12]

Blake rejected this, which he discerned as a deeply dangerous spiritual state. The figure of Newton, a founding father of the Scientific Revolution, features frequently in his work. In one print Newton is depicted seated on a rock at the bottom of the sea (traditional symbol of material creation) trying to reduce the world to a mathematical formula. We see him staring at a geometrical design; his left hand holds an open compass, symbol of limitation and restriction – of creation by the reason unenlightened by imagination.[13]

Until such a world view took over popular consciousness, human beings were not alienated observers of the cosmos but direct participants in its drama. One's personal destiny was bound up with its destiny, and this relationship gave meaning to one's life. This type of participating consciousness involves merger or identification with one's surroundings. Since the sixteenth century it has been progressively expunged. Now we have a pervasive feeling of total reification: everything is an object, alien, not-me; and I am ultimately an object too, an alienated "thing" in a world of other, equally meaningless things. The final stage of this development of *non*-participating consciousness is that state of mind in which one knows phenomena precisely in the act of distancing oneself from them.[14]

Extremes of non-participating consciousness have become the norm today. They are there in Mrs Thatcher's famous statement that there is no such thing as society, only families and individuals. They are there in the notion of a free market in which a City of London financier earns X and a Liverpool docker earns Y and the enormous gap between them is regarded as misfortune for the person in Liverpool and of no concern to the one in London. They are there in the distancing of chemical companies from the long-term effects of their products. They are there in the ways in which reproductive technology is pursued in a closed context of a particular species, either vegetable, animal or human, without reference to the effect on other gene pools.

They are startlingly evident in the general acceptance by establishment thinking in the "developed" countries that it is only a matter of time until we distance ourselves entirely from this planet and go off to colonize the moon, or Mars, or wherever outside of earth appears most suitable. A space station built with materials mined from the moon is being planned, and there is talk of sending families into space as the ideal "space buddies". I've even heard a prediction that the first space baby will be born on Mars. While "Space" is being filled with satellites and other junk, at the same time the exponents of chaos theory are telling us that the movement of a butterfly's wing this side of earth can begin a process which ends in a cyclone on the other side.

There is enough concern about this for the Brundtland Report to talk about the "management" of orbital space, centring on using satellite technology for monitoring planetary systems, on making the most effective use of the "limited" capacities of geosynchronous orbit for communications satellites, and on limiting space debris. It advises the international community to design and implement a space regime to ensure that space remains a peaceful environment for the benefit of all.[15] The assumption behind this advice, admirable and far-sighted as it may appear, is that all objects external to human beings, including those in the solar system, are "passive", "inert", "inanimate", that is, that they have neither consciousness, value nor purpose in themselves. They are there solely for our benefit, to be used for our benefit and "managed" by us.

This utilitarian attitude is endemic in our culture, and to a certain extent, we must all be utilitarian in order to survive. Since we cannot photo-synthesize the sun's energy for ourselves, we must prey on the animals and plants who do this for us. What is being decried is *total* utilitarianism, the principle that anything non-human has no value, only use. And even that qualification can disappear. It is possible to objectify human beings also, as units of production or of wealth or war, and treat them accordingly. The connection between the user and the used is either broken, or never made at all. There is no merger or identification, no sense of connection with the other's ecosystem.

Hierarchy and Dualism

These assumptions are part of the hierarchical consciousness which organizes reality according to the dualities of the Western intellectual tradition: the duality between nature and society, matter and mind, slave and free, female and male, sensuousness and intellect. The dualities acquired meaning only because they existed contrapuntally, each in opposition to and in conjunction with the other. Recognition of and adjustment to the tension between them was met by giving both epistemological and social priority to the second term in the duality over the first. This imputed priority was also the basis for attributing value to the second term rather than to the first. The internalization of inferiority by the first term (slaves and women), made possible and perpetuated the varying degrees of control exercised over them. Hierarchy in this sense is not merely a social condition or a system of classification: it is also a state of consciousness, a sensibility toward phenomena at every level of personal and social experience. It reaches into the core of the psyche by internalizing domination and subordination as eternal traits of human nature: by separating us from the subjects or objects presented to us on a hierarchical scale.[16]

Not everyone succumbed to this shaping of consciousness and lost the sense of participation in and connectedness with the whole. Obviously Blake did not, nor Wordsworth, nor Mozart, nor Hegel, nor Turner, nor Joyce; nor many other individual artists, poets and philosophers. Today, there are many in disciplines other than those normally associated with poetic vision who have correctly diagnosed the effects of hierarchical, non-participating consciousness and are trying to heal it with integrity, clarity and scientific commitment.

The following provisional outline of an ecological paradigm owes much to their work. It contrasts explicitly with the hierarchical paradigm discussed up to now. Awareness of the differences between them may help us to become conscious of the presuppositions of our own thoughts about the world and our relationship with it. It may also, it is hoped, provide theology with new ways of interpreting and expressing our relationship with God.[17]

Terms Defined

The paradigm will be expressed in words which have an accepted sense in other contexts, and it is necessary therefore to give their particular meaning within the context in which they are employed here.

The first word which needs clarification is the word "paradigm" itself. It can mean simply a standard model or an exemplary occasion. In a religious or philosophical sense it can mean the particular orientation or framework which guides the human spirit authoritatively. In its scientific sense it covers the whole constellation of meanings, opinions, values and methods shared by the members of a particular group.

In its ecological sense it is a construct of reality which sees across the boundaries between species and strives to give value to each in itself and in relation to the whole and not on the basis of a hierarchical concept of use to a dominant species, humanity. It carries with it a commitment to live accordingly.[18]

All these meanings have been present to some degree in the way in which the word has been and will be used here. It is qualified as an "ecological" paradigm because it draws its models, its exemplary occasions, its orientation and its authority from the non-hierarchical meanings, values and methods of those engaged with theory and action aimed at understanding the conditions of possibility for the sustenance and health of all who call Earth "home".

For us, humans who share that home, the basic unit of attention is our bodily system. The word "system" describes a unit of living space that is able to function as a whole. A person's body is the primary system, but it should be understood as the integrated total of soul, body and spirit, from and through which one relates to other systems. A body does not function of itself. It depends on and relates to an environment constituted by many other human and non-human systems. It appears divided from them by the clearly discernible surface of the skin. But the skin only divides the body from the rest of the world in thought. By nature, the skin is as much a joiner as a divider, being, as it were, the pathway through which the inner organs have contact with air, warmth, light and other earth systems. The epidermis is ecologically more like a two-way track than a wall.

This word "pathway" can refer to any channel of communication between systems. So our five senses are as much pathways of exchange as the path between our home and the one next door; our skin is as open a receptor as satellite television.

The word "exchange" is used for any kind of information or energy interchange which takes place along such pathways. This can vary from a letter to a change in cloud formation; from a hot drink to a blind person's white stick; from a scent released by an insect to a Renaissance painting.

The word "open" is used to suggest an unchecked abundance of possible exchanges between systems. This presupposes that other meanings are available than those immediately accessible to the primary system. The exchanges keep us "open" to the possibility of continuous learning from other systems and to newer, richer, shared enjoyment of the world.

An Ecological Paradigm

The main features of an ecological paradigm can now be briefly described. They will be expanded in various ways throughout the book with now and then a certain amount of recapitulation.

First of all, an ecological paradigm demands that we cultivate a sense of belonging to a system that functions as a whole, no matter how small or large the particular system one is engaged with at any one time. Then it demands that we extend our awareness to the other systems with which we interact and to their interaction with further ones. This extension of awareness leads to good solutions for environmental problems, for it assumes that a healthy organ in a body is not there to give health or be used for health as though it were a discrete object, but that it be seen as a *part* of the body's health. The health of organ and organism is the same, just as the sickness of organism and ecosystem cannot be separated.

The second feature of the paradigm to be noted is that the relationships between the entities within systems are described in a most inadequate fashion. This has a lot to do with the fact that this is, after all, a theological and not a scientific treatment of the issues. But it is not only that limitation which results in the less than satisfying description of complex relationships. It is also the case that no matter how exhaustive that description might be in terms of any one discipline or author's expertise, all the relationships within any system can never be fully described. We are touching here on the fundamental relationship between language and reality which by its very nature makes all description of that reality relative to the whole truth about it. This important factor in human interaction with the world will crop up again and again.

It directs our attention here to another feature of the paradigm. Since our language is always going to be a more or less adequate attempt at conveying the truth about something, then it helps to start with an identifiable entity in order to communicate perceptions or increase knowledge. So a leaf or a branch may have to represent the tree for us, or a whisker the cat. However, while such images are properly used to represent the entity in question, they do no more than that. Understanding Nature by means of thought and then translating the thoughts into words is like trying to make out the contours of a cave with the aid of a small flashlight casting a bright but very thin beam.[19]

The rock we focus on is not the cave. The leaf is not the tree. The map is not the territory. Furthermore, the representation necessarily excludes those features which make any entity unique. Only in the night of the imagination are all cats black. This gap between what we perceive, what we mean and what we can say will be discussed at some length in the chapter on metaphor.

As well as keeping us dissatisfied with what we can say, the gap keeps us constantly on the lookout for new images, new representations, new modes of speech. Therefore another feature of the ecological paradigm is its pressure on us to keep open the pathways to other systems, mentally and physically.[20] This is not only important for language. It is vital for sustaining the life of our own system, for the possibility of transforming it, for good or ill. Lack of input, of stimulus, of energy are all symptoms of a closed system which atrophies for want of interaction with those around it.

In contrast to this, the paradigm demands openness at all the intersecting pathways between the primary system and those accessible to it. It is these which convey the exchanges of information and energy which vitalize and revitalize that system.

But this is not one-way traffic. There is also an exchange of vitality from the home system to those connected with it, and this two-way exchange affects both the giver and the receiver. So when I learned that the women of the *Chipko* movement in India were hugging the trees around their villages in order to protect them from the chainsaws of developers, it affected my attitude towards the trees similarly threatened around my home, and my attitude in turn affected that of my neighbours. At a deeper level, my attitudes toward women, trees and development were also affected, as were those of my neighbours. (The *Chipko* movement will be discussed at some length in Chapter 3.)

Using the pathways to systems other than our own in order to learn from them is both easier and harder for us than it used be, since the media do so much to make other places and cultures accessible at a superficial level. But the very superficiality keeps us from entering into those systems in any real way. This is another way of stating the problem about having a moon's eye view of the world. The "nearness" of the television screen can actually be a way of distancing oneself from what is projected on it. The spectator attitude can encourage disengagement rather than commitment.

However, there is an allied feature of the paradigm which safeguards us here. We have to learn to recognize which openings to larger systems out of sight of our own are truly important for us. One criterion for this recognition is that of appropriateness: another is fruitfulness, the recognition of what is life-enhancing. While I had read of the *Chipko* women some time ago, their response had little relevance to my way of life until our own trees were threatened, and then it became fruitful as an example of how to react.

This was not the only aspect of my exchange with these Indian women which forms part of an ecological paradigm. There is also the fact that they did not know of their interaction with my home system, and yet there was an exchange of energy between us: not only between me and them, but between them and those immediately around me. The exchange does not end here, for how can I tell how many people and systems unknown to me will, because of reading this, be affected by *Chipko* in turn?

This fact links up with another element in the paradigm. We have to remember that the pathways we plot and maintain consciously are only part of the whole territory, and that they are affected by things that go on there unknown to us. Sensitivity to this truth can prevent us from mistaking the part we are aware of for the whole beyond our comprehension.

It can also keep us on our toes when there is a problem or an opportunity, ready to travel as many pathways as possible in order to find a solution or maximize the opportunity. It warns us to leave the way open for information to come down pathways as yet unperceived.

If these factors are consciously kept in mind, an important attitude can develop which I call *ecological humility*. This allows us to recognize the impossibility of gathering all relevant information, much less of retaining it. Such recognition of limitation keeps us from absolutism, either in identifying problems, proposing solutions or defining positions. The temptation to absolutize besets us all, and as we shall see, it is endemic in Christianity.

Taking all these features of an ecological paradigm together, the overarching effect is that of openness within constraints, which presupposes that we not only accept intellectually the interactive nature of our own and other ecosystems, but that we also behave in a way which fosters a healthy interaction between organism, society and the total systemic creature we call world. The important insight guides us that we live in a world of interdependent relationships, of seamless unity in which things are intelligible only in terms of each other. We are part of an immense complexity of subtly balanced relationships which, like an endless knot, has no loose end from which it can be untangled and put in supposed order.[21]

In all the examples that have been or could be given of bad environmental practice, these apparently simple ecological rules have not been kept. Systems have been treated as though they exist in isolation: the pathways to other systems have been blocked; the available information not taken into account. No compensation has been made for the fact that our individual human consciousness, which is necessarily partial, even distorted, has been taken to be the measure of the whole.

Underlying these mistakes at the organizational or theoretical level are two of the presuppositions of a hierarchical consciousness: first, that each system or part of it is not to be valued for its own sake but only in terms of its usefulness to those above it on the scale of value, and second, that relationships of domination and subordination are written eternally into human nature.

Looking ahead slightly here, it can be said even now that there is a need to change to an ecological paradigm in Christian theology. This is evident in that, within a world beset by global environmental disasters and eager for its "good news", traditional Christianity has behaved largely as a closed system of human salvation. It has treated the systems around it, of philosophy, art, science or religion, as though the information they had to impart was of little or no concern or value, or, as in the case of Galileo, as though it was opposed to and irreconcilable with that supposedly available only to the closed Christian system.

To a large extent, it has closed off its sacred system of worship within church walls, shut out the perception of sacredness in Nature. This has reinforced the harsh dualisms of Nature and spirit, body and soul, female and male which support hierarchical structures of domination. In modern times, when there is a growing perception of the damage done to women and Nature by exclusively male systems of government, Christianity has remained one of the few where female subordination is legitimized as God's will. The interaction between its accepted attitudes towards women and Nature, as we shall see, denies to both any possibility of representing divinity, and therefore of being spoken about or treated naturally with reverence.

The consequences of these closures, both for Christianity as a system and for its relationship with its environment, will be the subject of the second part of this book. It seems fair to say that they contain an element of apocalyptic judgment, in that "Christian" values, with their destructive lack of ecological wisdom, are no longer perceived by other systems of thought as having any positive role to play in the present world crisis. The religion of the native American Indians, of Jainism, Buddhism, Druidism or the Goddess are taken by many baptized Christians as more helpful pathways to living in harmony with the natural world. Is this common perception mistaken? Is God calling Christianity to account?

> We may say that the biological systems – the individual, the culture, and the ecology – are partly living sustainers of their component cells or organisms. But the systems are nonetheless punishing of any species unwise enough to quarrel with its ecology. Call the systemic forces "God" if you will.[22]

Chapter 2

Ecology and Feminism

In terms of the ecological paradigm outlined in the previous chapter, my own ecosystem is the context for my theologizing. The pathway between it and modern feminism has not only given me the possibility of thinking and feeling across the boundaries of the predominantly patriarchal system in which I live and work. It has also brought me the realization that a truly ecological society, culture or religion today must necessarily be open to feminine values or else it will continue to take one part of itself, the male part, for the whole.[1]

This distortion has been so hard-programmed into Western consciousness that it remained largely unnoticed and unquestioned until recently. The challenge to its supremacy is now perceived not only to have consequences for the integration of women into society. It is seen to be inextricably bound up with the fragmenting of the natural world into discrete objects to be manipulated for man's use. The same cloak of inferiority and unconsciousness was thrown over Nature as over women by Western rational consciousness. All of us tend to view Nature, the world we define as non-human, through the lens of social relationships. It is the unconsciously accepted relationship between women and Nature which is the basis for a specific sort of ecology called ecofeminism.[2]

Before this interaction of ecology and feminism can be used as a basis for discussing Christianity, it is necessary to establish that they do interact in a fundamental way. Before we can do that, we must decide on which ecology and which feminism we mean. There are many types of both. I have shared in an ecology workshop with a green anarchist, two deep ecologists, several Christian ecologists and others who didn't know what to call themselves but came along to find out what they could do to help save the world. Similarly I have shared meetings with Christian feminists, post-Christian feminists and militant feminists. So what are we talking about here?

24

Which Ecology?

Following on from the previous chapter, the specific ecology argued for in this book may be defined as *a consistent refusal to fragment the world into separate and independently existing parts*. It is therefore also a commitment to making connections in practical ways between what we think about the unbroken wholeness of the world and how we live in it. The connections are made between "eco" or "house" systems which function as wholes and the "metacontexts" of other systems interacting with them. Openness to change and assessment of it as it happens are part of this interactive process.

Such ecology refuses to fragment the world by separating human beings from inert matter and other living organisms in a way which distances them "above", "apart from" or "beyond" the natural systems of which they are a part. It regards the world as a whole, as an interconnecting non-hierarchical system containing diverse and cooperating equalities.[3]

Which Feminism?

The feminism in question can also be defined as a refusal. It is *a refusal by the original "other" in hierarchical human society, woman, to be reduced to silence or to be the "other" any longer*. Therefore it too is a commitment: to behave as women or toward women recognized as autonomous persons valued for their diversity of gifts, and to free them to speak on their own behalf. The refusal to be defined in relation to men or to be silent recognizes that, as other, woman is distanced from man in a way which inspires him with ambivalent feelings of dependence and desire for domination. On the one hand, woman reminds him of the helplessness of his early years and the fragility of human life; on the other hand woman as the "weaker" sex is a symbol of male strength and ability to dominate. Therefore male transcendence has been identified with a flight from dependence on the mother, on the body and Nature, and as control over them in their "weakness". Women have internalized this perception of men and themselves to the extent that they reject any attribution of dominance as unwomanly, and accept dependence on male strength, judgment and reason as their proper role. Feminism linked to ecology is committed to challenging both these sets of assumptions arising from men's social domination of sex, race and class, and to connecting them to human domination of Nature.

Such feminism refuses to accept the hierarchical fragmentation of the world in ways which distance powerful men from subordinate women. Therefore it refuses to settle for any social or theological system that is patriarchal: one in which men are perceived as inherently superior and are then accepted as rightfully more powerful. Such systems are sustained by and reinforce the dominance of male culture and decision-making "over", "apart from" and "above" the female. These patriarchal structures programme both men and women to regard themselves as "in control" of the rest of the world which is then distanced in order to exercise this control more effectively. The ideal human being is presented as the detached scientific observer who can make maximum use of whatever object lies passively before him, without value or purpose in itself other than as an extension of his power. In other words, the holder of a Newtonian worldview described in the previous chapter.

Such a worldview is held in place by the structures of patriarchy which are self-perpetuating, since they are closed off from other ways of thinking which would in any way question the foundation principles on which they operate. So access is barred to alternative values and beliefs capable of opening society to other possible life styles. There is little acknowledgement that a feminine culture or worldview exists other than as derivative from and of secondary importance to the dominant male one, even though it is found wherever imagination is present. Therefore the poet and the artist have been marginalized also. The denial of feeling, of intuition, of non-verbal communication is symptomatic of a world in which the symbolic feminine is unassimilated.

The exclusion of feminine consciousness from patriarchal systems makes them inadequate by definition. Against an ecological paradigm, their inadequacy can be traced to the lack of sound interactive monitoring which has feedback and open pathways built into it. In patriarchy, the partial male stereotype of objective intellect usurps power over the system and determines the accepted perception and expression of what it means to be human. Its understanding of itself and its development provides its members with male models only. The male norm and the human norm are made identical, and it is assumed that generic masculine habits of thought, language and research are enough. Therefore when women's studies *are* pursued, they are treated as marginal, as something to be fitted into the dominant worldview.[4]

The history of this impregnable male monopoly has been assessed from many different perspectives. They range from the anthropologies of Richard Leakey which trace the shift from a gathering to a hunting culture with its division of labour between the sexes to Virginia Woolf's writing on the differences in opportunities open to women of different social classes and at different periods of history.

Gender Inequality

Wherever one begins tracing its development, three elements can be singled out which have influenced attitudes toward women. The continuance and effectiveness of these attitudes will surface in different ways in the arguments of the chapters to come. Briefly here, the first is the uprooting of the male from the female context of early life and his forcible identification with the male community and its roles and functions, seen as separate from that of women. Here men are pressured to react and continually prove themselves unlike the stereotype of the female.[5]

The second is the division of labour between the sexes, which has reinforced the distinction between the male and female spheres of action, with the male seen as higher than the female.[6] The subordination of women throughout most of human history has depended on the freeing of males for cultural control by filling women's days with most of the tasks of domestic production and reproduction. Men learn to consider this work "beneath" them. The prized wise woman of the book of Proverbs labours for her household from before dawn, and this labour frees her husband to sit with his peers at the city gate. Much more is at stake here than a division of labour. A paradigmatic change is called for in the way we think about men and women and their individual and common tasks. The perceived relationship of men to work needs to be integrated into the human experience of care for living substance.[7]

The third important structure of female inferiorization is the reduction of women to silence: cultural, religious, political, artistic and philosophical. It is this silencing that feminism refuses to collude with. Women have not been able to give public form to their experience of themselves, of Nature, or of God. They have grown up in a world where Adam's "naming" of woman and animals is paradigmatic; where men's images, both verbal and non-verbal, have dominated cultural imagination. The majority of modern men live in a de-sacralized world of phenomena whose only meaning is either their quantitative relationships expressed in mathematical formulae or their material usefulness. We need a language rich enough in symbolism to build a bridge between us and Nature, one which walks "that edge between what can be said and that which cannot be said . . . The words stop but the meaning goes on."[8]

The mental struggle involved in bringing feminine consciousness to speech is perhaps best seen today in the debate about inclusive language for God (inclusive, that is, of women; not of Nature). In the strong words of one Jewish woman, the masculine and feminine have been torn asunder and the feminine dismembered and banished, both from the discourse about divinity and from the human community.[9]

The effects of this dismemberment are described as follows by a male theologian:

> If
> *every naming of God*
> *is a borrowing from human experience,*
> And if
> *language slants and angles*
> *our thinking and behaviour*
> And if
> *our society*
> *makes qualities labelled "feminine"*
> *inferior to qualities labelled "masculine",*
> *forming women and men*
> *with identities steeped in those labellings,*
> *in structures where men are still dominant*
> *though shaken*
> *and women still subordinate*
> *though seeking emancipation. . .*
>
> Then it follows that
> *using only male language*
> *("he", "king", "father")*
> *to name and praise God*

*powerfully affects our encounter with God
and our thinking and behaviour;*

So that we must then ask
*whether male dominance and female subordination
are seeing God only in male terms
are God's intention
or human distortion and sin.*[10]

Undeniable as the influence of these three elements in the
social and religious conditions of women's lives may have been,
and still are (the cultural separation of the male from the female
context, the division of labour between the sexes and the loss of
the feminine component in language), they are not singled out
here in order to suggest a patriarchal conspiracy theory. Rather
they hint at the many complex reasons why the culture we share
has located and maintained women in a position of powerlessness and silence, without access to public forms of knowledge,
speech or writing.

Comprehensive theories of the rise of male domination are
found in such classics as Simone de Beauvoir's *The Second Sex*
or Gerda Lerner's *The Creation of Patriarchy*. One interesting
collection I have read recently is *Women's Work, Men's Property*,
papers by French and British women anthropologists. As one
might guess from the title, they argue that the point of departure
for all explanation of gender inequality must be sought in social
rather than biological imperatives, for it depends on woman's
role in production, and not on her powers of reproduction. The
origins of male dominance, they say, were bound up with the
struggle to control women's labour and products, and control
of her reproductive powers followed from this. Specifically, the
authors agree on the "critical importance of post-marital resi-
dence rules in determining gender relations within unilineal kin
corporate societies". They argue that "patrilocality" – the system
in which women move to their husband's kin group at marriage
– enabled men to utilize and appropriate women's labour and
products in ways that ultimately enhanced the authority of the
senior males within the husband's family.

Patrilocal societies where women moved at marriage had
greater potential for expansion because they offered more
opportunities and incentives to intensify production beyond the
level necessary for everyday subsistence. The more productive

the society, the more expansionist it could become. Female subordination actually preceded and established the basis for the emergence of true private property and the state. The historical processes involved varied in time and place, but once set in motion, sexual and social stratification proceeded together. The oppression of women provided a means of differential accumulation among men, which in turn gave some men special access to the labour and reproductive powers of women, as well as to the services of other men. Women as a category were assigned to the juridical status of the propertyless in a system increasingly based on private property. The whole system rested on gender hierarchy: the notion that men have rights over women.[11]

The Emergence of Patriarchy

These anthropologists do not agree on whether or not male dominance was a conscious creation of men who wished to exploit female labour, or a less consciously planned outcome of social processes whose original dynamic did not rest on sex oppression. Those who read their researches are free to draw their own conclusions. The Frenchwoman Monique Saliou, a specialist in the history of religions, points to two forces in particular which shaped the processes which issued in our patriarchal culture: the emergence of the Greek city-state and of Greek philosophy.

The growth of the city-state depended on an identity between those who exercise power (right citizens) and those who transmit it (parents). Compulsory exogamy and the rupture between the woman and her family, expressed by the handing over of a dowry, placed her and her possessions physically in the hands of a husband. Then, in order to discount the notion of maternal parenthood, the Greeks denied that women played any part in the reproduction of the species. Apollo declares in Aeschylus's *Eumenides*: "It is not the woman who begets the one who is called the child: she is merely the nurse of the seed she has conceived. The one who begets is the male".

Therefore, in Athens, women had no civic identity: there was no feminine Greek word for Athenian, only women of Athens or wives of Athenians. They had no right to vote, or to bear a name and pass it on to their children. (The present Greek word for church, *ecclesia*, was used in Athens for the assembly of male

citizens alone entitled to vote.) The tragedies organized by the
city magistrates, such as the *Oresteia*, show the mother,
Clytemnestra, punished for having been a bad wife, either by
asserting her independence or by taking sides with her clan
against the interests of her husband. Athena, the city deity, was
featured as a warrior virgin, born without a mother out of her
father Zeus's skull.

From the second half of the sixth century onwards, says Saliou,
Greek philosophers endeavoured to build a rational system of
thought based on the opposition of contraries. Dualist classifications, inevitably symbolized by male and female, gradually
gained the upper hand. Woman became, in essence, all that is
most alien to man. For the pre-Socratics, the earth and water
were the lowest on the value scale, and they were precisely
elements with feminine connotations. Air and fire were endowed
with a superior value and were "masculine". Plato believed that
the body, the prison of the spirit, was earthly. Aristotle perfected
a structure which opposed Femininity/Matter to Virility/Spirit,
Passivity to Activity, Water to Fire. This was the beginning of
the development of the idea that slaves/women were inferior
not only because of what they did, but because of what they
were.[12] Sexism and racism share a common father.

It is not possible here to give an adequate anthropological
treatment of these themes, but they will recur in other contexts.
Those who wish to follow up the anthropological studies will
find ample references in note 12. For those not so inclined, it is
an enlightening literary exercise to go back and read the Greek
tragedies in the light of what has been said. Iphigenia's sacrifice
and Antigone's execution show them to be at the very least the
victims of masculine values; in Antigone's case one who was
not deceived by them. Reading the Bible, a similar drama is
played out in stories of virgin daughter sacrifice in Genesis 19:1-
11; Judges 11:30-39 and Judges 19:22-6.[13]

Staying with the Bible, the same themes of sacrifice to
masculine values are raised by Carol Delaney in a study called
The Legacy of Abraham. This will be taken up in more detail later,
but it is worth anticipating a little here in order to make some
connections between the cultural processes under discussion
and their reinforcement by Christianity. She also recounts the
story of the birth of Athena, noting that she was born from
Zeus's head because he had swallowed her mother, the goddess

Metis. She sets this in the context of Zeus's own birth. His father Kronos swallowed all his children as they were born until Rheia, his wife, deceived him by giving him a stone to swallow and so saved Zeus. These stories of the power of life and death over mother and child presume that such power and authority are the father's right.

Linking this with the Abraham and Isaac story, she draws attention to the fact that there Abraham is the founding father of a new religion, a new way of life, and that once again, the theme of killing a child and the male sexual organ (in this case circumcision) are associated and are dominant aspects of the story. They symbolize the religious idea that men have the primary role in conception. The Biblical mind interpreted semen as *seed*, the child in essence, the part for the whole. The woman served merely as the *soil* in which the seed is planted, and her value was derivative.

Delaney draws a conclusion which echoes and amplifies Saliou's on the development of Greek philosophy, and brings us back again to the connection between woman and Nature. The view of conception in which the male has the primary engendering role sheds light on the alignment of the *powers* of creativity and spirituality with the male principle and the *virtues* of receptivity and materiality with the female:

> As the idea of male supremacy in conception took hold, not only did female deities and women themselves lose the power and status they had once enjoyed, but the earth too became desacralized, it too became merely soil. The earth and the fruits thereof became the property of men, as did women and children. The seed is the father's, the father and the son are one, the woman is merely the vehicle through which this relationship is established.[14]

Such analyses of the rise of male dominance form a subject in their own right, as is clear from the copious references in the books cited. The themes highlighted here come up time and time again: the male as sole parent with powers of life and death over wife and children; the patrilocation of women; the appropriation of their labour and their children by their husbands; their downgrading as true parents and the consequent legitimation of all this oppression on the grounds that they were biologically inferior. What concerns us here is the way in which the perception of the male as superior has persisted in the mental evolution of Western culture. By disclosing the patterns of patriarchy and finding out how they closed off culture from feminine influence, we may be able to open it up again to transformation through a new perception of woman and Nature.

The Phenomenon of Hard-Programming

One way in which closure took place was through what the philosopher Gregory Bateson calls the phenomenon of *habit formation*, which sorts out the ideas that survive repeated use and puts them in a more or less separate category. These trusted ideas can be taken for granted; they become axiomatic assumptions on which no thinking-time or effort need be wasted. The more flexible parts of the mind can then be saved for use on newer or more pressing matters. So frequency of use guarantees the survival of certain ideas, and this survival is further promoted by the fact that habit formation tends to remove the idea from the field of critical inspection.[15]

Bateson says that it is usually the more generalized and abstract ideas that survive repeated use, ones that combine more or less readily with other ideas. These more generalized ideas thus tend to turn into *premises* upon which other ideas depend. These premises become relatively inflexible, or hard-programmed. This hard-programming means that the premises become nuclear or nodal within constellations of other ideas, whose survival depends on how they fit with the hard-programmed ones. The popular images used in art, in religion and in metaphor depend on such accepted constellations.

The Nature-Feminine Link

One such premise, that of femaleness, has made it normal to use images of maternity, of nurture, of fruitfulness, of passivity and of marriage when we refer to Nature. Visitors to art galleries see Nature portrayed as a naked, passive nymph in Lucas Cranach's *The Nymph of Spring*, while Botticelli's *Birth of Venus* and *Primavera* show the virgin in conjunction with the earth mother, covered with a gown and wreath of flowers. The famous sixteenth-century fresco on Mount Athos, in which heaven, the angels, the Magi, the shepherds, the desert and the earth bring gifts to the Mother and Christ, depicts earth as a kneeling,

garlanded woman. Schoolchildren learn from Wordsworth that
"Nature never did betray the heart that loves her". In churches
people sing of "Dear mother earth, who day by day, unfoldest
blessings on our way". When the Gaia theory of James Lovelock,
which revives the name of a female Goddess of Earth, is
discussed by scientists and lay people alike, the use of female
imagery is never questioned.

Together then, habit formation and image formation have
given us the nodal metaphor: The earth is our mother. This
gathers other constellations of metaphors around it such as
womb, nurse, virgin, seed, fertility and barrenness which imply
an active partner, man. Feminine nouns and pronouns are used
for Nature which internalize and reinforce assumptions about
its role vis-à-vis man. The closest relationship between him and
woman is used to describe his proper relationship with the earth:
"husbandry". The connotations of this word are carried through
when his work with Nature is described as that of the "husband"
penetrating virgin forest or soil, sowing seed and raising crops
from the fertilized earth beneath his feet.

Some of the origins of these metaphors can be found in the
prehistory of that same Athenian culture already discussed in
the context of the myth of the male as sole parent. In the aptly
named *Sowing the Body*, the literary scholar Page duBois
demonstrates, through a radical examination of classical sources,
how the female gender in the classical period was seen through
an elaborate set of metaphors which linked the female body with
production and reproduction in an agrarian system. She explores
one set of metaphors in detail: the field, the furrow, the stone,
the oven and the writing tablet. Beginning with Homer's epic
poems, usually attributed to the late eighth century B.C.E., she
shows from many realms of cultural and daily life that the female
body as a space for labour was the basis of women's status for
centuries. By the fifth century B.C.E., the period of Athens'
greatest literary productivity, the metaphor of the flourishing
field appears in texts and in ritual practices such as the *hieros
gamos*, the sacred marriage which celebrates divine sexual union
with the productivity of earth.

In Homeric texts the seed is planted in the earth without the
agency of another of the species. Earth is the receiver and nurse
but has no part in the determination of the kinds of trees that
grow: a sort of promiscuous receptacle that receives all seeds

and feeds all. When the once communal lands become privately owned fields, the produce becomes the property of the planter. Seed is sown in discrete plots of earth, in particular bodies: women's promiscuity is therefore intolerable, since the nourished product of the planting must be identifiable as the offspring of a particular seed.

DuBois quotes a passage from Plutarch which shows how the Homeric traditions about women and earth were evident three centuries later in Athens. He remarks that the Athenians observed three sacred ploughings: the first at Scirum, the second at Raria and the third near the base of the Acropolis. "But most sacred of all such sowings is the marital sowing and ploughing for the procreation of children".[16]

This text takes us on from the metaphor of the earth and the woman's body as a field into the related one of the furrow. Her body is marked, cut into, and ploughed in furrows by the cultivator; the body of the woman is not only the property of her husband but also the space in which he labours, a surface he breaks open and cultivates, the terrain where his heirs are produced. In fifth-century Athens, the women became the guarantors of citizenship for male lineages, and greater and greater emphasis was placed on their sexual purity. They were guarded as vulnerable household possessions, traded among citizen-families, hoarded within families without male heirs.[17]

DuBois reflects on the metaphors and asks a question which brings us back to the third element which has played a part in women's inferiorization. If the woman's body is like the earth, she asks, if she produces children like plants, if she is like an empty vase – an earthen container holding and giving up the goods of life - then how can she speak?[18]

These sources and consequences of cultural conceptions about women and Nature arose in and have been perpetuated by a male-oriented culture. Male attitudes toward Nature and woman have been accepted, consciously or not, as universally adequate, but can now be recognized as partial by feminists of both sexes. Ecologically, they need to be seen in the context of women's perception and experience of what it means to be defined, in every sense, by the dominant partner in a relationship. Images are always in dialogue with action. Constellations of behaviour are linked to those of language. It would be almost impossible to say a blessing over a person or object and kick it at the same

time. Just listen to the language of someone wrestling with a
recalcitrant piece of machinery.

Ecofeminist use of Ecological Paradigm

Therefore ecofeminism, in bringing an ecological paradigm into
play from a feminist perspective, sets out to disclose the intrinsic
link in a male-dominated culture between how one speaks about
women and Nature and how one behaves towards them.

Ecologists in general can take heart from Bateson's observation
that any change in the hard-programmed ideas may involve
change in the whole related constellation. They will also be
encouraged to hear from him that frequency of validation of an
idea is not the same as *proof* that the idea is either true or
pragmatically useful over a long time. They will assent gloomily
to his conclusion that we are discovering how several of the
premises deeply ingrained in our way of life are simply untrue:
and that they become pathogenic when implemented with
modern technology.[19]

Feminists will agree with what he says, and will point to
patriarchy as one false and pragmatically dangerous premise
which has been hard-programmed into the collective consciousness of the West. Because, as we have seen, patriarchy assumes
that the father figure does the naming, begetting, controlling,
ordering and giving, it polarizes human beings by gender into
roles and properties which prevent each from experiencing full
humanness. Feminists work on the assumption that if this
premise can be changed, then changes will occur in the whole
related constellation of ideas and structures in society which
have hard-programmed men into regarding themselves as in
control of the rest of the world.

Ecofeminists share both reactions. They endorse them by
demanding that the two basic cultural premises discussed here,
patriarchy and the femaleness of Nature, be connected systematically to the present environmental crisis through the consistent
use of an ecological paradigm resulting in a more inclusive vision
of the world. In this way we may be able to change the pathogenic
habits which are destroying us all today.

By its very nature this paradigm is a force for change. It is
gaining ground at a time of crisis in the life of the planet, the
very moment at which paradigm shifts occur by necessity. They

arise because the prevailing one is unable to integrate new theories or cope with the anomalies of accepted ones. The hierarchical paradigm which prevails in much of Western culture is now seen as inadequate by a post-Einsteinian scientific consciousness.

It is possible, therefore, for ecofeminists to use an ecological paradigm as a means of questioning very basic assumptions about the nature of human nature, about human gender relations and their effects on the non-human world, and to draw conclusions about the relationship between these matters and how we behave as organisms embedded in the systemic creature Earth. They do this through radical critiques of the prevailing gender hierarchies, which assume that men, by nature, have rights and power over women and the non-human world.

"Critique" is one of those words used so often nowadays that everyone presumes to know what it means, i.e. a sort of negative and rather abstract assessment of something. Therefore the word is sometimes used as a euphemism for what is more popularly known as a hatchet job. But what is intended here is critique in the Kantian sense: the recognition of limits, the limits of human reason which by its very nature is called upon to answer questions which it can neither ignore nor answer, as they transcend every faculty of mind. So a feminist critique is a consistent recognition of the limits of hierarchical patterns of thought, of the way in which our culture has been and still is dominated by the questions posed and answers given by male "scientific" consciousness. This consciousness rules our world in every sense and has closed off other perceptions of Nature. It is "delimited" according as its partial nature is recognized and acknowledged. Such a feminist critique calls for conscious input and receptivity from men and women alike. For both, the results can be frightening and enlightening all at once.

Tracing his personal mental evolution, the nuclear physicist Fritjof Capra wrote that his engagement with feminism and its radical critiques of society transformed his entire perception of social and cultural change. He realized that the full power of patriarchy is extremely difficult to grasp because it is omnipresent. It has influenced our most basic ideas about human nature and about our relationship to the universe, for "man's" nature and "his" relationship are taken as normative. But then patriarchy, as Capra remarks, had never been challenged until recently, and its preconceptions and structures are as yet only barely touched by feminist critiques.

Realizing the pervasiveness of patriarchy brought on a crisis of perception in Capra which he likens to the experience of the physicists who developed quantum theory in the 1920s. Like them, he found himself questioning his very basic assumptions about reality, about human nature, society and culture. He became aware of some of his own patriarchal values and behaviour patterns at the same time as he became fascinated by the radical feminist critique of them. It is the fascination one experiences, he says, on those rare occasions when one encounters an entirely new mode of enquiry. For him, the discovery of the feminist perspective was a challenge to redefine what it means to be human.[20]

My own feminist perspective has given me a new way of relating to what is there in the world, and especially to texts. It has made me aware of the pervasiveness of patriarchy in myself and in authors who would not consciously subscribe to it. A good example occurs, ironically, in Bateson's warning of the particular habit of mind most likely to destroy us:

> If you put God outside and set him vis-à-vis his creation and if you have the idea that you are created in his image, you will logically and naturally see yourself as outside and against the things around you. And as you arrogate all mind to yourself, you will see the world around you as mindless and therefore not entitled to moral or ethical consideration. The environment will seem to be yours to exploit. Your survival unit will be you and your folks or conspecifics against the environment of other social units, other races and the brutes and vegetables.
>
> If this is your estimate of your relation to Nature and *you have an advanced technology*, your likelihood of survival will be that of a snowball in hell. You will die either of the toxic by-products of your own hate, or, simply, of over-population and overgrazing. The raw materials of the world are finite.
>
> If I am right, the whole of our thinking about what we are and what other people are has got to be restructured.[21]

This powerful statement sums up much of what has been said so far. It also exposes the problem: the way in which *man* has placed himself outside the world and against it. However, the generic use of the word "man" sounds another responsive chord in ecofeminists, all the more striking since the author appears deaf to it himself. He describes *man* as one for whom the world is not considered entitled to moral or ethical consideration, and so it can be used and/or hated at will. (The metaphor of "hating" the world is hard-programmed into Christianity, and extended into Western culture.) Ally this attitude with advanced technology, he says, and you have a world dying today of the toxic by-products of that hate, whether around Chernobyl, among the steel works of Nowa Huta or through the green algae of the Mediterranean. Such examples in the 1980s prove how right Bateson was in 1971, although I would want to stress over-use rather than hate as the cause.

But ecofeminists see something more in his analysis. They begin the restructuring of our thinking that he calls for by de-structuring the very words with which he makes his plea. His sexist language about humanity and God not only properly reflects *on* the limitations of a male culture but is also a true reflection *of* the limited premise of that culture. It reflects the constellation of ideas which takes the male as signifying the whole of humanity and sole type of divinity. So when he warns of the *dangers* of thinking that we can put God outside *his* creation or that we are created in *his* image, ecofeminists may properly retort: "we told you so!"

Gender-specific language which either excludes women or includes them only as part of the male norm keeps pathogenic hierarchical structures in place. Moreover, if Bateson's words are taken literally they also reveal *why* they are destructive. Those who think of themselves in images of a male God and close off any possibility of divinity elsewhere are precisely those who arrogate all mind to themselves, see the earth around them as mindless and therefore as not entitled to moral or ethical consideration. This is not to attack Bateson personally. On the contrary. One can be certain he would insist on having his own premises and language constellations exposed in all their partiality and inflexibility.

A quick browse through a women's studies section in the library will give more than enough proof that attributions of "mindlessness" against women are part of our history. Why else were they denied the right to higher education, the right to vote, the right to their own property on marriage, the right to maintenance and/or custody of their children on divorce and all

the other manifestations of a lack of moral and ethical consideration only slowly being legislated out of existence? The women
of Liechtenstein in Europe were fully enfranchized only in 1984.

But, says Bateson, this lack of moral and ethical consideration
shows itself in the exploitation of the environment. So, say the
ecofeminists, what is true for it is true for women, and vice versa.
If you have no moral or ethical relationship with Nature and
you have an advanced technology, then poisonous by-products
which bring about the death of Nature cause you no qualms. If
you *say* you have a moral or ethical approach to women and
then, for instance, use advanced technology on their reproductive organs with no more qualms than if they were battery hens
or hybrid apple trees, then you must grant the ecofeminists their
case. "Earthly" bodies are there to produce and reproduce under
the control of men. In such a hierarchical society, women are
"lower" than men and Nature "lower" than women, which
leaves both subject to male control, "objectified" for experiment
in the name of science.[22]

Why are these trends not only condoned but hailed as major
and exciting breakthroughs? In the previous chapter we mentioned the phenomenon of non-participating consciousness and
the shift from the question of *why* to the question *how*. In the
case of the animal and vegetable worlds, the criterion of
usefulness to man rather than any value or purpose in
themselves is deemed sufficient. So prize cows, for example, are
induced to ovulate every two months, and their udder development and teats are measured together with their milk record in
order to obtain a basis for gene selection and to help produce
"better" cows.[3] One item alone, yield of milk, is targetted for
increased production, without consideration of the destructive
consequences on either the cows or the interlocking systems
around them.

In the case of women and reproductive surgery, we must look
deep beneath the mask of official statements about the tragedy
of infertility and back towards the idea of the male as primary
parent. Some women are manipulated to fear barrenness as a
cruel enemy which threatens the heart of their marriage
relationships, and to feel guilty that they cannot "give" their
husband a child. A Greek wedding agreement puts it bluntly.
The father says: "I give you this girl in the hope of a ploughing
which will produce legitimate children".

In this vulnerable situation for a woman, the reproductive scientist looms like a magician on her horizon, a distant powerful figure who is given total access to the intimate confines of her body.[24] The objectifying of women into "earthly" passive matter for manipulation deprives the "rational" technicians and surgeons of any participation in the women's consciousness, physically or mentally. Their bodies are treated as surrogates which "mechanically" carry the male seed to fruition, an attitude internalized by women and men alike.

In a Calcutta public hospital a team of biochemical engineers removed and froze embryos from the wombs of one hundred women "donors", later implanting them in the recipient wombs of one hundred other women. Unconcerned about their welfare, they were equally unconcerned about the defects and abnormalities they might have been producing. According to the Chief of Operations, they were not really worried about genetic abnormalities. "We [the male technicians] would rather have had an abnormal baby than no baby at all."[25]

The myth of the male as sole parent has survived also in marriage laws about the husband's sole possession of property and children. Such legislation depended on the premise that life actually originated within the man and that in the act of intercourse he placed a minuscule baby into the womb of the woman – the nurturer of "his" babies. "She became like the earth in which seed was sown." This concept made it possible for him to claim as his property anything born of woman and to treat it accordingly. Therefore he considered it his right (reflected in early Greek and Roman history) to kill all defective children, any female children he chose, all children who were not his, i.e. illegitimate, and even a woman who secretly aborted. Infanticide by the father was not considered a crime until the fourth century C.E., yet if a woman were found guilty of it she was tortured and put to death. Abraham, taking Isaac to put him to death without consulting Sarah, showed no doubts about whether or not he had the right to do so.[26]

The continued acceptance of the myth at subconscious level has particular significance now that advanced technology, allied with a lack of secure personal relationship, leaves the whole field of human reproduction as open to poisonous by-products as that of animal and vegetable reproduction has become. The word "maldevelopment" takes on harsh significance when uneducated women in poor countries are used by male researchers for reproductive experiments which gain funding and prestige for Third World research.

The suffering undergone by women who are the subjects (in the sense of objects) of male scientific techniques is hidden under the glossy presentation of this important "advance" in manipulative surgery. Those who witness the suffering become aware of why ecofeminists insist on stressing the irrefutable connection between the treatment of Nature and the treatment of women. Whether or not she personally experiences biological mothering, nothing connects a woman so profoundly with Nature as her reproductive system. Her menstrual cycle links her to the moon, the tides and the crops. She shares with the earth the experience and ability of bringing forth and nourishing life. There is no violence comparable to that which seeks to exercise absolute control over this ability.[27]

There are many ways in which latent misogyny functions in our social, political and religious structures. Collectively, they create a society in which men keep women mentally and emotionally at arm's length. Woman can be exalted as wife, virgin, mother, or deprecated and abused as temptress and whore. "Whatever way the male projection works, woman is object, nonequal, manipulated, *distanced*". She is not encountered as a contributing equal to men in occupational and civil life, in board rooms and centres of policy-making.[27]

Ecofeminism makes connections between such fragmentation of male and female sensibility within human relationships and within attitudes to Nature. It connects the exclusion of female perception and experience from patriarchal culture with rigid and unchanging structures of control over the natural world. It connects patterns of male domination of woman with those in which science and technology are bound to a conception of absolute mastery over matter. It insists on the inclusion of women's perceptions as corrective to a solely male and therefore partial view of the systemic creature, world. It relates natural ecosystems with human ones consistently and sensitively.

Ecofeminism stresses the connection between woman and Nature on the grounds that Nature, in our distanced, masculine-scientific culture, has also been made "other", something essentially different from the dominant human male who has an unlimited right to exploit "mother" earth.[29]

For both men and women working in ecology there comes a change in our perception of Nature when, by consistently linking women's history of oppression with the history of the environment, we affirm the natural kinship between feminism and ecology. Then we realize that in our readings of environmental crises we will compound the errors if we do not keep faith with the ecological paradigm, starting with our own lives and finding there the deepest manifestation of Nature-hating: our collusion with hierarchical structures. We belong to a society in which women, identified with Nature, have been objectified and subordinated. The attitudes we bring to Nature in our ecological work will reflect this, especially in an unwillingness to accord it autonomy or value in its own right. By becoming aware of patterns of domination in our own lives, we learn to connect these patterns with the domination of non-human Nature. This is the first step outside the common perception of ourselves as discrete static beings who must control others and the environment in order to survive. It is the first step towards an ecological society and sensibility.

Chapter 3

Ecofeminism and Dualism

Taking a closer look at the place where ecology and feminism interact, certain difficulties appear as well as new possibilities for enlarging our worldview. The greatest problem is implicit in the whole of the preceding chapter. Given that women have a hard time in a patriarchal society, and that Nature gets a raw deal also, why make matters worse for women by identifying them with Nature? If it is the case that men are "above" women who are "above" Nature, why pull women down instead of up? Both men and women wrestle with this problem. Some men resist the charge of being responsible for identifying women and Nature in a harmful way just as much as some women resent being identified with "natural" inferiority.

It is hardly surprising then that some feminists, aware of the connections between the treatment of women and of Nature, want to sever them. They want instead to devote their energies to being integrated with men in the creation of culture. They want to be identified with the transcendence of spirit rather than with the immanence of body and Nature. They want a self-image of independence and freedom from necessity rather than one bound to and bound by dependence. They want to be active makers of history rather than passive objects moulded by male historical-cultural agency.[1]

Some feminists holding this position insist that female subordination is culturally and not biologically determined, that it is not woman's biological role as mother which automatically relegates her to second place, but the lack of opportunity for education and public office. There is no innate reason why women should not equal men in achievement. The fact that they do not appear publicly to do so has nothing to do with their physiology and everything to do with the way in which men have exercised control over education in its broadest sense: that which we know in our society and how we come to know it.

Sex Roles/Gender Roles

One way in which this point is cogently made by feminist

44

thinkers from a variety of disciplines is by insisting that a distinction be made and preserved between sex and gender. Sex is a biological "given" which defines women as half of the whole of humanity, with men as the other half. Gender, however, is culturally determined, being the definition of behaviour appropriate to the sexes in a given society at a given time. Gender is acted out by both sexes as a set of cultural roles.

Since these distinctions are at best blurred in popular consciousness and more usually ignored, we in fact live within sex-gender systems, where culturally defined gender roles are institutionalized to the extent that resources, property and privileges are allotted on the basis of these roles. Thus it is sex which determines that women should be child-bearers; it is the sex-gender system which insists that they should be child-minders. It is sex which gives the mother the ability to sustain children with her body's milk. It is the sex-gender system which presupposes that the father should nourish his sons' minds by introducing them to the world of thought, travel, adventure, law and discipline. (See the extended references to this polarization of the parental relationship at the beginning of the previous chapter).

This brings us to the definition of patriarchy as just such an institutionalized sex-gender system, in which the dominance of one sex, the male, has allotted resources, property and privileges to men according to culturally defined gender roles. Feminist consciousness, in men and women alike, seeks to develop an alternative vision of society and so of the future, in which the culture will shift from an androcentric one to a truly inclusive one where women are equal partners in the shaping of events and in the thinking work of the world.[2]

The truth of this feminist analysis and the resulting goals set by emancipatory movements for women is being slowly accepted within the patriarchal culture they criticize, and both analysis and goals are taken as axiomatic in much of the argument of this book. But their truth should be seen within an ecological framework which does not see the achievement of equality within human sex-gender roles as an end in itself. The rights of some on the planet must be seen in the context of the needs of all, and the gaining of emancipatory rights for women must be consciously perceived as part of the struggle for survival of the whole. To go back to the analogy of health: healthy relationships between men and women are part of the total health of relationships within the world.

Within this larger context, it becomes clear that willingness to sacrifice the link with female biology at a personal and planetary level in order to realize one's potential as a human being is based on a nonecological way of thinking about oneself as a woman. It sacrifices the interconnections between the primary system of one's own body and those which surround it. It also ignores the fact that the education common to our society has made the connection between women and Nature a premise for some of the most damaging environmental ideas, images and behaviour prevalent today. If women are to exercise any control over future education they have to ask why their relationship with Nature has been a common source of their degradation, and be prepared to look at the connection in ways which might provide different premises, ones less inimical to themselves and the non-human world alike. Otherwise, to take a "worst case" scenario, they may find themselves equal to men without a planetary stage on which to enact the role of equality.

To limit the struggle for liberation from male oppression to the condition of women alone reveals acceptance of one of the main premises of the system feminists seek to change. It ratifies the assumption that the male human being is the dominant form of life to which all others gravitate and/or by which all non-human life is controlled. Behind this lies the further assumption that man is "apart" from all other creatures, which exist only for his use and benefit. His consciousness is separate from the evolution of the rest of creation.

Nature/Culture

The acceptance of male natural superiority shows absorption of other cultural premises which have created and fostered Nature/Culture dualism. There is an internalization of an epistemological dualism which supposes opposition between necessity, located in the natural habitat (*oikos*), and freedom, located in the public domain (*agora*, or more broadly, the *polis* itself). Underpinning the supremacy of the *polis* in Greek thought was a more universal dualism: the supremacy of order (*kosmos*) over meaningless desolation (*chaos*). To the Hellenic mind, order always had to resist disorder. This oppositional imagery is essential for understanding how the Greeks, and every European ruling class that followed them, were to think about the human condition. The predominant note was always a hierarchical organization of reality stated in rational terms, in which *chaos* had a very mundane and earthy substantiality which included slaves, foreigners, women and potentially unruly freedmen.[3]

There was also the notion that Nature, woman and body are material, irrational, passive, dependent and immanent, as opposed to culture, man and spirit which are immaterial, rational, active, independent and transcendent.[4] These dualisms have been internalized by both men and women alike, so that today we find some women trying to discard their identification with one half of them at the same time as some men are seeking to reclaim the half they presumably lack.

Lying behind this is the acceptance of the Nature/culture split as something given and not culturally created. Yet the United Nations Charter for Nature (1982) states unequivocally that: "Civilisation is rooted in nature, which has shaped human culture and influences all artistic and scientific achievement, and living in harmony with nature gives man [*sic*] his best opportunity for creativity, rest and recreation".[5]

On the basis of an ecological paradigm there can be no real break in the interaction between Nature and culture, for culture cannot rise or exist in a natural vacuum any more than cultural pursuits can be followed by disembodied minds. In the present context of the destruction rather than the rise of culture, the interaction between them can be seen very clearly in cultural centres such as Venice or Athens which are being destroyed because their natural environment is being destroyed. The planetary context of culture is there for all to see.

The acceptance of a supposed split between them, other than as an intellectual abstraction, both relies on and fosters another cultural premise of modern society: that Nature has no intrinsic value. It is either absorbed into the territory of female sex-gender or discounted as genderless, an object which exists without consciousness, there for the use of men and women alike. This too has been challenged in the United Nations Charter for Nature, which declares :"Every form of life is unique, warranting respect regardless of its worth to man [*sic*], and to accord other organisms such recognition, man [*sic*] must be guided by a moral code of action".[6]

The profound identity crisis lying below the surface of the

debate about whether women identify with culture or Nature is slow to appear in a patriarchal culture which publicly attributes its glories (whether political, military, religious, artistic, literary or scientific) to men and its baser elements to women and Nature. Enough of the crisis is manifest, however, to be perceived ecologically, that is, as a loss of confidence in the relationship between the whole of humanity and the rest of the planet. A general unease is beginning to appear about the consequences of separating humanity from and elevating it above the earth, even though for most people it is the consequences of this separation that claim attention rather than its philosophical sources.

Ecofeminism's Response to Dualism

Ecofeminists therefore, as part of the central thrust of our species' life towards more viable forms, refuse to sever the link with Nature in order to become honorary males, perceived as the makers of culture and forgers of human destiny in distinction from that of the planet. They choose instead to free themselves from the stereotyped patterns of behaviour between men and women which place them in opposition to each other, or in a relationship of domination/subordination. But this move towards self-emancipation is not intended to elevate them to a position of control over Nature, thereby doubling the ratio of human dominance over it. Rather it is intended to open up and keep open the pathways between the sexes, between their ways of living, working and responding to Nature. It is hoped that this exchange between them will compensate for the inadequacy of the dominant patriarchal view, for the tendency to value input from men alone.

This is no small agenda. Patterns of domination have become "natural" to the human male, and are now certainly part of our common culture. Since they have been allied with advanced technologies, they may well contribute to the extinction of our species. That fact too would be "natural". Therefore ecofeminism sees no reason for allying women with them. Instead, it seeks to change these patterns. To do so, however, we need to understand "not only the societal mechanisms by which they are supported, but also the central psychological 'adjustments' of which they are an expression."[7]

The type of adjustment required from Christianity will be the subject of the following chapters. At a more general level, some changes required of all of us became evident in the preceding chapter. There is no doubt for instance, that over-population threatens our survival. But it is not only societal mechanisms for population control in the poorest and most overpopulated countries that have to be looked at and adjusted, such as later marriage, lowering of infant mortality, the connection between large families in poor societies and the fear of no provision for old age, contraceptive programmes, and so on. There is also a central psychological adjustment to be made by men and women in the developed world. Men's right of sexual access to women, and the right of male seed to continue its intended course in the womb, must be seen in the context of male control over the reproductive powers not only of women's bodies but of the earth. The myth of the male as sole parent, which gives him the claim to and possession of both their fruits, must be dealt with in all its complexities. (See again the discussion in the previous chapter of the cultural matrix of metaphors which link the earth and the woman's body as the nurse of seed.) Issues like abortion, reproductive technologies, contraception and genetic engineering need to be debated within the global context of male control over Nature and its fecundity.

Then an ecological community might be possible in which we would ally ourselves with the natural environment and re-establish our sense of ecological wholeness, of diversity in unity.

In the pursuit of this wholeness, the connection between overpopulation, forest denudation, inappropriate agricultural techniques and indebtedness to the banks of the First World needs to be made explicit. The influence of multinational technologies, military aggression and monetary policies of unlimited growth in the First World also needs acknowledging. These excesses are now coming together exponentially, in a catastrophic relationship between human fertility and the earth's humanly imposed infertility.[8]

Wages Work/House Work

Another change in patterns of behaviour that is being publicly called for, with its attendant societal and psychological adjustment, is the reduction in harmful emissions into the atmosphere. Politicians are making pledges on behalf of governments to reduce emissions from car exhausts and power stations at the same time as environmentalists are exhorting us to cut consumption. Whether through policy, necessity or commitment, we cannot expect our life styles and living standards to remain unaffected by this.

One inevitable effect will be reduced mobility. Travelling by car will be discouraged by force of reason or simply by the prohibitive cost of oil. It is likely then that public transport will concentrate on peak hour passengers going to and from work. The reduced mobility will be most keenly felt by those women whose employment outside the home, because of family commitments, is at non-peak hours. It is also realistic to assume that in homes where the number of cars is reduced, the man's journeys to and from work will take priority. In housing estates which are not within walking distance of town centres, those women housebound with small children will feel the psychological effects of being isolated for long hours.

In effect, the split between the public male sphere of action and the female domestic private sphere will become more deeply entrenched. The Nature/culture divide will be reinforced unless, of course, there is a change in the pattern of relationships between work and gender. This would require a societal and psychological shift in the perception of the domestic sphere as solely the woman's realm.

It is already starting to happen. I know two homes where the husband remains at home with the children and the wife goes out to work. In both instances this has happened because the wife could get a job and the husband could not. It is also the case that modern computer systems are making the "electronic village" concept a reality, where work is not necessarily something you "go to".

But behind the decision to adapt to this situation and adjust their perceived roles, both sexes must make a prior adjustment in their definition of work: more precisely, in the way in which our industrial culture defines work, that is, as wage labour. This effectively reduces housework to non-work, and through a hierarchical evaluation gives it lower status.

This work tends to be cyclical – it has to be done over and over again without leaving a lasting product to be assessed in cash terms. Cooking, cleaning, sweeping, washing dishes and clothes all come under the heading of what the economist Hazel Henderson calls "entropic work", because the tangible evidence of the effort is easily destroyed and entropy, or disorder, increases again.

The jobs with status generally involve either work that creates something lasting (a building or a sophisticated machine), or is considered high-tech, or which endows the holder with professional status over others (politics, education, medicine, religious office). Ironically, jobs with perhaps the highest status, in marketing, finance, law, business and media administration, create nothing lasting either, but only generate electronic blips to be scanned as money, print-outs or entertainment. In all these categories, the jobs are male-dominated, with the executive operating from the top of a pyramid of female labour, both at home and in the office.[9]

Making connections, no matter how sketchily, between necessary reduction in atmospheric pollution and the need for assessing contemporary attitudes to work, opens the way to perception of a global malaise which concerns us all. This is the loss of dignity for the worker, whether in the home or on the work site. Even in well-paid jobs, the system grants independence of thought and action only to an elite. But for all workers, these included, their self-worth is inextricably bound up with their earnings, and when faced with unemployment, they too readily conclude that the inability to keep a job is their own fault. Therefore today's unemployed account for rising rates of suicide, alcoholism, first-time admission to mental hospitals, homicide, wife-battering and child abuse.

Simone Weil understood this better than most, since she chose to live and work for eight and a half months as a member of what was perhaps the most despised class in the French factory system – unskilled women workers. She found the experience almost unbearable. Her *Factory Journal* boils over with frustration with the time-keeping system, her anxiety at failing to make the daily rate, her impotent rage at the way she was treated. She also learned that economic inequality alone was an inadequate explanation of the problem of oppression. This was essentially maintained by the systematic humiliation and the instilling of a sense of inferiority in the oppressed.

Weil went into factory work with an ideal of what it *could* be. She wrote on the first page of the journal:

Not only should man [*sic*] know what he is making, but if

possible he should see how it is used – see how Nature is changed by him. Every man's work should be an *object of contemplation* for him.

She found that this was impossible. The worker does not know how each piece is used, or is combined with other pieces, or has successive operations carried out on it, or what the whole is for. This prevents him from being the one she had idealized – who exercises his mind correctly and comes to know both the world and his own true nature as a thinking and an active being.[10]

Such an interaction between work and human nature, human activity and raw matter, will remain an ideal as long as work is assessed only in terms of monetary value, as long as it is done in isolation from the rest of human activity in the home, and as long as it is cut off from the all encompassing activity of Nature. Such a split consciousness of work separates it also from relationship with the Creator, from any possibility of it being contemplation.

The theologian Dorothee Soelle expresses this very well:

Theologically we are trained to separate God's creation from human work. We do not see the relation between God and the worker mediated through work . . . For a long time I had separated creation from my own life. I had pondered creation in a purely aesthetic way, never in terms of my life and work. The theology of the bourgeoisie deals with work under the themes of curse and hardship. The secular ideology obstructs the emergence of a different theology of work in its reduction of the value of work to the pursuit of cold cash.[11]

Reconnecting Work, Home and Nature

The separation of male work from housework and human work from God's creation is symptomatic of the split consciousness ecofeminism tries to heal. Rather than endorse patriarchal errors of reducing work to the pursuit of money and status, ecofeminists choose to value their interaction with Nature, accept it and deepen it because of its importance as a personal relational rather than a technical image of our interconnection with the world. They connect our primary relationship, our home system, with those surrounding us and employing us. They connect these again with the rest of creation.

Making these connections helps us to realize our interdependence as a species, not only in woman/man relationships, but on
the raw matter which sustains life and makes work both possible
and necessary. We come to a new understanding of the fact that
far from being independent of Nature, we depend for our lives
on the plant and animal world. In spite of our large brains, we
cannot photo-synthesize the sun's energy for ourselves but have
to rely on the work of Nature to recycle it for us. We could not
live without Nature; it could live quite happily without us. We
could not work without Nature; but it works very well on its
own.[12]

Going back specifically to the problem of overpopulation, an
ecological assessment of procreation places female/human sexuality within the larger context of our relationship with the whole
of creation, as an integral part of being alive rather than solely
as gender arrangements for the production of children. The
emphasis shifts to communication and relating, to healing the
life-sapping split which in our case alone divides the basic activity
impulse that we share with other creatures into work on the one
hand and play on the other. This healing involves a process of
reconciliation between the rational and the intuitive ways we
think about our relationships with each other and with the
environment.

For humankind, sensual experience is embedded in a highly
developed mental life, the physiological basis for which is as
concrete a part of our biological equipment as our organs of
touch, vision and smell. Our most fleeting and local sensations
are shot through with thoughts and feelings shaped by our
personal history, our present awareness and our expectations
for the future. And when another sentient being is present for
us, even in fantasy, our thought and feeling are in turn shot
through with impressions of that being's state of awareness.

This relational state of awareness includes – actually or
potentially – some knowledge of our own sentient presence.
Sexual feeling thus radically transcends momentary and solitary
sensory pleasure or relief. The bodily complementarity of males
and females is something much more than a source of agreeable
sensation. It can be a central manifestation of the wider human
delight in existence, a focal point, symbolizing and providing
expressive release for the whole of our erotic connectedness to
the world. The *Song of Songs* is a sublime expression of this

constellation of feelings and ideas. Bach's Double Violin Concerto discloses it in sound. Poussin's painting, *Le Printemps*, focusses it for us in colour.

Soelle lists four dimensions of sexuality – wholeness, trust, ecstasy, solidarity. Under wholeness she includes multidimensionality and integration of our physical, intellectual, aesthetical, emotional and spiritual potencies.[13] Sexuality sensitizes the entire body to respond to all other forms of life in the world – person, animal, flower or river. "The force that through the green fuse drives the flower" is the same energy which drives our own system, our body, into interaction with all the other systems we encounter. When sexuality is set apart as a specially good or specially evil compartment of life, it remains an unspiritualized force, unspiritualized in the sense that it is divorced from the universal and concrete reality of Nature, from the total pattern of organism–environment relationship.[14] This requires acceptance of the fact that humanity alone does not engender children; it is the entire living environment which produces the child and keeps it alive – air, soil, plants and animals.

Innate Value/Instrumental Value

This truth gives a new dimension to the image of earth as mother. If the image is accepted positively as a nodal metaphor, in the sense of influencing behaviour, the world becomes for us a systemic creature, a living body in which we all participate, continually changing, merging and emerging in rhythmic cycles. The celebration of this in the seasonal cycle is not of mere "fertility", but of the establishment of balance among all the different communities that comprise the living body of earth. The Gaia hypothesis of James Lovelock is a scientific elaboration of this, demonstrating the geophysiological interaction of atmosphere, oceans, climate and the Earth's crust, which are regulated comfortably for life by living organisms using the sun's energy.[15]

Such views of the world clash fundamentally with current values. For to celebrate the living body of earth is to celebrate it as it is in itself, as well as what it is for us. Each being has a value that is inherent, that cannot be diminished, rated or ranked, that does not have to be earned or granted. This challenges current Western economics, for instance, which does not measure inherent value but only instrumental value, that is, usefulness for conversion into "wealth". The present economic order was shaped by the eighteenth-century thinking of Adam Smith who built on the ideas of scientists and philosophers like Bacon, Hobbes and Newton. Bacon reinterpreted Nature as a limitless resource to be exploited for human purposes. Hobbes reinterpreted wealth as power over other people in the incessant competitive struggle of human life, and Newton's atoms provided a model for individual humans interacting in an economic system.

There are some economists today who wish to create a different sort of economy. They aim at an ecological future, as opposed to a hyperexpansionist one.[16] In the face of widespread deficits and indebtedness, men like Senator Albert Gore are speaking out about the lunacy of rescheduling debts from the Third World to the First, when the latter is claiming back more in interest than it is giving in aid programmes. He describes this as a sick person giving a transfusion to a healthy one.

The expression "market values" (which includes such data as the Gross National Product, the Dow Jones Index and monthly inflation rates) dominates our culture and our power politics and is shorthand for all the factors involved in an instrumental view of the earth. Current assessments of the "value" of the rainforest are based on its potential as timber, as a source of usable drugs, as land for ranching cattle, as a source of minerals, as a quantifiable factor in the destruction/retention of the ozone layer, as a gene pool for countless "valuable"/rare/unknown species (including possible tribes as yet undiscovered), and so on. All these economic indicators of value are based on utilitarian motives. In classic utilitarianism, actions are right when they maximize human pleasure, or at least minimize human pain. This is a "consequentialist" doctrine, which focuses on the consequences or outcomes of actions in determining their value for humanity.[17]

In some sense, as I said before, we all have to be utilitarian in order to survive. But some philosophers are addressing the complex issues involved in our accepting dependence on Nature. Andrew Brennan, for instance, gives a succinct definition of the kind of outlook implicit in the ecological paradigm argued for here. One of the central pieces of ecological insight, he says, whether of scientific or metaphysical ecology, is that each thing is *what* it is in part by being *where* it is. Living things are complicated arrangements of only a small number of elements from their environment, and continued existence of each depends on being located in the right place on the great cycles of matter. But living things likewise bear the marks of evolution – having morphological features and behavioural traits critical in the past and still essential for the survival of the genetic material they carry. These are aspects of the truth that organism and environment are complementary, each inseparable from the other.[18]

Another philosopher, James Rachels, approaches the question of value from the perspective of Darwinism. He argues for a new ethic, in which species membership is seen as relatively unimportant for assigning value, and wants this replaced with some form of moral individualism, according to which what matters is the individual characteristics of organisms, and not the classes to which they are assigned.[19]

Hard Data/Soft Data

Ecofeminism too insists that another kind of value than the instrumental one must *also* be taken into account if we are to live ecologically, or continue living at all. This is the notion of *innate* value, of non-instrumental worth where one's concern for the rain-forest, for instance, is unrelated to whether or not it is a source of any material benefit for oneself. It is enough for me that it exists and ought to continue to exist for and in itself. It needs no arguments or apology for its existence. It is inherently valuable. This value cannot be quantified and it is inappropriate to try and do so.

It is recognized in the United Nations Charter for Nature: "Every form of life is unique, warranting respect regardless of its worth to man [sic], and to accord other organisms such recognition, man [sic] must be guided by a moral code of action."[20]

This inherent value, which exists whether anyone acknowledges it or not, sometimes comes under the heading of what information theory calls "soft" data, as opposed to "hard" data which is given credibility by the support of facts and figures (such as the economic indicators mentioned above). But for a balanced assessment of any situation both kinds must be taken into account: the subjective "irrational" relationship just as much as the "hard" data of objective calculations. (The distinction itself between hard and soft data *is* soft data – i.e *what the proponent feels to be significant and not significant.*)

The engineer to whom I owe this "hard/soft" distinction works on the development of exploration platforms for the oil industry. The hard data, he said, should be presented in objective graphs and figures (the number of houses, road capacity, types of tree, etc.) which are there for all to check. The soft data, (such as personal reactions in the community and possible effects on the environment) are subjective evaluations but none the less important for that, to be taken into account by "any respectable discipline".

An example of such a presentation is a book of anthropological research entitled *A Leaf of Honey*, by Joseph Shepherd. It is a linguistic study of proverbs recorded among the Ntumu people of Cameroon. The even-numbered chapters of the book provide the orthodox ethnographic content in the form of field-notes and drawings. The odd-numbered chapters are a narrative account of his life with the tribe, their beliefs and worldview. The "hard data" and the autobiography are thus formally kept separate but their interdependence is clearly shown.[21]

This excursion into the notion of value has given us another context for ecological thinking, one which impinges on us daily in economic reports of devaluing or revaluing wealth. The point about these is that they present only the hard data about instrumental value. The soft data which try to keep the notion of inherent value alive is ignored, or dismissed as metaphysical, unscientific, irrational or whatever pejorative term happens to be current. Joseph Shepherd reported his research in the way he did because some of his academic seniors were worried about his "academic objectivity" once he had announced his intention of looking into the tribe's beliefs.

It is unfortunate when those who present soft data, not following his example, mix soft with hard data in a way which makes it easy for those who work with "facts" to dismiss "feelings". This also works the other way, i.e., mixing "facts" with "feelings" so as to distort or overemphasize certain "facts" in favour of certain positions, which makes it difficult for those who work continuously with hard data to share discussion with those who apparently do not. This became clear to me at a conference organized jointly by ICOREC (The International Consultancy on Religion, Education and Culture) and the New

Economics Foundation, which brought together economists and representatives of the world's religions. It was there I met my friendly engineer. One of the economists told me that he was baffled by the idea of talking to "a religion". He could not even think of how to formulate a question that either a religious person could understand or he could answer.

Power-Over/Power-From-Within

This proves the point but at the same time proves the necessity for such conferences. They provide opportunities for the kind of ecological interaction between disciplines which can bring about change in those who participate by an interchange of information at many levels. Those economists who come with a perception of power derived from Smith and Hobbes think of it as "power-over" – over resources, over markets, over other nations – and view the world as a resource to be controlled. Those who come from a tradition which avowedly attaches value to the world because it belongs to God will supposedly think of it at the very least as a place of accountability to some power inside it or outside it, and certainly one not bound by local or international power struggles.

Some of those from the Hindu tradition attach a different notion of power to the earth itself. It is not "power-over" but "power-from-within". In India this concept of power is beginning to confront economic powers of every kind. Power-from-within is known as *shakti*. In its general sense *shakti* means the power or energy of the universe, understood as a female generative force basic to all action. It is thus both power and action, and both are female. (Compare this with the passivity of Nature/woman in Western thought, where the male is the active subject.) Its generative power appears in the power of the earth to endure, generate and transform. *Shakti* is also the power of the gods, the energy through which they act, for it is said "Shiva without *shakti* is a corpse." In a more specific sense this all-pervading energy is itself divinized as the Great Goddess *Shakti*. Within her all powers come together and are unified, whether they are the powers of procreation, development or destruction; the powers of enjoyment, perfection, knowledge or sacrifice; or the powers of cruelty, time and death.[22]

In what is now known in India as the *Chipko andolan* (hug-the-trees movement), we see the living power of *shakti* integrated with action and working in men and women alike against ecological devastation. It is a demonstration of the interconnectedness of "soft" with "hard" data. *Chipko* began as a protest movement in March 1973 at Gopeshwar village in Uttar Pradesh, though its philosophy and practice go back to Gandhi. Three hundred trees in the region were to be felled to make sports goods, and the villagers were very aware of the links between tree-felling and the tremendous soil erosion which had caused massive floods in the area. When the lumberjacks arrived, they were met by a procession of villagers beating drums and singing songs. They had decided to hug the trees that were to be axed. The agents of the company retreated.

A year later, in a neighbouring village, the men were all away when the employees of the lumber company reappeared on the scene. A little girl spotted them and ran to inform a widow, Gaura Devi. She organized a group of about thirty women and children and went to meet the contractor's men. She pushed her way forward and stood before a gun carried by one of the labourers. She defied him to shoot her first before touching the trees. "Brother", she said, "this forest is our *maika* (mother's home). Do not axe it. Landslides will ruin our homes and fields." She and her companions were successful in persuading the angry contractor to go away without his logs. Soon after, the government set up an official committee which reported that this Reni Forest was a sensitive area and tree-felling was banned there for ten years.

The importance of the *Chipko* movement is that it has spread from village to village, and women in particular take novel initiatives, such as tying sacred threads around the trees to symbolize their relationship as protectors. They have gone on time and time again to protect them at the risk of their own lives. The women of *Chipko* often describe their struggle as one aimed at protecting the "skin of the earth" which, when it is peeled off through erosion or damaged through loss of nutrients and moisture, leaves the earth wounded and diseased. They have progressed from saving individual trees and forests to mobilising a ban on overfelling of trees and excessive resin tapping. Beginning in September 1986, they started a movement to blockade mining operations in the Nahi-Barkot area, and, as we saw in chapter 1, they have also successfully fought against quarrying in Khirakot.

In a full account of *Chipko*, Vandana Shiva analyzes the Westernization of the Indian continent and the consequent worsening of life for women and for Nature. She quotes Itwari Devi, a village elder who has guided her local *Chipko* to blockade mining operations which have killed the forests and streams, sources of life for the village.

> *Shakti* [strength] comes to us from these forests and grass lands; we watch them grow, year in and year out through their internal *shakti*, and we derive our strength from it. We watch our streams renew themselves and we drink their clear and sparkling water – that gives us *shakti*. We drink fresh milk, we eat ghee, we eat food from our own fields – all this gives us not just nutrition for the body, but a moral strength, that we are our own masters, we control and produce our own wealth . . . Our power is Nature's power, our *shakti* comes from *prakriti* [Nature] . . . Each attempt to violate us strengthened our integrity. They stoned us on March 20 when they returned from the mine. They stoned our children and hit them with iron rods, but they could not destroy our *shakti*.[23]

The presence of a different kind of power than that expressed in economic equations empowers ecological action in India. It is beginning to inspire it elsewhere as well. In 1989, in Stroud, Gloucestershire, a group of local people gathered to hug thirteen beautiful and mature trees which the local Council had ordered to be felled in order to straighten and widen a road. The leader of the group, Ron Birch, described his feelings after a whole hour's tree-hugging. The full weight of a security man hired by the Council lying against his forearm ensured that it would bear the mirrored impact of beech-bark contours the following day. An hour later, he and his group watched in alarm as the tree surgeons left their vehicles, stretched stiffened limbs, picked up menacing chainsaws and advanced towards the trees. By now, he said, something was happening which gave the huggers the semblance of an advantage.

> We were no longer simply protecting the trees; we were protecting Our Trees. I was protecting My Tree. And My Tree was no longer just a beautiful and wonderful example of the plant world doing its indispensable job. I had now felt its warmth, its wrinkles and its life.[24]

The campaign was successful and the trees were saved. They had become, in Ron Birch's words, old friends to be hugged at any time.

The kind of data that comes from such a subjective relationship with Nature as well as any objective information about it must be taken into account in any environmental action. It springs from a multidimensional sexual response to the earth which embraces (literally here) the potencies of the world surrounding us without separating them out into different sorts of data on a hierarchical scale, so that only some can be used and others ignored.

Ecofeminism is not saying that women will supply soft data and men hard data. It is saying that up to now, only one sort has been valued, and that the conditions of a patriarchal society make this inevitable, for such a society awards precedence to the stereotyped male response of objective, rational, scientific, detached and supposedly value-free thinking. The proper attitude is assumed to be one which sees all sides of an argument and takes none. In contrast, a subjective response to the earth is seen as suspect, as it leaves us free to express our hopes and fears in language and actions which are discounted in patriarchy as female, intuitive, bodily, illogical, emotional and disordered. The ecofeminist critique of the limits of patriarchy is intended to take us beyond those limits into an interchange of objective and subjective data in our personal evolution and in our common mental evolution. It is intended to counteract the tendency in us to divide beings into *things* and *persons*, with things to be used and only persons to be respected.

Ursula King concludes her summary of the Indian idea of *shakti* by remarking that if female powers are properly controlled, they are considered a source of protection, strength and blessing; if unchecked, they can create havoc and destruction. Presumably this perception brings about what she describes as the contradictory situation in India where women are thought to possess inherently more power than men, yet remain subordinate to men who control them and their power.

Nature as Mother/Nature as Disorder

This presents us with another reason for the continuing patterns of subordination by men of women and Nature. In the development of Western culture there was certainly, as we have seen, the identification of Nature, especially the earth, with a nurturing mother, a kindly beneficent female who provided for the needs of mankind in an ordered, planned universe. But another opposing image of Nature as female was also prevalent: wild and uncontrollable Nature that could bring on violence, storms, droughts and general chaos.

Both, says Carolyn Merchant, were identified with the female sex and were projections of male human perceptions on to the external world. The image of the nurturing earth carried with it a value system of subtle ethical controls and restraints which functioned as constraints, for instance against pollution of the rivers. They were described as the mother's veins. In Spenser's poem *The Faerie Queen*, mining was described as an act of human lust, the basest of all sins for it treats its mother, earth, as a passive receptor of human rape in the rush to mine the gold from her womb.[25] The native American Indians had a similar response to being asked to sell their land.

But the other image, of Nature as disorder, called forth the opposing idea that has already been mentioned, that of power over and control of Nature. In an analysis which closely follows that of the development of economics, Merchant shows that under the influence of Bacon, Newton, Locke and Hobbes, the Scientific Revolution made this the core concept of the modern world. A participating view of the female principles in the earth, which paid homage to her nurturing power and our dependence on it, was discounted and replaced by a mechanically oriented mentality that either eliminated or used female principles in an exploitative manner. The female earth and virgin earth spirit were to be subdued by the machine.

The supremacy of images and attitudes of control functioned as cultural sanctions for the devaluation of Nature. The philosophical sanctions depended, as we have seen, on a hierarchical ordering of the duality between *polis* and *chaos*, society and Nature, man and woman, freedmen and slaves, with supremacy given to the first term. The notion of human equality was impugned by Plato on the grounds that the differences between them stem from differences in souls. He wrote that the few who are equipped to rule – the guardians – are born with "gold" and "silver" souls, and are destined by their spiritual qualities to be rulers. Plato did not exclude women from the possibility of being among their number. Aristotle gave a rational basis for slavery and patriarchy, in which innate intellectual qualities endowed the Greeks to rule not only the barbarians but also slaves and women. These were supposed to "benefit" from the superior rationality of their masters.[26]

These philosophies universalized hierarchy as rational, based on superiority of soul or intellect. There was to be another potent force to ensure its survival, a religious philosophy which held that the hierarchical relationship between man, woman and Nature, their souls and their intellect, was ordained because of collusion in sin between woman and Nature. On this assumption, Christianity went on to provide religious sanctions for patriarchy. One succinct expression of this is found in the Decrees of Gratian, the first systematization of Western church law, promulgated c. 1140 C.E. For example:

> Women should be subject to their men. The natural order for mankind is that women should serve men and children their parents, for it is just that the lesser serve the greater.
> The image of God is in man and it is one. Women were drawn from man, who has God's jurisdiction as if he were God's vicar, because he has the image of the one God. Therefore woman is not made in God's image.
> Woman's authority is nil; let her in all things be subject to the rule of man. And neither can she teach, nor be a witness, nor give a guarantee, nor sit in judgment.
> Adam was beguiled by Eve, not she by him. It is right that he whom woman led into wrongdoing should have her under his direction, so that he may not fail a second time through female levity.[27]

The interpretation of the Genesis text which lies behind this Decree also rules that Nature, in the form of the serpent, beguiled the woman, and through them not only was Adam led into wrongdoing but all his descendants as well. Francis Bacon prayed that his knowledge might be "discharged of that venom which the serpent infused into it".

This connection between present ecological apocalypse and Genesis brings us face to face with some of those dark and limiting aspects of a narrow Christian tradition which stem from a particular reading of the Genesis text as an infallible account of humanity's relationship with its own sexuality and with the rest of creation. This account has placed man above woman and Nature and legitimated this supremacy in the name of God. It has presented man's sexual relationship with woman as essentially one of domination. It has taught that work is a curse and hardship, and that raw matter is to be subdued into shape rather related to as an object of contemplation. It has separated the area of transcendence, the sacred, from that of immanence, the earthly here and now.

The following chapters will follow through ideas, imagery and behaviour in Christianity which have proceeded from these notions, and subject them to an ecofeminist critique. This will be done in the hope that the Christian Spirit at the root of the world tree may empower us to live ecologically: that is, non-hierarchically. Then we may value Nature not as opposed to culture but as a developing, creative and fecund complexity of forms and interrelationships.

PART TWO
A Christian Paradigm

Chapter 4

Apocalypse Now

The first part of this book, on the basis of an ecological paradigm, focussed on the relationships and exchanges between women, men and the natural world. This paradigm can be used by ecologists to analyze relationships between ecosystems, to propose solutions for present problems and to help shape the vision of an appropriate and fruitful interaction between future human needs and earth's fertility.

The critical question addressed in this part is whether or not the same paradigm may be or ought to be used by theologians to interpret the relationship between humanity and the rest of creation.

Theologians and ecologists already share one interpretative tool: the use of apocalyptic imagery (see the opening poem) to communicate their ideas about the present and future state of the world. An apocalypse, whether ecological or biblical, describes disaster and judgment now in relation to past actions, future solutions or further disasters. But theologians and ecologists share more than this orientation toward the future. In face of their community's present experience of disorientation and *anomie*, immediate and radical answers to a present state of crisis are sought for and given. Both speak from within a threatened community, and both call for action now (repentance and change of life-style) and hope in the future, at the same time as they warn of present judgment.[1]

In theology, the re-interpretation of prophetic texts castigating human behaviour provides prototypes for making connections between human conduct and God's present judgment on the land. Isaiah's words, for instance, will find echoes in many an ecologist's heart when he makes uncompromising statements about the results of human iniquity:

> The Lord has taken his place to contend,
> He stands to judge his people.
> The Lord enters into judgment with the elders
> and princes of his people.
> "It is you who have devoured the vineyard,

the spoil of the poor is in your houses.
What do you mean by crushing my people,
by grinding the face of the poor?" . . .

And now I will tell you what I will do to my
vineyard.
I will remove its hedge
and it shall be devoured;
I will break down its wall,
and it shall be trampled down.

I will make it a waste;
it shall not be pruned or hoed,
and briars and thorns shall grow up;
I will also command the clouds
that they rain no rain upon it (Isa. 3:13-5; 5:5-6).

In its religious sense, the word "apocalypse" usually refers to
Jewish, Christian and Gnostic literary accounts of "revelations"
(apocalypses) to a prophet or writer. Some of these are concerned
with hope for a divine irruption into a present state of affairs
which is on the verge of catastrophe. Allied with this is a longing
for a divine realm in which God will reign as king.

The adjective "apocalyptic" generally refers to a pattern of
thought which exhibits these characteristics of disaster revealed
and hope affirmed. In its ecological usage, emphasis is placed
on the catastrophic state of the world at this moment, with some
explanation of why things have reached such a state and what
this might augur for the future.

The Structure of Biblical Apocalypse

This sharing of apocalyptic thought patterns and imagery will
be taken as common ground on which to decide whether or not
theology can employ an ecological paradigm. To clarify the
issues, it is necessary to give an idea of how both disciplines
employ apocalyptic imagery, and how their usage differs.

In Chapter 12 of the *Apocalypse* (which is how I shall refer to
the New Testament Book of Revelation for the rest of this
chapter), Nature does not merely sympathize with the human
plight. It actively cooperates with the heavenly and the human
order in seeking a solution to it. The scene is described as follows:
heaven and earth are at war with the great dragon, that ancient
serpent who sought to devour the woman's child. He is thrown

down from heaven in face of "the salvation and the power and the kingdom of our God and the authority of his Christ". Finding himself on earth, the dragon pursues the woman, pouring water out of his mouth to sweep her away. Then, the text says: "But the earth came to the help of the woman, and the earth opened its mouth and swallowed the river which the dragon had poured from his mouth" (Rev. 12:16).

This is more daring than Shakespeare. He didn't try to have us believe that Birnam Wood marched on its own to Dunsinane in vengeance for Duncan's murder. But then the certainty of the writer of the biblical *Apocalypse* that the earth consciously took part in the cosmic war which brought victory to Christ the King is not part of the usual Western perception of Nature.[2] Nor is it usually part of a modern Christian theological outlook either.

The thought world of the *Apocalypse* and the genre of apocalyptic writing has tended to be a minority theological interest. Its imaginative landscape is foreign territory to most modern readers, and theologians are no exception. For those who do tackle it, its mixture of ambiguity and certainty is generally coped with by reducing it to one or the other. Those who plump for certainty are ready to interpret every sign and symbol with exactitude, and add up the results in ways which give support to a particular moral or political viewpoint. Those fascinated by the ambiguity use the text as a speculative tool, as a religious hitchhiker's guide to the galaxy.

The biblical accounts of the cosmic battle of the end-time issuing in victory to the good accommodate both these approaches. The battle will certainly take place, but there is ambiguity as to when and how. The whole cosmos, heaven and earth together, will certainly be involved, for the river of the water of life flows from the throne of God through the street of the city. But there is ambivalence about the numbers involved and the time scale. In some accounts the battles occur at intervals of a thousand years. There is talk of first resurrection and second death, but the chronology throughout is not historical.

The ominous sense of final ending in biblical apocalypses struck a responsive chord in some theologians who lived through the catastrophes of the First World War, Karl Barth among them. It strikes a responsive chord today in some ecologists' hearts, and so, like Adrian Farey in our opening poem, they borrow apocalyptic imagery, often unconsciously, to convey this sense of imminent cataclysm. For them, the political and religious structures once capable of sustaining life are now seen to threaten it, or else appear impotent or at the point of rupture. In Eastern Europe, for instance, the ecological devastation caused by policies of unlimited industrial expansion is now laid open to their horrified gaze. But the turbulent political scene there does not offer much hope of concerted and appropriate action to tackle the problems so exposed. Instead, the horror of Western ecologists is matched by the jubilation of Western expansionist interests at the prospect of more markets and even more industrial "development". The battle between these attitudes is a global one. Too often it issues in sterile confrontation. But this is actually defeat for the ecologist, since the ideological stand-off absorbs the energy that should be put into remedial action.

Like his ecological counterpart, the biblical apocalypticist can be described as someone standing at a dread threshold, who looks in several directions in an effort to explain the prevailing doom. A backward glance, often in the form of a resumé of history, discerns patterns and trajectories in human behaviour which explain why it is that things have reached such a pass. Careful scrutiny of the present focusses on signs of an imminent collapse, on possible reduction to a state of chaos reminiscent of primordial formlessness.[3]

Therefore this type of literature flourished at times of crisis in Judaism and Christianity. The bleak worldview of the apocalyptic vision in Isaiah 24-27, Isaiah 56-66 or Zechariah 9-14 stems from the turmoil of the late sixth and fifth centuries B.C.E. From the Roman persecutions came Mark 13, the *Apocalypse* and a considerable number of extracanonical writings like 4 Ezra. There was a belief that the history of the world is close to the dawn of a new age:

> For the youth of this world is past, and the strength of the creation already exhausted, and the advent of the times is very short. Yea, they have passed by; and the pitcher is near the cistern, and the ship to port, and the course of the journey to the city, and life to its consummation (Syr. Baruch 85:10).[4]

These apocalypses were written by those suffering persecution, and were circulated among them as a means of sustaining hope for a new and better life (here or in eternity). The writers used a symbolic code which substituted numbers and beasts, for instance, for people and places, and cryptic imagery like the above pitchers and ships to signal expected victory or defeat. The passage quoted could be read as the obituary of the Roman Empire, or certainly as a hope for its demise. The mixture of certainty and ambiguity is part of the problem of dating this literature and placing it geographically. Its symbolic codes are capable of many interpretations, and make it continually appealing to those who feel themselves threatened by enemies they cannot name.

The Structure of Ecological Apocalypse

It is not surprising therefore that shocking apocalyptic images arrest the attention of increasing numbers of thoughtful moderns. For them, themes of history's decline, imminent doom and a new order beyond the cataclysm are far more descriptive of the world we live in than the facile assurances of civil leaders that the future is bright if efforts at technological development, materialistic production and accumulation are merely redoubled. To listen as I have to the naturalist David Bellamy sharing his reflections on the atmosphere and landscape around and beneath him as he flew from England to Australia is a frightening and depressing experience. His vivid and factual account of erosion, pollution and deforestation on a global and seemingly irreversible scale conjures up compelling images of an ecological endtime.

Thus both the certainty and the ambiguity of apocalyptic themes are employed forcefully by those who come under the generic title "Green", whichever one of its forty shades they wear. They too are certain that a cosmic war is being fought (some call it an "Eco-war"). They are sure that if it is lost, there will be death, but are uncertain as to whether or not this will be preceded or followed by resurrection. Some think we are already engaged in battle. Others think we have lost all but the penultimate one, that for the rainforest. Some think this millennium will be decisive while others concentrate attention on the coming of the next Ice Age. But whatever the time scale, everyone is certain that none can escape unchanged: heaven and earth, man and beast, ozone layer and algae are all involved.

Examples of green apocalypse abound. A typical one spells out in some detail the grim death, disease and rivers of blood envisioned in the opening poem. In the 900 days between the first meeting of the World Commission on Environment and Development and the publication of its report in 1987, major disasters reported included the drought-triggered, environment-development crisis in Africa, which put 35 million people at risk, killing perhaps a million. A leak from a pesticide factory in Bhopal, India, killed more than two thousand people and blinded and injured over two hundred thousand more. Liquid gas tanks exploded in Mexico City, killing one thousand and leaving thousands more homeless. The Chernobyl nuclear reactor explosion sent nuclear fallout across Europe. Agricultural chemicals, solvents, and mercury flowed into the river Rhine during a warehouse fire in Switzerland, killing millions of fish and threatening drinking water in the Federal Republic of Germany and the Netherlands. An estimated 60 million people died of diarrhoeal diseases related to unsafe drinking water and malnutrition; most of the victims were children.[5]

This catalogue of disasters has some of the characteristics of biblical apocalypses. It too conveys the sense of standing at the threshold of disaster, of looking backwards and forward in an effort to explain what is happening. It situates us at the edge of a great hole in the web of life, a biological abyss which opens before us with the extinction of millions of species. In the report's own words, it serves notice that the time has come to take the decisions about human activity on the planet needed to ensure its future. As does Isaiah, it places the responsibility squarely on human shoulders. It places it in part on those institutions responsible for our cultural and spiritual heritages as centres for reinforcing our economic interests and survival imperatives.

Differences Between Biblical and Ecological Apocalypse

The pattern of ecological apocalyptic discourse fits that of biblical apocalypse in many respects, but there are five notable mismatches, one of form and four of content.

Firstly, green apocalypticists do not have to code their words, since (with the notable exceptions of "ecological martyrs" such as Chico Mendes, Dian Fossey, Fernando Pereira and Valery Rinchinov) their own lives are not usually in immediate danger. They can name names, give verifiable statistics and safely denounce villains, whether individuals, multi-nationals or governments. The ecological dispatches are circulated openly, and on the whole it is fair to say that they tend to engender gloom rather than encourage hope.

Secondly, in further contrast to biblical apocalypses, ecologists do not interpret the final cataclysm as the destruction of the old order so as to make way for another and better one in which chosen human souls survive. Ecologists do not want the earth sacrificed while we are saved. For them, the whole of creation is destroyed or saved together. In this respect, ecology keeps the perspective of co-operation for good or ill between the human and the natural order evident in Chapter 12 of the *Apocalypse*. Narrow theological interpretations discount or ignore it.

Thirdly, ecology does not look for or expect direct answers to its problems from God. While many ecologists echo in their hearts the cry of the unknown prophet in Isaiah 64 who pleads with God to rend the heavens and solve the many riddles of existence, they do not share the prophet's confidence that God will do so. The very word "apocalypse", which means "revealing" or "unveiling", meant for the religious authors the unveiling of the counsels of God directly to the apocalyptic seers and thence to their readers. They were offered a clear authoritative pronouncement from the mouth of God which claimed to solve inconclusive human debates about our world and its destiny. The key to this outlook is the belief that God reveals divine mysteries directly to us. This gives us knowledge of the true nature of reality so that we may order our lives accordingly. In the Bible, the apocalyptic seer speaks of things *as they really are*: that is, as God sees them.[6] In contrast to this, the report quoted serves notice on the world community on the basis of the latest and best scientific evidence, and expects us to make decisions accordingly.

Fourthly therefore, in direct contrast to the religious prototypes, very few green apocalypticists expect that there will be a heavenly deliverer directing the battle who will snatch victory for us from the jaws of death. An unprecedented act of international human will, rather than God's will, is what is hoped for. And equally, the villain in ecological apocalyptic scenarios is humanity, not some supernatural force.

Finally, green apocalyptic writers see this leading role for humanity as the hinge of ecology's dramatic conflict, of the ecologists' dilemma. For it is precisely humanity's dominance in relation to the rest of the world that they see as the problem.

By contrast, some theologians assume that human dominance is ordained by God, is a result of a unique relationship between God and us, and that "the earth belongs to both God and man – to God because he made it; to us because he has given it to us".[7]

The range of possible reactions, from total engagement to complete withdrawal, is part of the problem. There is no common perception of what must be done or how to do it. For ecologists, the advocates of action against carcinogenic pollutants probably command most attention, as they appeal directly to one of the greatest human fears, that of cancer. Those who take a longer view, and they argue, a more enlightened one, ask for action on the nuclear issue or the ozone layer. Others are in no doubt where the priority lies. It is in preserving the tropical rainforest, which has the immediate effect of saving innumerable and unknown species, and ultimately of keeping the crucial climatic balance of the earth intact.

Theology's Response to Ecological Apocalypse

My own view as a theologian is that we need to take up the challenge and opportunity set out in the World Commission's report, and put our theology into service as part of the spiritual heritage which can reinforce and give vision to the economic and practical imperatives the present situation lays on us. Therefore we need to identify the Christian behaviour patterns that have brought us to the state we are in, through an honest assessment of Christian doctrines and beliefs. Then we are ready to make connections between that and the surrounding systems which stimulate and sustain us.

This strategy is implicit in an ecological paradigm. As a theologian it demands of me in particular that I make a critical analysis of the dominant assumptions which influence Christian responses to the present environmental situation. I have to view ecology and theology as two complementary dimensions of my life that must both be taken into account if I am to meet the needs of the world as it exists. I cannot take refuge from it in some kind of certainty about a unique relationship between God and the Christian universe which absolves its members of responsibility for the actual situation in which all living being has a relationship with God. Furthermore, it requires acknowledgment of and repentance for some of the consequences of Christian premises about God-given human dominance now seen to contribute to the environmental mess in which we find ourselves. As an ecofeminist, it asks that my insistence that ecologists take soft data into account be matched with a theological commitment to acknowledging hard data from the "practical" sciences. Theologians must be committed to a post-Darwin, post-Einstein view of the world.

This brings me back to the opening question of this chapter, as to whether or not I can use an ecological paradigm. The mismatches between the use of apocalyptic imagery in ecology and theology point to some apparent problems with adopting such a paradigm. But do I have a choice? To use a criterion connected to the paradigm itself, is it not the most appropriate, life-enhancing and therefore fruitful one for the present time? At the very least, it forms part of the new dialogue between science and faith mentioned by Charles Birch in his acceptance speech at the presentation of the Templeton Prize for Progress in Religion. The prize itself recognizes that there is such a thing as progress in religion, that a living religion cannot remain static as the world around it changes dramatically day by day. Christian doctrines, he said, are good sign posts, but bad hitching posts. They are sign posts to the frontiers of modern science, to relations with other religions and to the ecological and political problems of our time.

Constricting Views of Revelation

Behind all the problems mentioned, real or imagined, lies a perception of the conditions of possibility for theological use of ecology's insights. It affects not only the theologian's perception of the possibility, but also the possibility of finding a partner in dialogue. Thus it is not enough for me to announce that I intend using an ecological paradigm if I am perceived as opposed to accepting its premises. This problem was touched on in the economist's dilemma mentioned in the previous chapter. It arises wherever there is an assumption that theology has some other basis for discussion than fundamental human knowledge and experience.

This was brought home to me when I found myself on a committee combating local development. One of the members, who knows I am a theologian, asked me would I stand as a representative on the local government council "if it was not against my principles".

The difficulties experienced by economists or ecologists talking to theologians, and vice versa, comes from the fact that theologians speak about the relationship between woman, man and Nature within a metacontext they mark off as a particular *revelation of God*. Moreover, theologians seemingly take for granted that the truth of this revelation will remain unaffected by any change in the hard data presented by ecologists or economists. So some will continue to insist that God has given the earth over to human domination even when such domination is manifestly destroying the earth. They may also claim that the relationship between God and us takes supremacy over all others, indeed that it belongs to an agenda different from that of God's relationship with the rest of the world. Some of them want to add that the relationship is not open to us through the usual pathways of the systemic creature world and all its interrelated systems. They hold that by its and our very nature we are incapable of even finding such a pathway there. A relationship with God is opened to us only through a special intervention from outside our world: God had to send us his divine Son Jesus Christ to show us the only true way to him.[8]

This brings us back to the differences between ecological and religious apocalypses. Ecology does not consider this world and our lives and relationships in it as of relative value to our continued existence in another world with God. It does not expect direct answers to its problems from God, or that it is necessary to supplement human understanding of ecological problems with divine revelation in order to deal with them. It does not expect direct intervention from God in the form of a heavenly deliverer to save us from our self-created ecological dilemmas, even if they include our annihilation.

But is it the case that we are *by nature* incapable of receiving knowledge of God through our primary human system, and must therefore be granted entry to another transcendent one beyond immediate conscious experience and expression if we seek such knowledge? What is it that limits our understanding of the world so that we need direct answers from God to the problems it raises?

These questions arise only if we accept the premise challenged by an ecological paradigm: that the person living in, reflecting on, writing or reading about the world, Nature and God can be or is separate from them. This notion implies that the world and its creator, the human person and Nature, the organism and the environment are disconnected, and that therefore we can and must choose between them. The Christian doctrinal assumption behind this illusion, and one which gives it a long pew life, is that this separation apparently cuts through humanity itself. Those who opt for "God" (the saved) are separated for ever from those who do not (the damned).[9]

With this understanding, the basic community premise of biblical apocalyptic writing has been lost. Instead of a communal judgment involving earth and river, man and woman, city and sky, the focus is narrowed down to the fate of the individual human soul. Instead of the communal action called for by an Isaiah, in which housing policies toward widows affect the quality of harvest in the vineyard, we have an emphasis on "souls", categorized as "saved" or "damned", separated from the communities in which they proved themselves to be such. The enthusiasm with which the poor communities of the "Third" World read these biblical apocalypses comes from a different perception of them: as part of their own communal experience of oppression, suffering and exploitation of natural resources. This is the arena of divine justice. The material world is the focus for salvation, rather than a hope which centres primarily on the individual and heavenly reward. On this reading, biblical apocalypse is an example of the conviction that the divine indwells the human and the process of human history. The experience of the everyday world is an essential part of the knowledge of God.[10]

In a narrow Christian reading of its own biblical apocalypses as well as contemporary ones, this world is treated as a stepping stone to the one beyond, or as a weighbridge to record our heavenly gains and losses. Its beauty is seen as a snare which distracts our senses, and since they are open to distraction, they must be distrusted as a pathway to God. Our work is considered a sentence imposed on us in punishment for sin, and is divorced from the activity of Nature. Sensuality and sexuality are to be strictly controlled, and their manifestations done away with as far as possible. So celibacy is "above" marriage, which is treated in some Christian traditions as a distraction from, and so an impediment to, the possession of spiritual power.

Wherever these presuppositions are accepted, the correct Christian response to world problems is seen as withdrawal in prayer in order to discern God's will for mankind, and mankind only, for non-human species do not rate prayers. This retreat from political and environmental problems is justified on the grounds that God has foreordained who is to be saved, and our job is to keep tuned in to the divine wavelength, to pray and work in the hope that we are among the fortunate few.

Broader Views of Revelation

The foregoing outline of a Christianity concerned with individual human salvation would appear to rule out the theological use of an ecological paradigm. But theologians must question its assumptions. In continuity with the author of the *Apocalypse*, we might well ask what the Spirit is saying to the churches *today*. If an alternative broad Christian response exists, how is it arrived at? Is Christianity able to learn from other religious systems around it? May it be taught by scientific meditation on the cosmos that the separateness of human kind from the rest of the world is the real illusion? May it not accept that we are part of a universe continuously created through a spiritual as well as a physical process? Such propositions open up a contemporary context for a new mode of religious understanding, and for fruitful Christian dialogue with ecology.

To arrive at this broader Christian context, there must be a constructive critique of the narrow view, both from within Christian theology and in response to ecology's challenges. This will be attempted in the following chapters. Here it remains to find out why the narrow Christian response to ecological problems has been perpetuated and so often justified by the mainstream churches.

Up to now, the churches have justified their non-participation in environmental issues in various ways, but the nub of their argument is that they have more important things to do than address ecological issues, that is, that they must look after "immortal" souls destined for an eternal life after this one. Religious priority is given to the "moral" as distinct from the material. The "spiritual" well-being of a fallen humanity takes precedence over the physical reality of the natural world.

Some church spokesmen place the blame for the present ecological crisis on the same factors as do many ecologists: on the dualism of Hellenistic philosophy; on the psychology of Descartes, which divides the universe into living subjects and dead objects; on the mechanistic world view of Newtonian physics; on the rationalism of the Enlightenment and the capitalist and communist exploitation of labour and resources. But while blaming these, they continue to proclaim that the only subjectivity acted directly upon by God, in Jesus Christ, is a baptized human being, and that the arena of this action is the soul. This is based on the philosophy of Platonic hierarchy, which awards overriding merit to a particular category of soul.

Ecologist and Christian alike can agree on the first part of the above analysis. But some theologians and those ecologists concerned about the churches' role require a significant amendment to its conclusion: the Christian idea of person must itself be included in the catalogue of blame. The proof of this, if needed, is the role played by ecclesiastical colonizers in the scandalous treatment of indigenous peoples, on the grounds that they were less than human, or "soulless". The hard data of the European churches' involvement in human and natural degradation in the colonies should be acknowledged by them as a matter for formal repentance, especially in the decade which "celebrates" the conquest of the Americas by Christian Europe, and the beginnings of their ecological devastation.

Also, Christian ecofeminists want an honest appraisal of the destructive effects of Christian teachings on the relationship between women and Nature. These implicitly and sometimes explicitly downgrade them both as corrupt and corrupting. (See the Decrees of Gratian cited in the preceding chapter.) This has turned Christianity into the one legitimate and sanctified bastion of patriarchy (with all that this implies for attitudes to the earth), since these teachings are made in the name of a God who cannot err. Invariably they are based on male biblical interpretation which claims to be infallible. The male monopoly over theology has ensured that the Scriptures were and are read through a male (often celibate) lens, which disposes the readers to concentrate on texts which reinforce patriarchal authority and organization. The God of Christianity then appears to be perpetually on the side of the dominant male.[11]

Ecologists and some theologians want to point out that in making their analyses of ecological problems, the churches seem to place themselves and their traditions outside the cultural and scientific history influenced by Plato and those who have interpreted his thought in succeeding generations. In other words, they separate themselves from the historic contexts of the Christian tradition.

Once again the notion of Christian separateness from the world surfaces as the source of its ecological apartheid. Christianity seems to see itself subsist in a closed system cut off from those around it: yet its formulations of this closure are derived from the world-view of late classical civilisation which it seemingly eschews. The influence of Hellenic philosophy and concepts is plain to see in Christian doctrines of the soul, in Christian theological language and dualistic concepts, and in a Christian spirituality which still accepts the anti-body, anti-feminine view of late antique religious culture.[12]

The Effects of Disengagement

Analyzing the churches' present response to the ecological situation, one becomes aware of a significant gap in the logic. It might be called the absence of a presence. All those who try to find causes for the present crisis in order to prescribe remedies can understand how Plato, Aristotle, Descartes, Kant, Newton, Marx, Einstein and their intellectual descendants have contributed to it. What the Christian and non-Christian ecologist alike want to find is the contribution of Jesus Christ. Since it is the fundamental tenet of Christianity that he was as historical a person as any of the others, what has he contributed *to the world*? What does Christianity teach about his relationship with the interacting systems which sustained his life?

Some answers to these questions will be suggested later, particularly in Chapter 12. The concern here is the myopia of the Christian churches who see the villains responsible for ecological devastation as outside their number. This merely proves the non-Christian charge that the churches are unwilling to take responsibility for the world. Where were *you*, the ecologists ask (in a replay of God's part as interrogator in Job), when the world was being turned into a burnt-out monster by human institutions?

Up to now, the churches have proved as deaf to this indictment as they are blind to the need for their own involvement. There are some late appearances in the dock. The World Council of Churches has produced evidence of its concern in its programme called "Justice, Peace and the Integrity of Creation" (JPIC). The U.S. Bishops' Conference has presented two weighty Pastoral

Letters, the first "The Challenge of Peace: God's Providence and our response" (1983), and the second "Justice for all: Catholic Social Teaching and the U.S. Economy" (1986). The German Churches issued a joint statement on the environment in 1985, entitled: *Verantwortung wahrnehmen für die Schöpfung* (Taking Responsibility for Creation).

But this has done little to change the general perception of the churches' role. As a simple test, ask how many sermons treat ecological issues, or try yourself to introduce the subject in a religious gathering. You may well be told, as I have been, that it has nothing to do with religion.

There are two main reasons for this. One, which has been discussed to some extent already, is the a-historical perspective with which some churches work. The other is an obsession with internal church politics.

The a-historical perspective requires and fosters a theology which regards itself and its deliberations as a pure deposit handed on in a social, political and cultural vacuum. It is essentially to do with the sacred and not the secular. This distinction lies behind the ongoing debate about Bonhoeffer's decision to be actively involved with the antiNazi movement. It lies behind Vatican strictures on liberation theologians for their involvement in political action. It is interesting in this context to read the debate on John Robinson's book *Honest To God*, which was attacked for its perceived "secularization" of Christianity. Indicative of this outlook is the fact that not one "secular" ecological or conservation body was invited to contribute to the debate at the major gathering of the JPIC network in Seoul in March 1990.

A theologian working on the JPIC programme, Douglas Hall, who has taken part in some preparatory interdisciplinary talks, defines the attitude responsible for this Christian separatism as the "almost exclusive preoccupation with the human *soul*, and a language of heavenly longing" which pervades Christian theology and piety. This has created, he says, a climate of opinion – at least among the peoples of the Northern hemisphere – which encourages human beings and communities to regard the natural world as a mere stage upon which to play out their historic roles.

It is this, he thinks, which has prevented the churches from devoting much time to the third sub-theme of the triad Justice, Peace, and the Integrity of Creation. Are we hesitant to embark on it, he asks, because we recognize at some level of our subconsciousness an awareness of how it might call into question whole segments of our dearly held doctrines, and challenge the very foundations of our faith? He goes on:

> For one thing, we have never been able clearly to make up our minds whether this world – this material creation, this earth, this flesh – should be for us a matter of "ultimate concern" (Tillich). Can we love both God *and* the world? If so, then why have we been able to inculcate in our members and adherents over the centuries so little by way of concrete love of this world, particularly its non-human parts?[13]

Another cause of disengagement from ecological concerns is an obsession with internal ecclesiastical crises. Writing in *The Ecumenical Review* in April 1988 on the future of the JPIC programme, the theologian Ronald Preston is gloomy about what he calls its potentially fragmented nature and the lack of commitment to it by the Roman Church (which took up only twenty out of fifty places offered to it at Seoul). He offers questions for clarification which would ease the way to co-operation. One will suffice: "What are the parameters of proper church commitments in areas of social ethics, as distinct from the role of the lay person as citizen?" Judged by the usual time-scale of ecumenical discussions, when we have an answer to this question which satisfies all the churches, there will be no one left to hear it.

Positive Theological Responses

In contrast to this disengagement, for some theologians the ecological crisis is seen to offer an unprecedented opportunity for global ecumenism. There will be no worldwide ecumenism without creation-centred spirituality. For ecumenism is not a pious duty or one more commitment: it is an overflow of the relationship we experience with all that is.[14] After all, ecumenism comes from the same word *oikos* (house/home/habitat) as ecology, and the *oikumene* means "all the inhabited world". All living creatures are born from the earth, nurtured from it and return to it. If this truth were taken seriously, then we might begin to see how it cuts through religious differences and touches spiritual points of convergence.

We might also live to worship in a global church which is not obsessed with Western/Eastern or Reformation/Counter-Reformation ideologies of Salvation and/or Atonement, and which separates out Christians accordingly. We might be able to join in praise with a church which does not set itself apart from the rest of the world faiths on the assumption that it alone has been picked out by God for salvation. Then it could gladly include other religions in its prayer and in its celebration of creation.

We might also learn to live ecologically in a church which teaches ecological disciplines as expressions of divine courtesy. The fourteenth century woman mystic Julian of Norwich speaks of the divine courtesy of God which places restraints on God's omnipotence so that he can be "familiar" with us. Because it does not dominate, this courtesy allows all creatures the freedom to grow and be themselves. Such imagery depicts God relating to the world as a being among beings.

Commenting on this, the theologian Grace Jantzen remarks that we think too easily of creation as the manifestation of God's supreme power, calling beings into existence. There is truth in this, she says, but it must be qualified. For a Christian, if the cross is the ultimate reference point, the supreme power is not domination but love. Julian came to understand creation as the self-giving love of God, and an immediate result of this was her appreciation that all created things are good in themselves.[15] This insight is of paramount importance in a culture which devalues other beings into "things", instruments of use or gain to humanity.

Not only that, Julian also thought that since all things are created and are preserved by the love of God, their natural state is to reciprocate that love as best they can. This belief persisted for a long time in Celtic Christianity. In his book of prayers, hymns and incantations collected orally in Gaelic in the Highlands and Islands of Scotland, Alexander Carmichael records the following statement from a woman crofter:

> My mother would be asking us to sing our morning song to God down in the back-house, as Mary's lark was singing it up in the clouds, and as Christ's mavis was singing it yonder in the tree, giving glory to the God of the creatures for the repose of the night, for the light of the day, and for the joy of life. She would tell us that every creature on the earth here below and in the ocean beneath and in the air above was

giving glory to the great God of the creatures and the worlds, of the virtues and the blessings, and would *we* be dumb?[16]

This text is worth pondering, not least for the mother urging her children to take their pattern for praising God from the non-human creatures around them. It takes us back to the view of the physical world in sympathy with humanity which was mentioned at the beginning of this chapter. Reflecting on Matthew's account of the death of Jesus, in which the veil of the temple is rent in two, the earth shakes and the rocks are split, we find the same unity between Jesus and all the creatures which God had created. Nature reacted of itself to his death.

This echoes Isaiah's prophecy that "the earth shall be filled with the knowledge of God" when the Messiah comes (Isa. 11:9). Yet how little that knowledge is accepted in Christian churches – which profess belief that the Messiah *has* come in Jesus.

If we believe that this world is full of the knowledge of God, we must also believe that it has intrinsic value, since it lives in its own relationship with God. Then it is an open pathway to that knowledge for us. For the God of Jesus Christ celebrated in Christian churches is perceived to be the same God known by the earth, praised by all its creatures and reverenced in work by ecologists.

Chapter 5

The Traditional Christian Paradigm: Hierarchy

The problems in dialogue between ecologists and theologians highlighted in the previous chapter arise not only when segments of Christian doctrine are challenged or adhered to. The problems are symptomatic of a profound disparity between the ecological paradigm outlined earlier and the hierarchical paradigm which supports Christian belief. This disparity manifests itself at many levels, as we shall see. In order to recognize it and understand it, we shall examine this hierarchical paradigm just as we did the ecological one. Its strong network of commitments – conceptual, theoretical, instrumental and linguistic – supports Christianity as it is commonly understood.

It also determines, to a large extent, Christian attitudes to creation, attitudes now seen as contributing to the environmental crisis. These have been enumerated by a number of theologians, and two representative lists of their findings are given below. The first is taken from a EuroAmerican theologian, Thomas Berry, and the second from a Sri Lankan, Tissa Balasuriya. Their different perceptions of Christianity and its impact are part of the picture.

Common Christian Orientations

Berry enumerates what he calls "a number of religious orientations that have taken possession of Western consciousness to an exaggerated degree". Gathered together here for convenience, they run as follows:

> — *a transcendent personal monotheistic concept of deity with severe prohibition of any worship of divinity in Nature;*
> — *the redemption experience as the dominant mode of Christian consciousness;*
> — *the Christian emphasis on the spiritual nature of the human over against the physical nature of other creatures;*

85

—the expectation of an infra-historical millennial period in which the human condition will be overcome;

—an over-emphasis on verbal sources, mostly Biblical, and a consequent loss of revelation of the divine in Nature;

—too quick a movement from the merely physical order of things to the divine presence in things;

—religious traditions too distant from our new sense of the universe;

—divine-human mediation as the dominant context not only of religion but of the entire span of human activities;

—the emergence of the church with the sense of having an exclusive universal role in bringing about the spiritual well-being of a fallen world;

—maintaining that other religions' experience of the divine is simply the consequence of natural reason and not valid revelatory experience communicated by the divine;

—an attitude that diversity should not be, that it is a hindrance to human well-being.

I would maintain that the above list, if its theological shorthand were transcribed and the notions behind it presented to an average Christian congregation, would be understood by them to include most if not all of what they have learnt as Christianity.

Balasuriya analyzes in a similar vein what he calls the orientation of Christianity since it was identified with male domination and the Holy Roman Empire. His list includes:

—theological and spiritual deviation from Jesus Christ and acceptance of the West European model of expansion for the church's growth until expansion became an ultimate value;

—the alliance with capitalism, which fostered many anti-evangelical values and practices, such as the destruction of the economy of a colonized people, the creation of dependence, the exploitation of labour and resources, unfair terms of trade and the plunder from natural resources, witnessed to in the decoration of basilicas and cathedrals;

—the churches not facing squarely the questions of population, land and racism motivating the Euro-American world system;

—the churches' buttressing of male domination that characterizes the present world system;

—the split between scientific and theological world-views, in which scientists tend to study the universe only with the instruments of

quantitative measurement and enquiry because they cannot find meaningful motivation for their investigation from the Christian thinking of their day, and theologians tend to study the numinous without a clear relationship to the earth and earth processes;
— *science, technology and communications are utilized for power and profit in disregard for ethical values and Nature itself is subordinated to the exigencies of a rapacious capitalistic appetite;*
— *the impact of religionism on Christianity tends to consider one religion an end in itself and superior to all others;*
— *the central message of Jesus Christ – that God is love, and that we must love God and one another even to the extent of self-sacrifice – has not been applied to colonized and exploited peoples, but the emphasis of the church has been on making Christians, just as the emphasis of capitalism has been on making profits.*[1]

Asked to describe the paradigm on which these attitudes and orientations are based, the average congregation would find it difficult if not impossible. By its very nature, it is clear that the Christian paradigm, no less than the ecological one, will be attributed to people who would not use the term paradigmatic of their own thinking, and who would not be able to explicate their Christian belief in an orderly fashion. They see it as a motivating force in their lives rather than a product of reflection or concerted intellectual effort. Bearing that in mind, as well as the historical diversity and complexity of the Christian tradition, I would still maintain that, like other discernible groups, Christians think about the world in a particular way and take for granted that it is ordered according to certain values. This affects the way in which they integrate the different aspects of their lives into a coherent whole. They work with an image of the universe which both validates and maintains a specific social order. It also authorizes a moral code which, as Godgiven, appears to be a construct beyond criticism or human emendation.

"Myth" is the usual term for such a construct in the religious sense. However, I do not use this term here as it needs too many qualifications to be helpful. Nevertheless, some of its many uses are included in what I am calling the Christian paradigm. Whoever lives mythically, she or he is experiencing life as meaningful. A meaningless life is one of disconnections. Myths function as the building materials of reality, connecting mind and body, matter and spirit, people and their experience.[2]

In the generation and regeneration of Christian identity, the language of Christianity is crucially important since it builds and uses images which shape thoughts and reinforce attitudes from one generation to the next. The boundaries of our imaginative structures are set by the common perception of what it means to be Christian. Through liturgy, teaching and assimilation of concepts, belief in an exclusive relationship between Christians and the transcendent God of the Bible is inculcated, which includes the assumption that we have the only perfect revelation of God in Jesus Christ.

The pattern of this belief was outlined in the previous chapter at the points where it mismatches the ecological view. Notably, Christians make a distinction between the earthly order and the heavenly in favour of the latter. The earth and all it contains are valued as means to an end: the human soul's survival in a new and better world. In contrast to this, ecology insists that the earth is to be valued for its own sake.

The Christian paradigm therefore, consciously or not, produces in those who live by it a sense of separateness from the world. Christianity perceives itself as and seems to operate as a closed system, protected from the earthly systems surrounding it by virtue of its special relationship with the God of Jesus Christ. Other living systems, whether religious, cultural or societal are measured against exclusive Christian norms, and accepted or rejected accordingly. So, living with souls in the clouds, as it were, Christians take account of the earth beneath their feet only in so far as it grounds them in their God-given place in the order of things.

This notion of divine ordering and its consequences for Christian thought and behaviour will now be examined in some detail. Its most salient feature ecologically is that it gives supremacy to man. This position is awarded to him in the belief that there is a unique relationship between him and God set within a hierarchical structure: God above angels above man above woman above animals above Nature. God is separated from Nature by graded orders of being, with man "supergraded" over other life on earth.

This sets Christian life within the context of relationship with a God who is transcendent, situated "above" and "outside" all earthly systems as their one and only God. This transcendent God has divine monopoly over all creatures and rules them as supreme monarch. Divine control on the one hand requires total obedience on the other.

Taking the notion of transcendence seriously, Christianity rightly insists on God's unknowability, on God's existence above and beyond our sensual knowledge or human powers of conceptualisation. But this truth has been trapped in a hierarchical concept which places God at the pinnacle of being, "up there", invisible spirit, separated eternally from the lowest in the hierarchy, Nature. The very word "hierarchy" (sacred government or rule) denotes classification in successively subordinate grades, based on the image of collective groupings of archangels and angels below God. These have been given telling names such as thrones, dominations and principalities, which automatically bring to mind the power of one group to rule over the one beneath. The concept of hierarchy has become a governing principle in secular affairs. It is Christianity's ruling principle also, where it is hallowed by use and sanctified by association with heavenly rule.

The Divine Hierarchy of Denys the Areopagite

The Christian mystic known as Denys (or Dionysius) the Areopagite is credited with first use of the word *hierarchia* (hierarchy), and it seems to be his own coinage. It is composed of two Greek words meaning "sacred" and "source or principle". He used the concept of hierarchy in working out a cosmic pattern of government described as follows: *Thearchy* (Trinity) presides above *Celestial Hierarchy* (three grades of angels) above *Ecclesiastical Hierarchy* (bishops graded above priests above laity). This ranking is more than order: it refers also to what this sacred ordering makes possible; knowledge and activity:

> Hierarchy is, in my opinion, a holy order and knowledge and activity which, so far as is attainable, participates in the Divine Likeness, and is lifted up to the illuminations given it from God, and correspondingly towards the imitation of God. Now the beauty of God, being unific, good, and the Source of all perfection, is wholly free from dissimilarity, and bestows its own light on each according to his merit. The aim of hierarchy is the greatest possible assimilation to and union with God.[3]

The knowledge mediated by hierarchies is conceived by Denys in terms of light: illumination flowing out from the supreme

Godhead and irradiating the whole created order. The threefold
movement in this irradiation he calls purification, illumination
and union. These are operations that happen to us: we are
purified by God, illuminated by God, united with God. We
depend on God's gracious movement towards us. Relationships
within the earthly hierarchies depend on and reflect that between
the members of the supreme One: the Trinity. The mystical
relationship of Father, Son and Spirit proceeds from the
monarchy of the Father who sends his Son "down" into the
world. This pattern of derived spiritual authority is replicated
through the orders of angels and human beings. Angels are
literally those who are "sent": messengers from God. In
Christianity, apostles are those sent by Jesus even as he was
sent by God.[4] Denys' understanding of hierarchy is of the
overflowing of God's love, of God's active search for humankind
and gentle persuasion of fallen human beings. The members of
a hierarchy are a community seeking to draw near to God and
draw others near to God. It is a community being saved and
mediating salvation. Its presence expresses the transcendent love
of God made immanent.

However, the language in which his vision was described
spoke of low, middle and high orders of being and movement;
of graded stages of divine knowledge and spiritual activity. The
basic Platonic structure of this movement was between the One
(God) and the material world, in which an outward movement
of progressively diminishing radiation from God is met by a
movement of yearning on the part of all beings for unity. Reality
itself is perceived as arranged in graded levels that mediate and
relate one to another, as hierarchies linked up with one another
through a cosmic sympathy that embraces the whole.[5]

The basic structure of hierarchy carries through, according to
Denys, into the human order. In his book *Ecclesiastical Hierarchy*,
he sees the orders in the church as the extension of spiritual
reality, a hierarchy of sacraments, ministers and those to whom
they minister. A further manifestation of this ordering ranks
different locations in church buildings, with primacy given to
the sanctuary. The ordering of those who used the building
follows suit, with the ministers in the sanctuary separated from
those outside it.

Commenting on this, Andrew Louth says he is struck by how
masculine a picture this ordered arrangement is. Presumably

women were included in the laity outside the sanctuary, but there is not a word of it.[6] This masculine mystical vision of Denys, his apprehension of God's love for the world and its mediation in communities of beings has remained a force in Eastern and Western Christianity. Orthodox liturgies still resonate with this sense of the Oneness of being united in love. The ordering has been formalized in Western Christianity, inwardly, liturgically and publicly. The systematic application of the hierarchical principle has become normative and has been used as a framework for subsequent theological and church systems. This has determined their character to the point where this "divine" order of things is accepted and adopted *as divine*, rather than as the expression of one gifted individual's insight into the mystery of God.

The Vatican II document on the Church, *Lumen Gentium*, takes this "divine" character of hierarchy for granted. It contains a long and important chapter on "The Hierarchical Structure of the Church" (Chapter III), which says unequivocally that the divine sending by Christ of the apostles

> will last until the end of the world (Matt. 28:20), since the gospel which was to be handed down by them is for all time the source of all life for the church. For this reason the apostles took care to appoint successors in *this hierarchically structured society* [italics added].[7]

Such an orderly concept of the universe had and continues to have great appeal. It offers the security and certainty we all crave. It has been accepted as the master pattern for Christian thinking and metaphor right down to the present day. There is not much time spent on the place and role of the angels, but the pattern of the sending Father, the sent and sending Son and the sent Spirit holds sway over Western theological imagination. Attempts like Moltmann's to break the mould by using Byzantine concepts of the interactive roles of the Trinitarian persons have not percolated into either Catholic or Protestant consciousness in any meaningful way. Some of the reasons for this are directly linked to the threat felt when dearly-held doctrines are questioned. For example, the *Filioque* controversy between Eastern and Western Christendom, which seeks to absolutize the place of the Holy Spirit within their respective hierarchies, has been sustained throughout the centuries by the reactions of those hierarchies to any change in their perceived roles.

So the pattern of hierarchy continues to shape Western Christian consciousness, which in turn affects its attitudes to Nature, to all that is ranked "below" man, to all that is "outside" the sanctuary. It is a world-view which *separates*: clergy from laity, humanity from Nature and the world from God. It has endured because it invests man with superiority over all that is supposedly below him on the scale of being.

The God at the apex of this structure (for the notion of pulsating outward movement in Denys was gradually reduced to vertical motion from "above" to "below") appears accessible only to those human souls who purge themselves of the things of this world, that is, who "ascend" by separating themselves from everything "below" them:

> God wishes to be known, and it pleases him that we should rest in him; for everything which is beneath him is not sufficient for us. And this is the reason why no soul is at rest until it has despised as nothing all things which are created.[8]

The Hierarchical Grading of Reality

Asked to depict his relationship with the world, the average person would probably give a sketch of a detached observer vis-à-vis the globe. This goes back to the split consciousness which was discussed earlier. If the same test were given as a theological exercise, and the average Christian asked to include his relationship to God, the odds are that the picture would be that of a pyramid or hierarchy. In it, the earth and its creatures would be placed at the bottom, supporting man in the middle who is reaching upwards through space in the direction of a God enthroned above the angels. Such pictures are common in children's religious books.

The most succinct and memorable verbal expression of this comes from Psalm 8, which addresses this God and asks rhetorically: "What is man that thou art mindful of him? Thou hast created him a little lower than the angels and hast put everything else under his feet".[9]

There are some, myself among them, who would protest that such hierarchical patterns or images together with their spoken and unspoken inferences do no justice to the concept of God's transcendence as it has been properly understood by poets, mystics, philosophers and theologians. It certainly does not do justice to Denys. But we are talking about the common perception of God's transcendence which has been systematized into visible ecclesiastical hierarchies, hard-programmed into Christian consciousness as doctrine, reinforced by religious education and canonized in sermons.

John Robinson made precisely this point when his critics denounced him for his exposition of the distorted and common-place view of God's transcendence which he encapsulated in the phrase "God up there". It provoked the reaction: "But that's not what I mean by religion at all. It's a caricature". Of course it's a caricature, he replied, if by that is meant that no intelligent Christian or deeply religious person of any period has *only* had this understanding of religion. Of course, by itself it's a perversion, and it is possible to quote from every classic of the spiritual life that this is not what the masters or indeed the ordinary faithful have said or meant. But such views have been accepted and continue to be recounted as part and parcel of the usual Christian way of looking at the world.[10] In particular, this defective notion of transcendence has affected Christian attitudes to Nature and has created clusters of popular metaphors and images. Singing to a God "enthroned on high" and praying constantly for the Holy Spirit to "descend" on us reinforces the idea that all that is good, just, holy and powerful is "up there" somewhere. So that is where our gaze is usually fixed in prayer, figuratively anyway, not "down" on this earth. There is an intrinsic link between the accepted structuring of reality, our language and our behaviour. One can only imagine how differently Christians would relate to the earth if Hildegard of Bingen's image of the Spirit of God as the root of the world tree had been hard-programmed into us instead. How truly revolutionary it would be to turn our gaze on the earth as we invoke the Spirit's power.

Both the usual Christian picture of a hierarchical order and the imagery of Psalm 8 give the illusion that reality is ordered according to rank. This is implicit in "grading" levels of being. Things are then valued according to whether they are "up" or "down" on the scale. Not only does this give the impression that some things are more valuable than others in relation to God, but it also implies that what is more valuable on this scale, that is, nearer to "the top", has dominion and power over that which is lower and therefore has less "value". In the hierarchical/patriarchal system out of which Christian theology has emerged, only the child ranked beneath the woman. But the girl child was considered of infinitely less value than the boy child. The only human creature lower than the girl child was the boy child who had no father, no name, no lineage – a bastard.[11]

Images which place some things above or separate from others are conveying messages about value, about power, about relationship. These are not always open to reasoned exposition but nevertheless influence us and our conduct enormously. And any fair-minded reader would admit that the images and metaphors of transcendence which have been hard–programmed into common Christian consciousness have played a part in licensing attitudes to those "below" us on the scale of value which are a continuing scandal to the world.

This becomes even clearer when the hierarchical paradigm is contrasted with the ecological one. In the latter, a system is a unit of living space in which everything affects everything else. The differences between things generate energy and keep the system going. Large and small, round and square, heavy and light, symmetrical and odd, each thing contributes its particular character to the whole. *You can't rank the diversity that maintains a system* because each element has its part to play. All are important in sustaining life. In the strict sense of the words, there is no such thing as self-sufficiency. Yet hierarchical thinking encourages man to believe that he is "above" or "in charge of" his ecosystem. In truth, he now seems to be in charge only of its destruction.

When the diversity within creation is not valued, then devaluation of difference occurs. Differentiation at the human, animal and plant level is no longer a cause of wonder and joy, but something to be eliminated by adherence to and application of norms. These supposedly ensure the maintenance of what is ranked "superior" on the hierarchical scale and the discontinuance of whatever is ranked as "inferior".

In contrast to this, at the Faith and Ecology Conference in Canterbury in 1989, Dr Ruth Page from Edinburgh Faculty of Theology was asked to sit in on the practical workshops and then make some theological comment on them. She said that as a result of all that she had heard about the necessity for biological diversity, she began to understand what it means to say that God enjoys diversity. Our God is the God of all species, not just the human one.[12]

The application of norms works in different ways and at many levels throughout Western culture. They are established according to the hierarchical context. Eugenics for example, has physical, intellectual and psychological norms which aim to eliminate the deviant and the disabled from the human race. In agriculture, some Western-style "development" programmes in Sri Lanka decided on norms of high crop yield which separated out "superior" strains of rice for intensive cultivation. The elimination of "inferior" ones left the people with twenty to thirty varieties instead of about three hundred. It also left them with soil exhausted by monoculture.

Within Christianity, ingrained hierarchical thinking contributes to the devaluing of human diversity and to the exhaustion of theological imagination. When personal differences are perceived, this differentiation is not seen as a source of joy and energy to either God or the Christian, but is contrasted with the supposed norm of a perfect man, Adam "before the Fall". There is a kind of eugenics in reverse at work, in that we keep looking *back* to what we are supposed to be. Our perception of ourselves as "below" the norm makes us dissatisfied with our diversity (perceived as inferiority). Human life *as such*, as we actually live it and experience it, is devalued. And so is the place where we are forced to live out our sub-standard lives, the earth.

Where do we get the low self-esteem that keeps so many confessors, doctors and therapists busy if not from some feeling that we fall below an imagined norm? This unhealthy state is quite distinct from an actual experience of sin or ill-health. It relies to some extent on what we might call "the Paradise Factor": the hard-programmed Christian interpretation of Genesis which turns the expulsion from Paradise into the "Descent of Man" from his privileged place next to God. Now an angel with a flaming sword separates them one from the other. In many artistic representations of this scene Adam and Eve gaze back with longing at Paradise lost; and so too does the Christian viewer.

Furthermore, insofar as this premise of the inferiority of present human life is accepted, Christians may despair of their own ability to tackle the massive problems connected with global environmental devastation. They identify the results of human actions with the consequences of "original sin", that is, with an innate tendency to destruction. Not only that, they categorize Nature itself as "fallen" through man's sin. That which is higher on the scale of being has power to affect that which is lower.

The Pope's message for World Peace Day, on 8 December 1989, speaks of Adam and Eve's call to share in the unfolding of God's plan of creation, in which they were to have exercised their dominion over the earth with wisdom and love. "Instead, they destroyed the existing harmony by deliberately going against the Creator's plan, that is, by choosing to sin. This resulted not only in man's alienation from himself, in death and fratricide, but also in the earth's 'rebellion' against him. All creation became subject to futility".

Christians are taught to live with this imputed futility by believing that "the death and resurrection of Christ accomplished the work of reconciling humanity to the Father. Creation was thus made new . . . When man turns his back on the Creator's plan, he provokes a disorder which has inevitable repercussions on the rest of the created order. If man is not at peace with God, then earth itself cannot be at peace". The means of reconciling us to God here and now are found through baptism into the second Adam, Jesus Christ. This is the definitive and exclusive Christian norm. It supposedly enables us to live on a level "above" ordinary human nature (super-nature) and therefore above non-Christians.

The patriarchal language of this teaching assumes that the male relationship with God and earth is the norm. But what of Nature? Is there any reconciling baptism offered to it by Christianity? Evidently there can be none, for baptism is only offered to those human beings who profess belief in Jesus Christ.[13]

It is now becoming clear how hierarchy works as a principle of separation and subordination: between God and angels, angels and man, man and woman, baptized Christian and unbaptized pagan, humanity and Nature. Corresponding to this is a progressive devaluing of the second member of each class of being, and an increasing sense of powerlessness as one descends the scale. The whole structure is based on the premise that God created some beings inferior to others. We seem to be ranked by divine decree.

It should also be becoming clear how unecological an outlook this is. If one species is intended to dominate another, and that species the human one, then man can continue to control and exploit all those "below" him.

His supposed supremacy does not consist in this alone. The putative move upwards on the Christian scale of being, baptism, brings him closer to the life of the transcendent God, the Father. Proportionately, it moves the unbaptized down on the scale of value. A lower form of life, they are seen as expendable or saveable, depending on the era or their place in Christian expansionist policies.

The history of the Crusades, of the Inquisition and of the European colonies records Christianity's righteous hatred of diverse creeds and cultures: its extinction of those peoples devalued because they do not have a "normal" Christian relationship with God, Father of Jesus Christ. Indigenous races were reduced to perpetual slavery and their kingdoms and all their possessions appropriated with full religious legitimation through no less than sixty-nine pontifical Bulls.[14]

In general, the Christian desire to move ourselves "upwards" has been internalized and sanctified as an endeavour to be Godlike. The record of this aspiration in Christianity is a long one, going back to the seminal utterance of Irenaeus endorsed by Athanasius: "God became man, so that man might become God."

Luther tried to correct this when he said: "God became man so that man might become fully human". But his correction has never been absorbed into the Christian psyche in the same way as the original misconception, one reason being that a hierarchical perception of man presupposes the urge to climb upwards. It is not enough to be "merely" human.

It is not only in the individual's relation to God that human diversity is devalued in a hierarchy. At the social level, diversity among people according to colour, race, gender and sexual inclination is measured against supposed human norms of whiteness, maleness and heterosexuality. Such are the usual standards establishing one's place on the ladder. Others, such as class, education, health or creed, are all part of an "upwardly mobile" society, and, one must add, Church. The way to be accepted in ecclesiastical structures is to conform to such norms. Those who don't are devalued, ignored or rejected outright.

Reactions to Hierarchical Grading

There is, and always has been, based on the example of Jesus, a reaction within Christianity against this inferiorization of certain groups. The liberation theologies of to-day, wherever they are articulated, spring from the refusal of devalued people to accept their designated place on the hierarchical scale. Their theologies express the liberating experience of realizing that these hierarchies are *not* divine structures. They are man-made – and therefore they can be changed by human action. The rules which constrict our lives and vision are inherited from those who have gone before us, and are not handed down by divine decree. Therefore liberation theologians give voice to their belief in the love of God for each individual being regardless of human norms, and express the hope and determination to live accordingly.

Feminist theology refuses to accept the male relationship with God as the human norm. By insisting on the value of the female relationship and the importance of its expression, it frees women to speak about and to God on their own behalf. Ecofeminist theology broadens this liberative outlook by refusing to accept the devaluation of Nature within the Christian hierarchy. In community with those devalued by race it says with the black poet Aimé Césaire:

> I would come to that country, my country, and I would say to it:
> "Kiss me without fear . . . And if I do not know what to say, it is still for you that I speak."
> And I would say to it:
> "My mouth shall be the mouth of misfortunes which have no mouth, my voice the freedom of those freedoms which break down the prison-cell of despair."[15]

The self-perception of black people, not only in the "Third" World but also in America and Great Britain, is subverted by white ecclesiastical hierarchies. Until very recently, white clergy, liturgy and congregations were the standards by which all others were judged. White Christian Europe sees itself as the norm in a hierarchy where, as *First*, it rates Second and Third Worlds on descending scales of wealth, resources, technology – and religious authority. Césaire cries out for all those devalued by norms, whether of maleness, whiteness, sexuality or the possession of a baptized soul. Images in traditional myths, art and Christian theology have tended to depict light as good, dark as evil. And it is a very small step from there to the idea that white is good and black is evil. The negative connotations in this dualism go all the way back to the Pythagorean philosophers who taught that maleness and goodness belong to the light, but femaleness and badness belong to the dark.

Therefore those devalued by Christianity, consciously or not, may be women who, in a male Christianity, find themselves supposedly made in the likeness of the devil and not in the likeness of God, as Gratian decreed. They may be blacks who are baptized into a Church where to be a Negro is like being a second-grade clerk, waiting for better things but with no hope of promotion.[16]

Both blacks and women have been associated with all that is furthest from God on the hierarchical scale, with materiality and corporeality that must be purified, refined or baptized by white men to achieve union with God. Césaire and ecofeminist theologians speak also on behalf of the voiceless earth, for matter, soil, materiality. This is thrice condemned to misfortune: through association with human villainy, whether by direct action or through supposed involvement in man's sin; through the lack of common redemption from that villainy; through being associated with all that is furthest from God hierarchically. Ecofeminists identify with and speak for Nature in its oppression; for its right to be valued for its own relationship with its Creator; in the knowledge of its goodness which is a source of joy to God regardless of whether or not it is acknowledged by the human race. They refuse to accept the reality imaged in an unjust God who sentences Nature to "futility" because of its involuntary relationship with man, and then extends a reprieve to certain chosen men alone.

Through this lens of the enjoyment and valuing of diversity, hierarchical norms within Christianity are seen as sanctified devaluation of women and Nature. Those churches which publicly order themselves on hierarchies, with male clergy "above" laity, inevitably manifest characteristics of dominion over those "below", and in this way the religious devaluation of the latter is both accepted and internalized. Their powerlessness is assured and legitimized when they are taught that the male ecclesiastical hierarchy is the reflection and the instrument of a celestial one where God the Father reigns supreme. The hierarchical principle of A talking to C through B is implemented so that the male ruling body of a church (B) claims unique possession of the Spirit (A) and sole power to speak to the laity (C) in its name (as in the Vatican II Document already mentioned).[17]

Patriarchy and Hierarchy

It is a moot point here whether hierarchy precedes patriarchy or merely sanctifies it. The inferiorization of women has been justified throughout western religious history by their classification as "deficient" males. Debates were held as to why they were created at all. It was concluded that they were necessary for procreation. Augustine is the classical source of this type of patriarchal anthropology transformed into Christian teaching. Aquinas continued the Augustinian tradition, but added to it the Aristotelian definition of woman as a "misbegotten male". According to Luther, her punishment for being the cause of Adam's fall was that she lost her original equality with him and became inferior in mind and body. Therefore she is now subjected to the male. This is divine justice, to be accepted by her without cavil. She must not deepen her reproach by rebelling against her subordination as one whose sinfulness brought her to this state of subjugation.[18]

Through such teaching Christianity reinforced with its spiritual authority all that was oppressive of women in the hierarchical culture that was the context for the rise of Christendom. Its institutionalizing of sex-gender roles perpetuated patriarchal structures of authority.

The same sanctified tyranny was and is endured by those who are not "normal", i.e. heterosexual, males. Homosexuality is defined by church authorities as a *dis*order, a form of illness or retardment. Its practices are usually condemned as sinful. The present attitudes of some Christians to Aids sufferers is particularly offensive in that their suffering and rejection is being justified as divine punishment. Some sermons and synodical debates adopt the "high" moral ground, giving homosexuals the added burden of being condemned because they supposedly offend not only against human norms but against *God's* norm. In the present debate about repealing the law in Ireland which makes homosexual activity a criminal offence, the late Archbishop of Dublin is quoted as saying that mankind makes a serious error in determining sexual values *independently of God*. In other words, God has given us the norms.

This hierarchical imposition of norms embodies a refusal to consider the diversity of creation as a source of joy to the Creator and enrichment for the whole systemic creature earth. It presents it instead as a threat. Christian hierarchies operate by excluding, in the name of Jesus Christ, those who deviate from an inferred divine norm whether of gender, conduct or creed. Yet this same Jesus lived and died embodying the scandal of inclusiveness for his time.[19] This hierarchical exclusion contrasts with an ecological system, where it is recognized that the greater the diversity of a community, the greater is its resilience and adaptability, and that its survival depends on a balance of diversities, not their elimination. This is extended into a religious perception by Native American peoples, who see difference not as alien or abnormal or threatening, but as another reflection of spirituality.[20]

Consequences for Nature

Christians are as much part of the prevailing hierarchical non-ecological culture as any other group. They have inherited notions of separateness from Nature and scientific attitudes of detachment and experimentation. They too endorse the instrumental value system that operates globally and fosters non-participating consciousness in other citizens of the world. They go along with hierarchical structures in family life, in government, in the Army, in corporation management and the professions. The university "processions" at Degree ceremonies, the legal processions at the opening of Sessions and the State procession at the opening of Parliament are accepted by them unquestioningly as proper demonstrations of hierarchical civic order.

So when Christians use natural terms pejoratively for human conduct they are indistinguishable from the culture around them. Common metaphors for devaluing people are those which associate them with animals: "silly bitch", "clumsy ass", "stupid cow", "greedy pig", "brute" and "beast". The lowest standard of living, the dirtiest behaviour, are associated with Nature rather than with "normal" human aspiration. "Offal", "dung" and "worm" describe the nadir of existence. When Job collapsed onto the dung-heap, his degradation was complete. When the Psalmist wanted to express anguish at being despised, rejected and assaulted by his fellows, he spoke of himself as a worm, not a man.

But uniquely in the Western world, Christians take the supposedly divine hierarchical structuring of cosmic reality as justification for unecological attitudes to Nature. The dominion of man over fallen Nature is taken for granted. This expresses itself in a Christian constellation of dualistic ideas and attendant metaphors in continuity with the Greek philosophical ideas considered earlier.

The premise for these in Christianity also is the fundamental hierarchal form of a notional ladder rising from the immanent (this worldly) to the transcendent (other-worldly). Its function is to provide a way of climbing up, rung by rung, from the immanent to the transcendent. The rungs keep those above separate from those below. As we climb up on to each one, we are able to wield power over those below, and must bow to the authority of those above. The higher we go, the fewer people we find (Plato's Guardians). So a smaller number exercises power over a much larger mass. Those at the top are separated not only in power but also in value from those beneath them.

If we take the ladder as a whole, then the top can be opposed to the bottom in a judgmental manner. It always "comes out on top" in power, in value, in transcendence.

This logical manoeuvre gives the basis for Christian dualism. God and the world, the spiritual and the material, the sacred and the profane are apparently locked into eternal opposition. They seem to exist in separation from each other, and therefore one can and ought to opt for the "top" rather than the "bottom". Christians are exhorted to "choose the things that are above". We saw this kind of logic at work in the apparent choice to be made between ecology and theology, which seemed to present a Christian with an either/or situation: to choose to work for this world or for God.

There is an underlying suggestion here that even though God is all–powerful, yet the spiritual, the sacred and the light are always in danger of being overwhelmed by the material, the profane and the dark. This echoes the Greek dichotomy between the realm of necessity, *chaos*, and that of freedom, *kosmos*. A lot of energy is put into marking off their separate territories, or "kingdoms", and defending the "higher, valuable, Godlike" ones. So the pathway of Christianity can appear closed off from all the systems around it, or as one which exists on a "higher" level than all the others in our lives. It seemingly follows that God has nothing to do with dirt, sex, natural functions or anything which connects us to the animal world or the earth.[21]

This cosmic dualism apparently keeps God on the far side of the gulf which separates him from the world he has created. He transcends, stands independent of all material bodies. In so far as this world is material, it is utterly other than God. Thomas Aquinas wrote categorically: "God and prime matter are distinguished: one is pure act, the other is pure potency, and they agree in nothing."[22] This is often taken to mean that we have a split between God and the world of such magnitude that we could not learn anything about the nature of God from the nature of the world. A further implication I see is that for Christians the world is then perceived as not worth knowing: compared to God, that is.

The distinction made between God and the world to the total disadvantage of the latter has been a major influence on the Christian idea of person. The human mind is identified as the bearer of the image of God, and the body identified with the world. The body is opposed to the mind, and is to be subordinate to thought or reason. It is characteristic of the patriarchal shaping of Christian consciousness that reason is generally considered a masculine principle, ordained to rule the material body. This has only instrumental, transient value compared to the innately valuable, eternal soul.

The God of this Christianity is not only transcendent and male: He is One, and there cannot be any other for a Christian. There are severe prohibitions against worship of divinity elsewhere, and no allowance made for any residing in Nature. Man's unique situation on the ladder between earth and heaven brings him closer to God than any other living being. This proximity to transcendence is the presupposition for the supremacy of man. He is considered to be the only being capable of knowing God (*capax Dei*), or of being like God (*imago Dei*). Therefore he is the only bearer of soul in the Christian sense. "*Man* is like to God in his soul". Augustine wrote: "For not in the body but in the mind was *man* made in the image of God" [italics added]. The Neo-Platonism he bequeathed to Christianity used the concept of soul and mind interchangeably.[23]

This idea of person as an amalgam of body (earthly) and soul (heavenly) creates another religious hierarchy of values which gives absolute control to human beings *of a certain kind*, namely, those with souls chosen to enjoy an exclusive relationship with the one God through the essential and exclusive Christian norm of baptism. Those who are baptized Christians are separated from all other human beings by having their souls marked forever. These souls, and these alone, are capable of knowing God properly or being Godlike. (This is reminiscent of Plato's 'golden' souls.)

The colonization of other continents by Western Christendom was accompanied by the extermination or enslavement of indigenous peoples, as we saw above. This was often given religious legitimation on the grounds that these had no souls. Or, if they had, then the priceless gift of baptism was more than compensation for their bodily and material destruction as slave labour.

But whatever time was spent on debating their possession of souls, none was wasted on considering the sacredness of their lands. These had been kept in ecological balance and continuous fertility by "savages" who respected the spirits of air, fire, earth and water. Christians who could not acknowledge any immanent divinity in Nature exploited and devastated native homelands without debate and with greedy enthusiasm. They distinguished themselves from non-Christians (and other religions like Jainism) by arguing that this is how God has made us (or should we say left us after Adam's sin?), graded in hierarchical order of importance and value. On this grading, the natural world is so far alienated from God on the scale of being that it has no soul. Therefore it is incapable of knowing God. Therefore it is valueless. This extrapolation from the "fallenness" of Nature is linked to the notion that man can be redeemed through baptism while Nature cannot be.

Hierarchically man is considered "above" woman on the scale of Christian being, and woman is linked to Nature. The Council of Macon in the sixth century debated her humanity. Three hundred years later, the revered and influential Abbot Odo of Cluny taught that hugging a woman was like embracing a sack of manure. It was during his lifetime that a Church Council decided, by a majority of one, that women had souls. Nevertheless, grave doubts continued to be expressed about this. Nine hundred years later, in 1854, an opposing speaker at the Philadelphia Woman Suffrage Convention said: "Let woman first prove that she has a soul, both the Bible and the Church deny it".[24]

The charge of "mindlessness" against women discussed in the opening chapters was only a post-Enlightenment variation on expressed Christian doubts about their having souls. Women's supposed lack of soul implied that they could not be Godlike, while males could, and male language for God was therefore appropriate. It is no accident that the theological discussion in this chapter uses male language for God and our relationship with him, since this is the norm in all the standard textbooks on the subjects raised. By now I hope my discomfort with this will be shared by my readers.

The slavery of non-Christian savages and women shared a common justification, their inferiority to white men. It is no accident then that modern feminism arose within the debate about the rights and wrongs of slavery. In the emergent abolitionist movement a few white women began to stand up and attack as idolatrous and unthinkable the notion that black people were soulless, created by God to be inferior to whites. In rejecting the notion that blacks are "naturally" inferior, these white women began also to hear, in their own words, a message that should also apply to themselves and their position and rights in society. For the first time they began to ask: "Is woman's nature really proscribed by God as *different* from and *inferior* to men?"[25]

In spite of the abolition of slavery and women's franchise, the desouling process of all non-human forms of life has never been reversed in Canon Law. In Western political institutions, the nearest we have come to it is the United Nations Charter for Nature. But the churches continue to give a religious and political impetus to the Cartesian model of human knowledge which denies soul and consciousness to the non-human world.[26]

This confines subjectivity to human persons. Only they are permitted to be subjects, to be agents and doers. The Christian idea of person as the true focus of the divine and the only carrier of soul is basic to this world-view.

Religious Utilitarianism

Therefore the natural world continues to be seen by Christians as a vast and infinitely resilient reservoir from which to garner the raw materials for empires, an inanimate and unfeeling "thing" at the bottom of the hierarchy of being over which we have been granted unqualified "dominion" and which indeed we have a duty under God to "subdue". It has no intrinsic worth, only instrumental value for achieving the end for which man is created, the saving of his soul. It is not seen to possess rights or subjectivity or legal status, or as constituting with the human a single earth community.

A succinct expression of this attitude is found in the "Fundamental Principle" of the *Spiritual Exercises of St Ignatius*, a text which has had incalculable influence on recent Christian spirituality, and indeed on Western scientific consciousness also. It reads as follows:

> Man has been created to praise, reverence and serve our Lord God, thereby saving his soul.
> Everything else on earth has been created for man's sake, to help him to achieve the purpose for which he has been created.
> So it follows that man has to use them [*sic*] as far as they help and abstain from them where they hinder his purpose.

Later on in the Exercises, Ignatius explains the hierarchy of being on which the foregoing principle is based. God lives in his creatures, he says: giving matter existence, giving plants life, giving animals consciousness and giving men intelligence. "So he lives in me [man], giving me existence, life, consciousness, intelligence. More, he makes me his temple, since I have been created wearing the image and likeness of God."[27]

This presupposes that A (God) only communicates with C (the earth) through B (man). Those who believe and teach that the earth has been created *for man's sake* are "self-ordained" to communicate God's will to the earth. And in Christian teaching, that will has usually been proclaimed as man's right and duty to subdue it, have dominion over it and use it for the good of his soul. God seems to be distanced from earth entirely, and is only concerned with the end-product of its interaction with man, the salvation of the human soul.

The frightening overtones of *hubris* in this remind us of how potentially disastrous it is. Yet the model of "steward", in which man acts as intermediary between God and creation, continues to attract Christian interpreters. This model accepts hierarchical scales of power, value and control. It implies that man has been given a free hand with the earth, for good or ill, and that God is the prototypical absentee landlord who never visits the land but is only interested in banking the returns from it, i.e. human souls. "Good" stewards accumulate credits and are saved. "Wicked" ones squander and are damned. In contrast to this, the land restoration movement consists of people who see themselves as healers, rather than stewards. Stewards seek to optimize profits for themselves or their bosses. Healers seek to restore their own integrity as part of, not apart from, the integrity of the land. The model of stewardship is unecological.

The continuing influence of such models and the attitude to the world behind them makes understandable, if not excusable, the lack of Christian response to ecological imperatives. It is not always so clearly and unambiguously expressed as in the Ignatian Exercises, but it is illuminating to re-read some standard theological texts in the context of an ecological paradigm, especially those which are supposedly "green".

For example, the much-vaunted final document from the European Conference on Justice, Peace and the Integrity of Creation held at Basle in 1989 contains the following statement:

> Christian hope is the most dynamic stimulus to work courageously and ardently to render humankind more peaceful, more just, more filled with brotherly and sisterly love, more responsible for the stewardship of the creation *for the benefit of all men and women* and for the future of creation, living in universal solidarity [italics added].

The Secretary of the Conference of European Churches drew attention to this paragraph in a letter circulated to friends of the Conference, and went on to speak of the new post-Cold War Europe as the context "which challenges the churches of Europe to make their specific contribution to the *humanisation* of our societies and to the defence of *all humanity*" [italics added].[28] This Conference is the vanguard of the official Christian ecological response in Europe.

Differing Christian Orientations

Within the Christian tradition, the predominance of hierarchical thinking with its devaluation of everything natural has led to the neglect of other possible approaches to creation. Three examples follow.

1. The history of the cosmic Christ theme and terminology illustrates the long neglect of a particular religious orientation which could have helped give a positive bias to Christian consciousness of the environment. This theme, stemming from the New Testament cosmic perspective of John's Gospel, Ephesians, Colossians and Philippians is grounded in the Wisdom tradition of the Hebrew Scriptures. It was taken up by Origen in the third century, was rediscovered in modern times and has had its most powerful exponent in Teilhard de Chardin.

Its central tenet was summed up by Teilhard in 1916, about a month after he had hit upon the term "cosmic Christ". He wrote then that in coming to save mankind, Christ had to animate the whole universe which bears it. For mankind is not a group of isolated monads but, with the universe, makes up a single totality, consolidated by life and matter.

The term "cosmic Christ" was used in an address by the theologian Joseph Sittler to the Faith and Order Movement at New Delhi in 1961, when he announced that for the Church seeking unity the more effectively to bring light to the world, the way forward is "from Christology expanded to its cosmic dimensions". This takes account of the goodness that God saw in creation and of the command that men are to care for the earth. From Augustine onwards, said Sittler, Western Christendom has been marked by an inability to connect the realm of grace with that of Nature. Grace has been looked upon as operative only within personal morality and history. Redemption conceived as an "angelic" escape from the cosmos of natural and historical fact bespeaks a dualistic split between the spiritual and the temporal which is both inappropriate to the organic character of biblical language and unintelligible in the present state of man's knowledge and experience. For an age that has known Hiroshima, damnation threatens not just individual men and societies, as has always been the case. It now threatens physical Nature, the foundation of life itself.[29]

Sittler's address evoked a response of near incomprehension from most of the delegates at the New Delhi Assembly. Those few who were enthusiastic about it saw it as a pioneering vision urgently needed to inspire the ecumenical inter-church task and its mission to the non-Christian world *as non-Christian*, not as world. The controlling category remained church identity, the preoccupation saving souls.

2. Another eminent theologian of this century, Albert Schweitzer, made a valiant attempt to re-think the Christian's relationship with the world. He called this theology "Reverence-for-Life". As in the ecological paradigm, he begins with the fact of personal consciousness within the world surrounding it. From there, he says, man must decide what his relationship to life around him will be. The great fault of ethics hitherto, he says, is that they were believed to deal only with the relationship of man to man. But the real question is what is his attitude to the world and all life that comes within his reach:

> A man is ethical only when life, as such, is sacred to him, that of plants and animals as that of his fellow men, and when he devotes himself helpfully to all life that is in need of help . . . The ethic of relation of man to man is not something apart by itself: it is only a particular relation which results from the universal one.[30]

Schweitzer began work on this religious philosophy in 1915 and spent the rest of his life until 1958 working out its implications and putting them into practice. He went on to connect it to what he called the essential element in Christianity as preached by Jesus: that it is only through love that we can attain to communion with God. He pondered on the great question of how, in God, the will-to-create and the will-to-love are one. (There are echoes of Julian of Norwich here.)

3. There is another strand in contemporary theology which has great potential for helping to engage Christianity in fruitful dialogue with ecology: process theology. This addresses itself to redefining the relationship between God and the world in the light of the philosophical science of Alfred North Whitehead and the process philosophy of Charles Hartshorne. Process theologians see the universe as "part of" God in the same sense that bodily happenings – pleasures or pains – are part of our psychic life. Just as what happens in and to our bodies happens in and to us, so process theologians say, what happens in and to the universe happens in and to God. Yet just as we, as psyches, are more than our bodily happenings, so God is more than the happenings of the universe.[31]

These complex and different theological approaches are possible ways of breaking the hierarchical mould into which Christianity has been set for so long. The use of an ecological paradigm as a critique of hierarchy and then its adoption as an accepted Christian framework is the way explored in this book. The refusal to accept the prevailing paradigmatic hierarchical structures in church and world is in fact an attempt to take the transcendence of God seriously. For if God is ultimately beyond all categorization or human conceptualizing, then hierarchical concepts are no more adequate than any others, and should be subjected to the same kind of critique. The dangers of living within this particular conceptual trap for so long are becoming apparent as it closes in on our earth community in deadly ways.

The liberation theologian Jon Sobrino speaks of doing theology differently. For so long, he says, we have concentrated on the *Sitz im Leben*, the life context. Now, he says, theologians must work in the *Sitz im Tod*, the death context. He is speaking of theologians and civilians murdered in El Salvador, and of how theology is lived when one is surrounded by this human slaughter.

But his words are no less applicable to the threatened death of the planet. This is the context for a theology which will have to find courage to break out of the conceptual trap of hierarchy, to give up the illusion that we are separate from Nature, to defend and rejoice in the relationship between the whole of creation and its immanent and transcendent God. It accepts that the opposite of hierarchy is not anarchy. The opposite of both is ecological community.

Chapter 6

Fundamental Christian Questions

In discussing the problems posed by dialogue between ecology and Christianity (chapter 4), the question was raised (but not answered): "Do we know anything 'above' this world, and if so, how?" The usual Christian answer given to this is that, through Jesus, we do know about a world "above" this one. Therefore it seems to follow that Jesus belongs with the transcendent, with all that is "above" what is merely human.

In the previous chapter there was a further question implied: "How do we know the transcendent God?" The classic Christian answer to that is: "through baptism into the death and resurrection of Jesus". So what we might call the "transcendent" Jesus appears to be a person whose human life is inferior to his state after death, a state we can share through the power of that death. Jesus' journey to death is then viewed as the result of a divine plan which called for his death, so that sin, the obstacle to our knowledge of God, might be overcome. The primary effect of this divinization is the de-historicization of Jesus. He appears as the origin (Creator) and end (Recapitulator) of the whole universe, apparently insofar as he appears to be above and beyond all the ephemeral conflicts of history.

Yet, the most reliable historical data in the Synoptic Gospels caution us against any such superimposed interpretation of the reasons for his death, pointing instead to causes that are bound up with the actual way he lived his life.[1]

To ignore his life means, in ecological terms, that the hard data recorded of it are ignored or discounted in order to use the hard data of his death alone. Then the hard data of that death, its circumstances, its justification in the political and religious context of his time and its personal horror and desolation, are in turn ignored or discounted by treating them not as of value and significance in their own right, but solely as the divine answer to the problems of human sinfulness. This devalues the humanity of Jesus in favour of a utilitarian interpretation of his death. It denies history and condemns Christianity to the kind

111

of fall/redemption theology which ecological theologians warn against as the dominant mode of Christian consciousness.

This consciousness owes its dominance to a specifically Christian interpretation of the opening chapters of the Genesis narrative as the story of Adam's sin (called Original Sin). This is offered as explanation for human inability to know God through the world or human information systems. This inability is set within a hierarchical framework of explanation which interprets it as a symptom of our inferiority relative to a norm of human perfection: Adam before he sinned.

Redemption: The Fundamental Answer?

The antidote to Original Sin and its consequences (inability to know God or to be fully human), is offered to Christians as Redemption/Salvation through Jesus Christ. In this context, as Thomas Berry notes, the church emerges as having an exclusive role in bringing about the spiritual wellbeing of a Fallen humanity, since, within the hierarchical framework, its ministers have the power to baptize. This sacrament is understood, as in the New Testament, as rebirth and as death and resurrection. Through it the love of God is seen to give us "a divine beginning, a divine birth, and enables us to move towards the divine".[2]

Baptism then is seen as restoring our ability to know God, and remedies our human deficiencies by giving us a "superior" nature. Therefore within the Christian church baptism "into" Jesus is often seen as the answer to fundamental questions about ourselves, the world and God.

The questions are raised, as I have said, on a premise called "Original Sin", or "the Fall of Adam", presumed to destroy our natural ability to know God. Attempts to answer them have produced in the Christian tradition constellations of ideas and images which have "Redemption" or "Salvation" as their generic title. Together, question and answer have been hard-programmed into Christian consciousness as Fall/Redemption or Sin/Salvation themes. Theologians concerned with ecological issues claim that an undue emphasis on this complex of ideas is a major limitation in the Christian view of creation. (See chapter 5, note 1). The rest of this chapter will be devoted to finding out why this should be so.

Christian answers to human problems which cite Jesus as *the* answer have developed through the ages on the basis of a fundamental Christian doctrine often called "Atonement". The positive content of this doctrine is related to Denys' vision of the pulsating love of God overflowing on creation through various mediations. Jesus' mediation of divine love is counted most significant for Christians. The union between Jesus and God throughout his life is seen as exemplar for ours, and as part of the knowledge and activity of being Christian. This in turn presupposes that the knowledge and activity emanating from God are the ground of our oneness with God. This is the given – that God reaches out to us in answer to our yearning and that the exchange between God's overflowing love and our desire unites us. So the blanket term "Atonement" signifies that through the mediation of Jesus we are at one with God (at-onement). Not only that, but it includes the dazzling prospect that this union extends to the world in all its relationships, "whether things upon the earth, or things in the heavens" (Col. 1:19).

The traditional usage of the word, however, presupposes that primarily we are not at one with God because of Original Sin, and secondly, that the mediation of Jesus takes place through his death for us.[3] Thomas Aquinas said succinctly that since the passion (death) of Christ was sufficient and superabundant for the sin of the human race and the penalty incurred, his passion was a kind of ransom by which we were freed from both these obligations. It is these combined notions of the death of Jesus as mediation and expiation for sin which are commonly understood as Redemption. This relationship with the death of Jesus leans, as it were, on the notional ladder of hierarchy by stating plainly *why* we need at-one-ment. We are separated from God, from each other and from the world because Adam sinned and "fell" from full relationship and life with God. Human nature moved *down* the scale. Being merely human was no longer enough for being one with God. However, through the death and resurrection of Jesus, Christians alone, through baptism, can rise up above their deficient human nature and be re-united (atoned) with God.

Such a contracted form of the doctrine of Atonement is the accepted one in traditional Christianity. As I was starting work on this chapter, my eye was caught by a lengthy review in *The Tablet* of three new books on this doctrine. The review is a very good example of the point I want to make. On the cover of the magazine it is billed as "Gabriel Daly on doctrines of salvation". Inside the editor heads it "Approaches to the Cross, source of our redemption". Daly himself, in the first paragraph, tells us that there is a credal confession that what happened "on Calvary happened for us and for our salvation". The three books are titled respectively: *Responsibility and Atonement*, by Richard Swinburne; *The Actuality of Atonement: a study of metaphor, rationality and the Christian Tradition*, by Colin Gunton; and *Past Event and Present Salvation: the Christian idea of Atonement*, by Paul S. Fiddes. The review goes on to show that the authors' approaches are as diverse as the titles suggest.

Nowhere, however, is it suggested that their focus is other than on the death and resurrection of Jesus for us. The past event of the cross of Christ and its creative power in the present are the object of attention. Daly mentions some images used to speak about "how God comes to our aid in and through Jesus of Nazareth". If, he says, with many of the Eastern Fathers we take our models from the sickroom, we shall tend to think of God's saving work in terms of healing. If, with many of the Western Fathers, we turn to the law courts for our models, we shall tend to think of Salvation in terms of obligation, merit, penalty and satisfaction.[4]

Daly assumes that there is universal Christian acceptance for the Sin/Salvation hypothesis, and he is right. At the other end of the theological spectrum, a priest friend of mine told me how two of her parishioners passing their church on a bus mentioned it in conversation. Another passenger broke in and asked: "What do you learn in there?" The unhesitating answer came back: "That Jesus died to save me from my sins". This is the way in which many Christians express belief in the doctrine of Atonement.[5]

Such confessions of Jesus as Saviour, ranging from the academic to the popular, take as axiomatic that what happened on Calvary happened for the sake of sinful humanity. God came to our aid and solved our problems through the death of his son: the Father sent the Son down into the world for our Salvation. This presupposition distinguishes Christian reading of the Bible, whether of the books written before Jesus' death or those written after it. Christians look back, as it were, to Calvary, see it as "the source of Redemption", and then read the books from that standpoint. Indeed, the whole Bible is often subsumed under the title "Salvation history". The focal point is Jesus' death, suffered "for us" that we might be one with God again.

Some of the ramifications of this treatment of the death of Jesus in the history of Christian doctrine will be taken up in the closing chapters of this book. The focus here is the contraction of the doctrines of Atonement and of Incarnation into that of salvation from sin through Jesus' death; and the way in which that has become the overriding interpretative principle in Christian reading of the Bible.

Absolutism in Christianity

This reading easily allies itself to the absolutist approach mentioned already in which the word of God is identified with the human words written down in the Scriptures. This sustains the illusion that one can find direct and infallible communication of God's will for the world in these books alone. The further illusion follows that certain people have found there just such a disclosure of divine intent and have passed it on to others. And as it is usually read and handed on, this will is that the death of Jesus should save mankind uniquely out of a Fallen world into union with the transcendent God.

An "absolute" in the sense used here is something we can treat as a changeless graspable object. Therefore it is something we can cling to for support against all doubt. It presupposes ultimate, undoubtable criteria which decide which object shall be treated as absolute.[6] In the Christian context, certain beliefs about and attitudes towards God have become absolutes through the processes of hard-programming, and through the fact that they enable Christians to worship and interact with each other in a meaningful way.[7]

Looking at them from another viewpoint, they could be said to yield answers to questions raised by experiences which have already been interpreted in a particular way. The experience of human inadequacy, for instance, or the suffering of animals, or the devastating cataclysms inflicted on us by Nature have much to do with the dominant interpretation of the Genesis narrative as an account of "Original Sin" and its punishment. If you experience personal failure, suffering and guilt, and if you interpret this in the context of Adam's Fall, then certain questions can be asked about our relationship with God which will ensure that a particular kind of answer follows. On the assumption that the relationship is flawed, questions will be asked about how it can be improved or mended. So the criterion of Adam's Sin decides that Salvation from it becomes an absolute.

The theologian/scientist Arthur Peacocke gives alternative readings of the texts, but has to conclude that, in spite of the wisdom of biblical scholars distilled in them, Christian theology is still "deeply tinctured with the assumption of an 'original righteousness' which man lost at a point in time, of an original innocent state, from which man 'fell', and which it was the role of God in Jesus the Christ to restore". Such ways of thinking, he says, are no longer plausible in the light of what we now know about man's evolution. Yet they still hold the Christian imagination in thrall.[8]

Another such Christian way of thinking, as we have seen, is that God reveals himself through the words of the Bible. Implicit in that is the conviction that this revelation was made to certain men who received it absolutely correctly, and handed it on infallibly to others. And there is a consensus that what they handed on is the absolute truth: that Jesus was sent into the world to save us from the consequences of Adam's Sin. When these three absolutes (Sin, biblical inerrancy and redemption) are indissolubly linked, as they usually are in Christian teaching, they reinforce each other to the point where they block off other possible interpretations and beliefs.

The theologians who voice concern about undue emphasis on this conjunction of ideas are saying that it has become an absolute which excludes all other approaches to the mystery of God, humanity and the world. Whether it is called "the heart of Christian faith" or "a changeless graspable doctrine", it functions as an absolute in that it is appealed to as the ultimate criterion for assessing Christian experience and attitudes to the world.

One such theologian, Dietrich Bonhoeffer, voiced this concern in a letter he wrote from prison in May 1944 on the occasion of his godson's baptism:

> Atonement and redemption, regeneration, the Holy Ghost, the love of our enemies, the cross and resurrection, life in Christ and Christian discipleship – all these things have become so problematic and so remote that we hardly dare any more to speak of them. In the traditional rite and ceremonies we are groping after something new and revolu-

tionary without being able to understand it yet. That is our own fault. During these years the Church has fought for self-preservation as though it were an end in itself, and has thereby lost its chance to speak a word of reconciliation of mankind and the world at large. So our traditioonal language must perforce become powerless and remain silent, and our Christianity today will be confined to praying for and doing right by our fellow men. Christian thinking, speaking and organization must be reborn out of this praying and this action. By the time you are grown up, the form of the Church will have changed beyond recognition.[9]

Nearly fifty years later, the form of the church seems to have changed very little. Atonement and redemption remain problematic and remote. In themselves, these concepts are an integral *part* of the Christian tradition, a valuable insight into the possible interaction of human suffering, love and healing to be found in the mystery of Jesus' life and death. But when they take over the whole tradition as excluding and exclusive beliefs, then the tradition is impoverished, closed off from the rich diversity contained in other readings of the Bible.

The main victim of this process, from a purely theological point of view, is, as we shall see, the person of the Holy Spirit. The person of the Son is accorded supremacy in the mediation of redemption in its role as the primary mode of experience of the love of God. The traditional theology of salvation, certainly in Western Christianity, has no place for the Spirit. It is Christocentric through and through. God is revealed by Christ and Christ is made known by the church – meaning by this the church hierarchy. The Spirit features only as an aid to the hierarchy in their task of making Christ known.[10]

Effects of Absolutism on Dialogue

This narrowness debilitates dialogue between ecology and Christianity. Some of the ways this happens have already been mentioned in other contexts, but it is worth summarizing them here:

Firstly, by definition, absolutist approaches to the Bible and belief are unecological, since they close our minds to new or contradictory information. Openness is impossible. All the characteristics of a closed system are not only accepted but encouraged.

Secondly, an absolutist reading of the Bible is usually given from within a hierarchical structuring of reality, in which the divine has to "come down" into our world and bring us up from a demeaning relationship with Nature. Therefore the concept of God's transcendence is atrophied. It is no longer useful for keeping our thinking supple and open to all the heights, depths and riches of God revealed to us through the Spirit (1 Cor. 2:9-13). Instead, our thoughts on transcendence are curtailed by certain concepts and images and these alone. Their absolute claims to be revelatory discount and devalue all other attempts to speak about and know God. A conceptual trap builds up which undergirds many others, not least a refusal of Nature's capacity to reveal the divine.

Elizabeth Dodson Gray says that such traps are to the thought world of the mind what the astronomers' black holes are to the universe. Once inside, there seems to be no way of getting out or seeing out. Once inside, you cannot imagine a world outside. It is extraordinary that as I write, the world is watching the conceptual traps of Communism and Apartheid crumble, and political commentators praise Gorbachev and De Klerk as great statesmen who are prepared to announce that concepts and policies by which they have operated all their lives are utterly mistaken and must be reversed. The uncertainty and danger that attend their courageous decisions remind us of why these traps remained locked in place for so long, and why it requires so much courage to dismantle them – from the inside.

The same kind of accolade greeted Pope John XXIII when he convened the Second Vatican Council. It is a matter of opinion whether or not he succeeded in dismantling as much as he intended before he died. But certainly some external architectural patterns were broken, with altars moved and simplified. Some conceptual configurations too were shattered, including a few in church language. No longer do Roman Catholics pray for "perfidious" Jews on Good Friday. But inclusive imagery for God is still not accepted. "His" transcendence is still bound up with masculine concepts and metaphors.

Now ecology is pressing on Christianity for some further dismantling from within. Those Christians trapped into a narrow hierarchical view of God's transcendence vis-à-vis the world have the difficult task of breaking out of it. Ecofeminist theologians feel the constricting limits most acutely, and so are particularly aware both of the urgent need for this break-out and the difficulty of making it. They are in a unique position to evaluate Sobrino's challenge: for them theology already has a new context, the death of male-dominated Christian absolute concepts about God, Jesus Christ and Nature.

A third way in which ecology finds dialogue inhibited by Christian absolutism is in its narrowing down of our sense of divine revelation to verbal sources, written or proclaimed. Christians seldom notice how much we have lost contact with the revelation of the divine elsewhere. The numinous has become an object of study in standard texts. Printed rituals are carried out in sacred spaces marked off from the earth and earth processes. This non-participating consciousness is at the heart of a dominant relationship with Nature. The kingdom of God may indeed be among us, but one's gaze is directed normally on to the written or spoken word. Those who are usually called "Fundamentalist", that is, committed to an absolutist use of the Bible for directing their lives, are only an extreme case of a common Christian fixation.

Consequently, the diversity of other records (even written ones) of human encounters with the transcendent God is not seen as enrichment. Instead, diversity and dissimilarity are seen as a threat to be eliminated, so that the Bible can reign supreme as the only true divine revelation. The Vedic Hymns, the Upanishads, the Bhagavadgita, the Koran, the Lotus Sutra, the Way of Lao Tzu, the Tibetan Book of the Dead and all the other sacred writings are "marked down" as less valuable than the Bible, if not downright misleading. Poetry, music and the arts are also devalued as pathways to God.

Yet in fact all of these are open to authentic exchanges with the divine from within other religious, cultural and natural systems. Otherwise we are asked to believe in a God who has wilfully denied knowledge of the transcendent to the major portion of the human race.

A final example of a pervasive characteristic of Christian absolutism which hinders dialogue with ecology is the belief that Jesus died to save only sinful humanity, and exclusively those baptized sinners who come to God through his death and resurrection. Part of the problem of Christian identity is the fact that Christians identify themselves with Christ by exclusion, by negatives, what they are *not*. Worldwide, being a Christian excludes being a heretic, a Jew, a Moslem, a Hindu, a Buddhist, a witch, a pagan. Within Christianity itself, being Catholic excludes being Protestant, being Orthodox excludes being Reformed, being Monophysite excludes being Mennonite, being a Syrian Catholic excludes being a Lutheran and so on. At best the effort involved in overcoming this bias toward exclusion absorbs much inter-church energy and fosters ecclesiastical introspection.

But there is a darker side to this negativity which the too familiar phrase "sectarian murder" reveals, or rather conceals by its numbing repetition in the media. Thomas Szasz comments: "The moral aim of Christianity is to foster identification with Jesus as a model; its effect is often to inspire hatred for those who fail – because of their origins or beliefs – to display the proper reverence toward him. The Judaeo-Christian imagery of the scapegoat – from the ritual of Yom Kippur to the Crucifixion of Jesus as Redeemer – thus fails to engender compassion and sympathy for the Other."[10]

Failure to engender compassion and sympathy for those "others" who by birth or belief do not reverence Jesus Christ is a significant factor today in Christianity's failure to take up the green gauntlet. At a relatively harmless level, it makes possible protests from some Fundamentalist groups about Christian leaders joining with non-Christians in prayer for justice, peace and reconciliation with creation. At a policy level, it allows church authorities to make distinctions as to where resources will go. One distressing example of this was the decision of some missionary societies in famine areas to give relief only to those who asked for baptism in their sect. More sinister still is the attitude of some "Christians" to the genocide of pagan indigenous tribes and the exploitation of their homelands.

The denigration of those who do not honour Jesus Christ by birth or belief has a profound effect on official church attitudes toward nonChristian philosophies and cultures. Whether dismissed as "primitive", as in the case of the Australian aborigines, or "materialist", as with Marxists, any suggestion that they might have something to contribute to the Christian world view is anathema. Even to mention liberation theology and Marxism together is enough to condemn the former. The force with which some of the theologians themselves deny the charge as conduct unbecoming to a Christian, and claim shelter behind the teachings of Jesus to justify their social analyses of oppression, shows that they share the same prejudices as their accusers.

Christian Fundamentalism

In general, these anti-ecological characteristics are most evident, or are found in their most extreme form, in the type of Christian absolutism usually known as Fundamentalism. This conceptual trap is hallmarked by an exclusive use of the Bible as the sole authentic revelation of God's will. Stamped on it is the belief that Christians alone are saved through Jesus. There is an interaction between these two elements in all Christian thinking. But an absolute emphasis on them, together with a doctrine of sin which consistently devalues human nature, distinguishes so–called "Fundamentalist" from mainstream churches. They hold absolutely to the three elements of sin, biblical inerrancy and salvation through the death of Jesus. To avoid confusion with those traditions which have fundamentalist leanings but are not so rigidly exclusive, this absolutist version is here spelled with a capital letter "F".

No matter where on the Scripture/Tradition spectrum any individual Christian church is located, its unique relationship with biblical texts as God's word inclines it to Fundamentalism. This inclination is due in part to the fact already noted, that literate Christianity tends to overrate verbatim repetition or record. The illusion is widespread that if one has the exact words someone has uttered, one has by that very fact his or her exact meaning. The distance in time and context between the original culture of the Biblical texts, their setting down and transmission in writing should act as a corrective to this illusion.

Various attempts have been made to break out of a constricting approach to the Biblical texts. For instance, Barth's appeal to make faith in Christ a personal relationship, and Christ the true and only revelation of God, seems at first to give Christians more elbow room. But since according to Barth the Bible as we have it is the unique witness to that revelation, and the preaching of the church witnesses to Christ on the basis of the scriptures, we can find we are still concentrating on two elements: the Bible and salvation through baptism into Christ.

Within the Roman Catholic Church, since Vatican II's Dei Verbum (the Dogmatic Constitution on Revelation), there has been an unprecedented surge of interest in the scriptures. There is a new emphasis on the exposition of biblical texts within the celebration of the Eucharist. But the necessity of relating traditional faith with an understanding of the Bible involves a process of interpretation. So a conflict is felt between modern individual or scholarly readings and those which have always been accepted as infallible. This difficulty is met by officially transferring the absolute certainty that Protestant churches attach to the words of Scripture to infallible interpretations made by ordained men. The transferred authority is known as the *magisterium* (the mastery of official doctrine).

The interpretative circle of text, context and reader is always prone to hardening into an exclusive and therefore unecological one. This is the case when the circle is set within the trio of absolutes: literal biblical inerrancy, sin and salvation through the cross of the divine Jesus. The Fundamentalism which results will now be summarized and some of its theological and ecological consequences noted. It is characterized by:

> — *a very strong emphasis on the inerrancy of the Bible, the absence from it of any sort of error;*
> — *a strong hostility to modern theology and to the methods, results and implications of modern critical study of the Bible;*
> — *an assurance that those who do not share this religious viewpoint are not really "true" Christians at all;*
> — *a distrust of "liberal" churches on the grounds that they have failed to preserve the gospel or message given in the Bible;*
> — *an anxiety about the guarantees of pure doctrine, which makes it possible to distinguish between "nominal" and true Christian faith, and so to contrast the true Christian with the nominal one.*

The claims to absence of error and to a *guarantee* of pure doctrine are the binding forces which make Fundamentalism perennially attractive and Fundamentalists determined to resist any critique or challenge. Certainty triumphs and everyone feels secure. The consequent restriction of spiritual and intellectual movement and vision is considered a small price to pay for guaranteed membership of "true" Christianity, that is, those who are saved by the blood of Jesus from their sins. (See Chapter 4, note 9 about Fundamentalist experiences of this kind.) They define themselves by holding certain excluding and exclusive principles which positively identify the saved and, negatively, the damned.

First Fundamentalist Principle

Firstly, Fundamentalist faith holds as a basic theological principle that the true gospel is a message which in its simplest form announces salvation from sin through the blood of Jesus Christ and through personal faith in him. This, as was argued already, is a contraction of the doctrine of atonement. Its contraction is worsened by narrowing salvation down to those alone who profess personal faith in Jesus Christ.

Salvation thus is primarily the removal of that barrier (the flaming sword) which sin has set between God and man. It is the renewal of that relation of fellowship, righteousness and obedience which had been destroyed by the first Adam. In this view of salvation the essential step up the ladder is something that has already been accomplished by the work of Christ. Paradise has been regained "for" us, that is, for those who hold rigidly to this belief.[11]

Some effects of this focussing on fall/redemption spirituality within an ecclesiastical hierarchy were mentioned in the preceding chapter. The knowledge of one's weakness and sinfulness leads to desire for security and certainty based on the absolute authority of ministers. They have right of access to salvation for themselves and those who accept and implement their interpretation of scripture and their power to baptize. They (B) possess the Spirit (A) which speaks to the church (C) through them. Fundamentalist churches generally characterize this as a "leading" from the Spirit through their elders which calls for absolute obedience from the congregation.

It is characteristic of those I have encountered at first hand that this "leading" denies any authority to women. My attention was drawn just this week to a letter which states unequivocally the reasoning behind this denial. The writer, Rev. Dr Peter Toon, says that he is part of the historic tradition of Protestant exegesis which affirms the true equality of men and women in dignity and honour. This insists that "in the divine order of patriarchy [sic], centred in Jesus Christ [sic], men and women do not have identical vocations since sexual difference is part of the divine order and not merely a matter of human consciousness".[12]

On this evidence, there is scarcely any need to ask where Nature is placed in this "divine patriarchy". Indeed, such a question would hardly arise, as there is a constant internal dialogue in Fundamentalist churches about sin and redemption which keeps minister and congregation preoccupied with personal salvation: within a church presented as its guarantor. "Outside the church there is no salvation" corresponds to the biblical Fundamentalist insistence that "no one comes to the Father (i.e. is saved) except through Jesus". This religious introversion neglects or ignores the importance of creation in itself, seeing it only as a means to an end, the salvation of humanity through the divine Christ. This distorting lens held over the world was examined in the previous chapter.

But the Fundamentalist notion of instrumental value for salvation does not simply distort our Christian views and maps of the world. An enormous distortion occurs within theology itself, noticeably in its treatment of the incarnation, God become man in Jesus Christ. This brings us to the second principle.

Second Fundamentalist Principle

A second Fundamentalist principle is an exclusive focussing on the supremacy of divinity in Christ. This seriously distorts the mystery of the incarnation. Christianity holds that Jesus Christ is both God and man.[13] But the emphasis of Fundamentalist religion falls heavily on the divine nature of Christ. The ordinary Fundamentalist believer "knows nothing of the idea that Jesus Christ is equally God and man. What he or she believes about him is that he is *God*. He is God walking about and teaching in a man's body".[14]

This is a way of systematically stripping Jesus of everything which, from the standpoint of an ideal, could be regarded as weakness, limitation, or concession. It is the continuing application to him, in the name of his divinity, of false kinds of transcendence that end up turning him into a dehumanizing factor.[15]

This is part of the systematic stripping of any significance from the life of Jesus as a mediation of God's love for creation. The incipient utilitarianism present in this approach begins to surface when one asks *why* there is such an emphasis. It has to do with the assurance to the Fundamentalist that he or she alone has the correct reading of the Bible. His or her interpretation is guaranteed as infallible because it comes from God, i.e. Jesus, who handed on the correct reading to us through the Spirit. The body of Jesus was useful in that it conveyed, as in an envelope of flesh, the good news that the Christian believer is saved. The divinity of Jesus is used as *the* guarantee of salvation.

The biblical scholar James Barr warns of the corrosive effect of this on one's religion. In particular he points to its effects on the reading of the New Testament. Because Fundamentalism insists that its central affirmation is that Jesus is God, it is forced into a major harmonizing operation. All passages which fail to say that Jesus was God, and had been so from the beginning, are read as if they do say so. (This is a variation on reading the whole Bible from the standpoint of Calvary).

I had an interesting example of this tendency in a Roman Catholic Trinity Sunday liturgy where the first reading from scripture was taken from the book of Proverbs. In this the female figure of Wisdom raises her voice to proclaim her work in creation. But the sermon interpreted this passage, on the authority of the Church Fathers, as referring to the pre-existent Christ.

The most powerful effect of this Fundamentalist distortion is that it views the Bible as a whole as grounded upon the *divine* teaching of Jesus. (See again the letter quoted above in which patriarchy is claimed as a divine order centred on Jesus Christ.) In order for his teaching to be infallible, it has to come from God. Jesus' teaching recorded in the Gospels was infallible because he was God and shared in God's infallibility. Therefore every word recorded as his in the Gospels is treated with absolute reverence, and such pronouncements attributed to him as "no one comes to the Father but by me" are used, or rather abused, as divine exclusion clauses.[16]

This mindset manifests itself unconsciously in those Christians who would not consider themselves "Fundamentalist", but who insist that because Jesus called God "Father", then presumably that is what God wishes to be called. So it must remain the normative Christian mode of address in prayer, and "Jesus becomes, according to this picture, more like God dispensing eternally correct information through a human mouth than a man speaking under the conditions of his time and situation."[17]

A corollary to this in the Roman Catholic Church is the way in which the doctrine of the Immaculate Conception of Mary is preached. It is treated as a specific intervention of God, which, in anticipation of the birth of the divine Son of God, removes any "normal" human inclination to sin from his mother. The fact that Fundamentalists within Protestantism seldom make this extrapolation should not cloak the fact that both churches rely on the same exclusive insistence on Jesus' divinity. This, and this alone, is treated as the controlling factor in the incarnation.

This imbalance in treating the mystery of God made man, which reduces it to divinity without the reality of humanity, automatically downgrades the life of Jesus even as it elevates his death as the divine Christ to supreme importance. This divine death guarantees salvation.

Several anti-ecological strands come together here. By divorcing Jesus from the contexts and meta-contexts of his time, such as the Roman occupation or the hatred between Jews and Samaritans, he is taken out of his normal human surroundings and therefore out of contact with "the world". Unlike us, he supposedly exists in a closed-off divine system of union with the transcendent God. Therefore his life loses its relevance. So does the world around him.

In contrast to this, modern biblical studies necessarily take full account of his humanity. They take seriously his growth in understanding both of the Father's will and of his own mission. They accept as true the statement attributed to him, that the Son of Man did not know when he would come in glory to gather his elect (Mark 13:32). They are prepared to admit that he does not always practise what he preaches, so his rudeness to the pagan Syro-Phoenician woman is read as just that, and his use of insults, his impatience and fomenting of hatred in his enemies are not explained away as "divine" judgments.[18]

Such an approach is abhorrent to Fundamentalism, which does not allow that Jesus had to learn through what he did and suffered, or was ignorant of anything. So the relevance of his life, work and preaching is divorced from its social, political and religious context. What matters is his death "for" sinners. The fact that he lived in such a way that he was reckoned *with* sinners and died a despised outcast is dismissed as irrelevant. *His life and death are valued (or rather devalued) only as the price of an individual Christian's salvation.*

This religious utilitarianism pervades the usual Christian interpretation of Jesus' life. It ignores his life as having any value other than that it was necessary for him to be born in order to die: that we might live forever.

In this way, the relevance of Christian living today can equally be divorced from its natural and political setting. The dualism of divine/human is used to interpret both scripture and life, with inherent value attributed only to divine life. The type of sensibility required in ecological systems, of the felt awareness of our intrinsic interdependence with all around us, cannot easily be cultivated in a religious structure which divides the world into two storeys, with everything divine "upstairs".

There are correctives to this if scientific approaches to Jesus' life are seen as pathways to the mystery of incarnation. The starting-point is the recognition that God was unveiling meaning in the whole of creation and could not be more or less present in some parts of it than others. So the *continuity* of Jesus with the rest of humanity, and so with the rest of Nature, is stressed more explicitly.[19]

Third Fundamentalist Principle

A third Fundamentalist principle shows up specifically in its reading of apocalyptic, whether biblical or green. When Fundamentalists are faced with the problems of effective human decisions in world affairs, divine determinism takes over. Apocalyptic is read as if a whole series of earth-shaking events will be brought about by direct divine agency, with little or nothing that we can do about it. One of the greatest bestsellers of all time in America (it is said even President Reagan read it), *The Late Great Planet Earth*, puts it like this:

> After the Christians are gone God is going to reveal Himself in a special way to 144,000 physical, literal Jews who are going to believe with a vengeance that Jesus is the Messiah.[20]

Commenting on this, Barr points out that no one can be a Christian without making a free – and therefore unpredictable – decision for Christ. But according to Fundamentalists, in the events which end the world everything will work in another way and God will simply arrange that the requisite number of Jewish believers in Jesus will become available.

This belief in divine interventionism sees the death of the planet as the final stage on which the salvation epic of the human race is brought to a triumphant conclusion. It excludes the necessity for Christian action which might postpone the end-time, or the making of any effective decisions which would affect the life or death of the planet as a whole. With Voltaire, it is enough for us to cultivate our gardens.

Not only that, this modern *deus ex machina* syndrome ignores what is now the case in the world. For the first time in history, *human* hands and *human* decisions have the power to "assure" mutual and total destruction of human life on earth.

In his important book *The Fate of the Earth*, Jonathan Schell explores the implications of nuclear "capability" and the fact that mankind as a whole has now gained possession once and for all of the knowledge required to make nuclear weapons. Regardless of treaties between the super-powers, once this know-how has been acquired it will never be lost. "So there will never again be a time when self-extinction is beyond the reach of our species".[21]

Even with Schell's irrefutable evidence that we now live within this death context as a result of human activity, Fundamentalism reduces human responsibility for deciding the world's fate to zero. Therefore it loses the valid theological core of evangelical discipleship: the centrality of Christ as saviour *of the world*. The disciple is no longer one called to proclaim the good news "to the whole of creation" (Mark 16:14). Instead,

> The centre lies increasingly in the working out of a sequence of future events, in which Christ appears no longer in the role of a saviour calling all men to him but rather as a kind of automaton or switch, whose actions introduce each new stage of the apocalyptic sequence.[22]

Ecochristian Responses

As the Fundamentalist leanings in the Christian structure begin to appear, the scaffolding of a Christian ecological theology must be raised. It is constructed by keeping intact the mystery of Jesus' humanity as well as his divinity. It is held together by the refusal to accept a hierarchical view of the Incarnation, which downgrades his humanity in order to use his male divinity as an absolute on which the certainty of human Salvation can depend. It is necessarily open to the wider world with views across cultural and religious boundaries. It is supported firmly by the earth, but is not embedded so deeply as to be impossible to move to a better position if lopsidedness occurs.

In this view of the Incarnation, Jesus of Nazareth does not "do something on our behalf" but, far more importantly, manifests in his own life and death that the heart of the universe is unqualified and inclusive love. If one takes clues from the parables, Jesus' table fellowship and the cross, all add up to a perception of Jesus as model-*breaker*, as one who encouraged maturity in his followers rather than an immature dependence on supposed absolutes.

In particular, an ecological reading of the Bible discerns and values Jesus' breaking down of the hierarchical structures of his world by taking seriously the contexts of his life and teaching. He was born into a patriarchal society and religion, in which the supposed inferiority of women and sinners was unquestioned. His non-hierarchical behaviour throughout his public life was strikingly evident in his relationship with those religiously downgraded: women, the poor, tax-collectors and sinners. Against all the accepted and sacred norms, he chose to share food, life and healing with these. His reversal of the usual hierarchical perception of master and disciple was taught in response to the disciples' quarrel as to who should be the greatest in the kingdom, and acted out dramatically in his washing of their feet.[23]

In a society which regarded wealth as a sign of God's favour, and poverty and sickness as the result of sin ("Who has sinned, this man or his parents, that he should be born blind?" [John 9:2]), he praised the poor widow and counselled poverty. The shattering effect of this is obvious in the dialogue after the rich young man goes away sad. Jesus exclaims how difficult it is for the rich to enter the kingdom of God. "Who then can be saved?", asked the amazed disciples (Mark 10). If the rich can't make it, who can? In a society which ranked women and children with slaves, when he noticed his disciples arguing as to which of them was the greatest, he put a child in front of them as a model.

In his teaching in parables about who would be saved/rewarded by God, he shattered expectations and destroyed cherished religious securities in those who heard him. His parable of the "last judgment" (Matt. 25:31f.), names those inheriting the kingdom as the ones who feed, clothe, nurse, visit and liberate anyone in need: activities in no way confined to pious Jews. On the contrary. There is no mention whatever of "the blessed" keeping any religious observance.[24] The effects of such teaching were described by the religious hierarchy demanding his execution on that account as "perverting the people".

Perverts, then and now, are threats to "normality" and authority. In the dispute between the man born blind and the Pharisees, their indignation mounts at being challenged and worsted in argument by "a sinner". So threatening is this that they cast him out of the synagogue. Those who challenge or dismantle conceptual traps do so at their peril.

Both Jesus and his challenge were rejected from the beginning of his public ministry. In the narrative in Luke 4:18f., paralleled briefly in Matthew 13:37, in the synagogue in his home town, in the same words which will be used in the Passion narrative, his brethren lay hands on him and lead him away to kill him. For what? For proclaiming the good news to the poor, a synonym for the sinner, the disabled, the captive – all the "outsiders".

Towards the end of his life he is pictured weeping over Jerusalem and its warring and separated people. In the light of his own rejection as a prophet, he mourns over their killing those like him, who "would have gathered them together", but they would not have it. Jews have nothing to do with Samaritans; Pharisees do not eat with sinners or pray with publicans; the sabbath is kept sacred for worship and is not to be used for healing disabled women or men, or for gobbling corn in the fields; holy bread is set apart for priests.

When Jesus' rejection by entrenched hierarchies is seen in the context of his times, a new picture of him begins to emerge. He is a Jesus who lived *in* the world of his day in a scandalous, non-hierarchical way simply because he lived and died *with* the sinful and shared powerlessness with them unto death. There is never, except in the case of the Syro-Phoenician woman, any indication that he thought of himself apart from the motley crew (*ho ochlos*) surrounding him. And she won her argument with him and broke down the one barrier he had tried to keep between them, that between the chosen Jew and the pagan.

He put no safe or sacred distance between himself and anyone else. This is instinctively recognized, as was remarked in the last chapter, by all those who are consistently downgraded today for not living up to the white, male, heterosexual norms of our hierarchical church and society.

Set within the context of his life, nowhere does his death appear as separate from it. He lived and died *with sinners and as a sinner*, with all the misery and rejection that entailed. Looking back at that death, we are able to hypothesize about its meaning.

But never to the extent that we separate it from the humanity which brought him to it and endured it. He did not live or die "for" those around him, cocooned from them by divinity. He was identified totally *with* them, in life and in death.

A reading of the Bible more concerned with Jesus' life would seek to preserve the mystery of incarnation. Therefore it would not separate the humanity and divinity in Jesus. It would not regard them hierarchically, so that his divinity excelled his humanity in importance and value. On the contrary, the way into the mystery would be through the primary system of his body in relationship with those surrounding it. The "joyful exchange" between that humanity and the divinity of Jesus would be seen as part of the same exchange between the human and the divine, the immanent and transcendent revealed in the whole of creation.

Such a reading would not separate his life from his death. They were in continuity and flowed naturally one from the other. The way he shared life with sinners and outcasts determined his death as a sinner and outcast. There is no question then of emphasizing the usefulness of his death apart from his life. Both shattered the absolute convictions of those about him, especially his disciples, and so opened them up to the mystery of the reality of God.

Such a reading would perceive that for Jesus, much of the intervening cultural strata in Judaism with their hard-programming of social and psychic habit appear to have collapsed like so many floors. We may take as illustrative his appeal back to Moses, to the "beginning of creation" in the words assigned to him in the dispute about divorce (Mark 10:6). This depth in the sanctions of Jesus explains the implicit universalism in his position, as in his attitude to the Samaritans; his appeals to reason, common sense and the processes of Nature; the quasi-secular tone of his parables and much of his teachings.[25]

The Gospels would then be read in the context of Jesus' time and not as though he lived in some a-historical zone where his life and what he did with it ceased to have meaning. Therefore we would take seriously his interaction with all the other religious and cultural systems that characterized his surroundings, especially his relationships with people "closed off" from his, such as Samaritans, or below accepted norms, such as the sinner and the sick.

Therefore we would take his non-exclusiveness seriously, remembering his own dictum: "And if you salute only your brethren, what more are you doing than others?" (Matt. 5:47). This non-exclusiveness would open us up to interaction with all the other ways and paths to the divine known in the world.

Through such readings, certain questions would surface which would not be raised by the sin/salvation hypothesis. We would wonder why, as far as we know, Jesus himself never wrote a recorded word.

We might dwell on the fact that he was born into a religious people who did not have to wait for his birth in order to have a living relationship with the God they knew as transcendent. Therefore we would accept the widest possible view of that transcendence and its revelation.

We would not ask anyone to believe that this God is separated from any part of the world being created at any time, because the will-to-create and the will-to-love are one and without limit (infinite) in God.

Through the openness of Jesus' humanity, we would learn to take his divinity seriously: not as the guarantee that we are saved from sin out of this world, but, on the basis of his non-rejection of sinners, as a guarantee that we are loved by God in this world as sinners. As Jesus did not reject, separate himself from or stop loving sinners, neither does God. This would require a different reading of the Genesis narrative than as one of humanity banished from God's presence because of sin.

We might then value the divinity of Jesus differently, as part of the transcendence embedded in the world, in that as his soul was one with his body, and that body was buried in the earth, so is the transcendent embodied and embedded in the immanent. This insight lies behind Bonhoeffer's insistence, which echoes that of classical Christian spirituality all down the ages, that Christ must be met at the centre of life – *but at the centre of a life where a religious sector can no longer be presupposed as a special point of entry or contact.*[26]

We would not take his divinity for granted, as an escape route from the pain and sin of the world, but remember it was rejected by those who could not discern it because of hierarchical expectations of the Messiah. What kind of divinity is it that suffers bodily?

We would rejoice in his life, death and divinity, because it means that God is present in the processes of life and death we share with the rest of the planet. We would accept that the Spirit of God has always been present in these processes, even before they yielded up the human life we share, in a relationship between Spirit and matter which quickens and sustains all living being.

PART THREE
Ecofeminism and Christianity

Chapter 7

Ecofeminism and Christian Imagery

The traditional Christian paradigm raises particular questions for ecofeminists, some of which started to appear in preceding chapters. Most of them spring from the realization that Christianity has institutionalized patriarchy as *the* paradigmatic form of our relationship with God. Therefore, say ecofeminist theologians, Christianity must be challenged to respond positively to a radical critique of both its theology and its institutions. For what if the subordination of woman and Nature is not simply a matter of surrounding cultural and social attitudes, but is in part created and sustained by the Christocentrality of hierarchical Christianity?

Such challenges have been raised in recent years by feminists who see patriarchy and androcentrism as different but related aspects of the same basic problem: a hierarchical ordering of reality falsely thought to be intrinsic to reality itself. This falsification is now radically confronted by ecology also. So far, most critical discussion of the religious institutionalizing of patriarchy has come from women in the Jewish and Christian traditions, but critical feminist consciousness is growing everywhere around the globe among Hindus, Buddhists, Moslems and women of other traditions. Many of them include in their concerns the relationship between patriarchy and the destruction of Nature.[1]

Experience of False Hierarchical Ordering

The preceding chapters have gone some way toward clarifying what is involved in falsely assuming that reality is intrinsically patriarchal, but the following exercise in Christian self-awareness may help readers reflect on their own experience in order to understand the kind of falsification women are speaking about. It centres on the specific context of church liturgy, the commonest experience of the Christian tradition and one in which subliminal messages about sex-gender roles are given an illusory aura of sanctity.

Suppose that you are a man, a member of a predominantly male congregation. All through your church life you have heard only women's voices lead in prayer and only they have preached. You have seen only women preside at rituals in the sanctuary, and only they have blessed or absolved the living and the dead.

You have heard only feminine words used for yourself and your fellow worshippers. You have been assured that these are intended to be inclusive of both sexes; that whenever the officiating woman says *womankind* she means all humanity. You are presumed to understand that when you sing of the Motherhood of God and the Sisterhood of Woman you are praying that all men as well as women come to experience true sisterhood. Your son is baptized, and the congregation thanks God that he has been reborn as God's daughter.

How do you feel when you notice that feminine words and imagery alone are used for God? You ask about this and are told that these are merely semantic forms, and that of course, since God is transcendent, there is no question that She is female in a sexual sense. If you persist, and find the nerve to protest about the exclusive use of "Mother God", saying that it does something to your sense of male dignity and integrity, a learned lady cleric may explain that in the matriarchal society which formed the tradition the wording of scripture, liturgy and theology could emerge only in matriarchal language.

You may press on and ask why, when there is a real effort now in society at large to redress the effects of matriarchy, little or nothing is being done in Christian churches. Then you will be told that while Christians believe that God is ultimately beyond sexual categorization, She sent Her Daughter down into this fallen world to make God known to us, and that we know that God is fully revealed in Her. Furthermore, this Daughter called God "Mother" and told us to do the same. During Her life, She passed on Her intimate knowledge of God to some chosen women friends, and they passed it on to others. This means Christians can be sure they are right when they speak about God and claim a special relationship with Her. This relationship is made possible through the power of Her Spirit handed on to chosen women who hand it on to others.[2]

If you still persist with your questions you may ask why,

if God is asexual, have females only been chosen to represent this God. Then you will be told that as in Eve all women sinned, then through God's Daughter all womankind will be redeemed. As Adam and Nature led Eve into sin, so they are to be subordinate to her. As ordained representatives of the Daughter Who has saved us, women have the power to baptize men into a new relationship with God whereby they also are made God's daughters. This is the relationship we should all aspire to. The link with Nature led to sin, and is to be discarded in order that we may be raised to new life in this world and after death even as God's Daughter was raised.

The hierarchy which has subordinated men, you will be taught, established matriarchy as the way in which God can be correctly related to and spoken about. Primacy is given to female bodies and imagery since they are associated with the revelation of God in Her Daughter and our Redemption by that Daughter. There is no divine revelation or redemption associated with Nature.

This exercise, whether it is done by women or men, at the very least brings us to the point of understanding the great "What if?" questions posed by ecofeminism to Christianity. What if the divine figure of Christ sustains the subordination of women and Nature? What if their devaluing in Christian ministry and language reflects a theology which ultimately legitimizes this subordination by appeal to the male divinity of Christ? What if a doctrine of biblical inerrancy leads to the canonization of patriarchy?

Re-Imaging Transcendence: the Challenge

The exercise may also help to disclose the double bind in which Christian women have been held for so long. On the one hand, they are constantly assured that God is transcendent, above and beyond all gender, concepts and categories. On the other hand, they are told that male categories *alone* are properly used for God, since Jesus, the divine Son, was God.

Yet we know that if we take transcendence seriously, we must acknowledge that there is more to God than Jesus, that Mary's son is not God without remainder. To hold that he is would make the accepted Christian doctrine of the Trinity redundant by excluding Father and Spirit from divinity. To hold that he is not is the starting point for a truly inclusive ecological Christianity. For the Spirit of the one God is not only the crown of the world tree but also its root. It fills both the daughters and the sons of God with power and the earth with knowledge of the divine, the unifying knowledge expressed in the Hebrew word for the union of a wife and husband who come together in the deepest fleshly and spiritual interaction of marriage.

This expansive logic is too threatening for those trapped behind the exclusivism of Fundamentalist doctrines of the incarnation. Their constricting power over Christian imagination makes itself felt with renewed force whenever women's view of transcendence is articulated, that is, that it should not be contained solely in male imagery and language. Even if this is accepted at a theoretical level, on the rare public occasions when female images are used today to speak of God in Christian services they are more often than not received with embarrassed sniggers or snorts of outrage.

Carol Christ explains why female imagery for God provokes these reactions. Those who have learned to think of God exclusively as a white masculine presence are bound to be shocked when, for instance, the Black American woman writer Ntozake Shange states bluntly: "i found God in myself// and i loved her/ i loved her fiercely".

> Though most sophisticated Jewish and Christian thinkers would deny that they think of God as an old white man in the sky, the unconscious association of deity with maleness is perpetuated by language and symbol. The African tribal woman has long had her body and skin color affirmed as the image of divinity. But to the Black woman raised with pictures of a blond, blue-eyed Jesus, Shange's affirmation of the God in herself is a revelation of a new way of viewing the world and being a woman. To say "i found god in myself// and i loved her/ i loved her fiercely" is to say in the clearest possible terms that it is all right to be a woman, that the Black woman does not have to imitate whiteness or depend on men for her power of being.[3]

This vision of finding God in herself, this "new being", is for a black woman a new way of viewing the world. It discounts the hierarchical blond, blue-eyed Jesus who, if taken as the norm for either humanity or divinity automatically devalues her twice over. A different pattern has focussed in the kaleidoscope. This is not to be taken as the new definitive pattern either, for then the kaleidoscope of language would only have frozen once again. But the shock of using feminine images for God makes all of us question normative masculine images and prepares us to accept others. Most pertinently, if women can find God in themselves, love her fiercely and speak of her openly, can they do the same for Nature?

The magnitude of the task must not be underestimated. Even without the dimensions of blackness or earthiness, any signal of change in the accepted imaging of God stirs up reactions at all kinds of levels. One of the best examples of this in recent years was the response of churches and public to John Robinson's book, *Honest to God*. The furore that greeted it was triggered off a week before its publication by an article about the book in the *Observer* newspaper written by Robinson and entitled by the editor: "Our Image Of God Must Go!" What image was it? In Robinson's words, "a picture of the world in which the reality of God is represented by the existence of a God in some other order or realm of being 'above' or 'beyond' the world in which we live". What is in question, he said, is not the truth of the transcendent and unconditional as such, "but simply the particular model by which this dimension of reality is given expression".

Robinson went on to argue against the rejoinder that this image of a God "up" or "out" there is a crude parody, partly because his post-bag confirmed that many popular religious ideas are still more incredibly naive than anyone supposes, but more importantly, he said, because the biblical and mediaeval picture of the world, which determines almost all popular theology, liturgy, hymnody and art, *was* supranaturalist (and, the ecofeminist would add, patriarchal). That was the way in which the world was pictured when God was included – if not a three-decker universe, at any rate dualistic in terms of a natural realm (inhabited by humanity and Nature) and of a supernatural order (inhabited by God and spirits). It was when this picture was threatened that Christians became "jittery and defensive."[4]

The massive response to Robinson, triggered by the provoca-tively titled article, bears out the truth of what has been said in preceding chapters about any challenge to the coherence of the traditional Christian paradigm. The shattering of long-held securities based on constellations of ideas and images assumed to be God-given and beyond human emendation subverts not only our image of God but also of ourselves. Any change in the structure of belief requires change in our behaviour. So if God is no longer perceived as "out there" at a safe distance, or as a benevolent old or young white man, then we are forced to ask ourselves where or who God might be. What if God is here, in woman and man and Nature? What if this world is open to transcendence? What if transcendence and immanence are both integral to the earth? What if there is no intrinsic inferiority in Nature?

The problem is that we view transcendence through the distorting lens of a certain Christian conception of reality as a hierarchy of being. Through this, Jesus is regarded not only as a normative human male, but as *the* normative *divine* male. Through this, women and Nature are demoted to a subordinate position not only because of what they do but because of what they are. This, as was said earlier, is the basis of racism and sexism. In our relations with non-human species, a similar assumption of their innate or divinely ordained inferiority is sometimes given the name speciesism. In Christian imagery this is evident in the refusal, or at least the reluctance, to use natural images for what is ranked most highly in the Christian order: God.

Christian women today in common with their sisters else-where are asking fundamental questions about the way patriar-chy may have formed/deformed Christianity's view of them-selves and Nature. In response to this, even at institutional levels, there is now a growing perception that this is not actually how the Christian perception of God's transcendence or Jesus' divinity should inform Christian practice.[5] Even though there is no consensus as to whether or not patriarchy was an accepted part of early Christian society, or was imposed on it as a means of minimizing women's spiritual power, it is becoming clear that male theology served to legitimate and stabilize future social and religious structures of subordination. Women, slaves and Nature were kept under male domination throughout Christendom by the compelling and authoritative force of religion. The prevailing Christian ideology affirmed that God's will had mandated and sanctioned this state of affairs. The Bible's own rhetoric provided the concept of theological primacy, that is, that such structures originated in God's command. (See again the letter quoted in chapter 6, note 12.)

There is now a conscious effort to break out of this conceptual trap. As feminist theologians of both sexes grow in understanding of how it is maintained by a Fundamentalist insistence on divinity in Jesus to the total exclusion of it elsewhere, they try to counteract its effects with an insistence on the importance of his life, its contexts and relationships. No more and no less than any other human being he lived in relationship with the systemic creature earth, sustained by natural elements and stimulated by their diversity, energy and beauty.

Ecofeminist theologians insist that the debate about language and imagery for God be brought out into the open, so that the reduction of real transcendence to a distorted absolutist male version alone is no longer acceptable. Those images of God which sanction domination, which distance God from the world, must go. What if, ecofeminists ask, the images by which you live are not only supposed to be but are shown to be limited? Would you be willing to have them shattered in order to let the truth about God and Nature emerge into consciousness? What if, when we take our Christian traditions ecologically, we find ourselves closer to Nature than we realized, and not unecologically separated from it?

A single-sex religious language structure continues to impoverish the wealth of formulative notions with which Christians learn to relate to the world and articulate their feelings about it. So any image of "Goddess", for instance, if it is acknowledged at all, is treated in pejorative terms as "primitive and/or pagan", or as "profane" rather than "sacred". In the latter comparison, dualistic shaping of Christian perception usually applies the pejorative word "profane" to Nature.

This chapter and the next will argue, therefore, that if we can reclaim images of the divine for women, we can do the same for Nature. The familiar equation of woman with Nature will then no longer serve as an excuse for making women inferior to men in religious rituals and theology. Instead, what will be claimed for women in respect to God will be claimed for Nature also. The questions raised on behalf of one will require answers acceptable for both.

The Feminine and Nature Excluded from Transcendence?

One such question asks what there is about our tradition that requires this downgrading, that insists upon Nature being kept "down" in the place where God "is not" as opposed to "up there" where God "is"? This seemingly forces us to separate ourselves from Nature in order to be close to God.

A hierarchical tradition necessarily positions beings in order of power, rank and value. Its accepted relationships between being and authority imply associated value judgments. The higher you go in a hierarchy, the more power, rank and value you have. Correspondingly, going down the scale automatically decreases value until you arrive at the most devalued: in this instance, Nature. In the "civilized" world, the identification of women and animality with a lower form of life often relies on the distinction between Nature and culture. Nature-culture dualism sets culture above and apart from all that is symbolized by Nature. These two arenas of life are then equated with a general division between two kinds of activity. The private or domestic sphere revolves around the home and the reproductive processes that originate there. Female identity is linked with the "natural" functions taking place in domestic contexts. Males are then more closely identified with supradomestic "cultural" life. (See again the discussion at the beginning of chapter 3.)

In America, Carolyn Merchant points out, this distinction was basic to the tension between civilization and the frontier in Westward expansion and helped to justify the continuing exploitation of Nature's resources. After the Virginia massacre of 1622, Indians were described as wild, savage, slothful and brutish outlaws. They had "little of humanity", were "ignorant of civility, of arts, of religion", and were "more brutish than the beasts they hunt". These animal passions believed to govern the Indian and to be present in all human beings were also symbolized by the lust of women and the disorder wrought by the witch. The blame for the bodily corruption of the male was attributed directly to lust and temptation by the female.[6]

In so far as Christianity has been defined in male terms, women and Nature have been kept out in the place of the desacralized, beyond the frontiers of the holy. Denys' hierarchical ordering of church buildings has been preserved intact, with the sanctuary still kept, in some of the major denominations, for solely male representatives of Christ. The function of this male preserve was described in the Anglican Archbishops' Commission Report of 1936 on the ordination of women: "We maintain that the ministration of women will tend to produce a lowering of the spiritual tone of Christian worship". What is there about a female body rather than a male one in the "sanctuary" which would lower the spiritual tone? Some men are honest enough to say that it's because female bodies make them think of sex and not of God. But that begs several questions about sex, about bodies, about churches, and about the relationship of one sex rather than another to God. These can only be raised within a dualistic framework which separates women and men rigorously and subordinates one to the other.

The "What if" questions raised about Christian patriarchy expose the notional hierarchical ladder which makes this imposed dualism respectable by insistence on Jesus as the only normative divine male. If you rely on him alone as the only access to God, then downgrading of all the levels "below" him is inevitable. Which is where women and Nature cling together. From there, in the Christian churches where only men have the right to speak for God, their voices are stilled. Yet is there any reason to suppose that God cannot still address us out of a whirlwind, in the laughter of women or the sigh of a wave? Can God be restricted to male pronouncements?

The ladder, as we have seen, does not only support and give access. It also separates: men and women, spirit and sex, heaven and hell, God and Nature. The opposing dualisms that assume that this is a divine structuring of reality ensure that Nature is identified with all that is "not God".

R. C. Zaehner's book, *Mysticism Sacred and Profane*, is an instructive example of this dualistic tradition, beginning with the title. In it he writes:

In strictly religious mysticism, whether it be Hindu, Christian, or Muslim, the whole purpose of the exercise is to concentrate on an ultimate reality to the complete exclusion of all else; and by "all else" is meant the phenomenal world or, as the theists put it, all that is not God. This means a total and absolute detachment from Nature, an isolation of the soul within itself either to realize itself as "God", or to enter into communion with God. The exclusion of all that we normally call Nature is the *sine qua non* of this type of mystical experience.[7]

Behind such exclusion lies a perception of Nature, conscious or not (and as we shall see, it is conscious in Zaehner), which identifies it as feminine. In a hierarchical/patriarchal religion the female is excluded from the territory of transcendence. At the same time, there is a stress on detaching, isolating "the soul" from Nature in order to enter into communion with God.[8] If this tradition in Christianity is taken seriously, then it certainly requires separation from Nature, from "not-God".

Consequences of Such Exclusion

Such detachment for the sake of communion with God has far-reaching practical effects. If Nature is seen as "not God", then this licenses human control over it. This is one type of Christian legitimation of male dominance in society discussed in the first part of this book. Carolyn Merchant's analysis links the mechanistic world view and the patriarchal ideal of "man" dominating Nature. From the works of Bacon, Descartes, Newton, Hobbes and other founding "fathers" of modern science she brings to our attention the extremely violent anti-feminine language used by them. Bacon wrote that Nature has to be "bounded in her wanderings", "bound into service" and made a "slave". The aim of the scientist was to "torture Nature's secrets from her". Although a female's inquisitiveness may have caused man's Fall from his God-given dominion, he said, the relentless interrogation of another female, Nature, could be used to regain it.

Today Bacon's appeal to Genesis is considered superfluous in a scientifically oriented society which applies interrogatory techniques to Nature's reproductive faculties as a matter of course. Now the whole science of reproductive engineering extends them to women's bodies as well.

So there is nothing innocent or arbitrary about the exclusion of female and natural forms from God-imagery. By promoting the use of the symbol *man* at the expense of *woman* the visibility and primacy of males is supported. This provides positive reinforcement of male identity in Christianity while that of the female is muted. Women have to make an extra effort not required of men to include themselves somehow under the "generic" umbrella. As members of the dominant group, men are not required to modify their understandings: they are never referred to as *she/woman*. Most traditional Church communities today are made up of dominant/muted groups, in which the dominant can take for granted what is problematic for the muted, and so they continue to be muted.

Let women learn in silence with all subjection. But I suffer not a woman to teach, nor to usurp authority over the man, but to be in silence (1 Tim. 2:12).

The consequences of canonizing such practices were basic to the exercise at the beginning of this chapter. They were in mind when the silencing of women was named as the third element in their inferiorization (see chapter 2).

They operate *a fortiori* in regard to imagery for Nature in Christian language. The dominance of the male, reinforced by theology and culture, not only silences Nature, but distances her from male self-understanding and all too easily from the modified self-understanding of women. In so far as male language alone is perceived as proper discourse for relating to God, men understand it to include them and exclude the female. For themselves, this places them in the dominant relationship with God. In regard to women, it places men of conscience under an obligation to try to include them in theirs. But this still avoids acknowledging female relationship to God in its own right. In regard to Nature, it allows both sexes to assume that their dominance *as human beings* is a divine right, and that their ability to speak to and on behalf of God indicates their unique relationship with God, one denied to "dumb" Nature. Therefore it need not be reverenced but used/abused.

As we saw from the passage quoted in chapter 4, the Celtic strand of Christian tradition, and the psalms and the Wisdom tradition in the Bible, have, to some extent, granted Nature her own voice and exhorted us to listen to it. Nature's form of praise to the glory of God is recommended as pattern for ours.

However, insofar as traditional Christian language has excluded the possibility of reverencing Nature, it has sanctioned its exploitation. It has conditioned us into an acceptance of man alone as the one who inhabits the pure high realms of the will and of reason, from whence he rules above the earthly and the irrational (the places occupied by women and Nature in the hierarchical language game). This world-view has been reinforced by the interpretation of Genesis which makes causal connections between sin, woman, Nature and the legitimation of their oppression.

Carol Christ, who describes herself as a thealogian (the spelling of this word is automatically corrected by women and men who have absorbed the convention of using only the masculine form *theos* for the subject of talk about God, a usage she has forsaken), writes compellingly of the reasons for the obverse of this phenomenon, of women's own acceptance of identification with Nature. Women's intense perception of their own nothingness sometimes gives them acute insight into the larger forces of nothingness, domination, death and destruction that operate in a world dominated by "male" values. They may have very clear visions of the way in which the destructive power of men operates not only in their own personal lives, but also in the larger worlds of Nature and society (as with the experience of the *Chipko* women). Even when they cannot articulate them fully, women may sense connections between their own victimization and the relentless technological devastation of the environment, the exploitation of the poor, or the bombing of villages. Women's sensitivities to the forces and currents of violence may also lead them to entertain apocalyptic visions of an ultimate destruction.[9]

However, the cultural forces which encourage women to seek equality with men according to the stereotype of masculinity can numb this sensitivity and encourage women to take on violent roles. In the present crisis in the Gulf, it is being reported with pride that there are 10,000 women soldiers present in the United States armed forces. When interviewed, the women themselves stress that they are there on equal terms, ready and eager for action: including blowing away the Iraqis with massive guns.

Ecofeminist Critique of De-Souling Women and Nature

If a patriarchal culture "de-natures" women, a patriarchal/ hierarchical Christianity effectively de-souls them, in so far as they apparently depend on a male hierarchy for re-souling in baptism in order to know God. Women are not considered to be *capax Dei* by nature. This was stated bluntly in the debate on women's suffrage quoted before (see Chapter 5, note 24). It is implied in the traditional Christian insistence that men alone are capable of enacting the role of God towards the soul and reclaiming it from sin and death through baptism. They offer no "sanctifying" rebirth to Nature.

These implicit assumptions behind traditional Christian baptismal practice lay bare, once again, the limits of the incipient Cartesianism of our religion. This divides the universe into living subjects with souls and dead soulless objects. There is no space for anything intermediate, ambiguous, and metaphorical. Writing of the dissemination within Christianity of this form of Cartesianism from the end of the sixteenth century to the middle of the seventeenth century, the psychologist James Hillman remarks:

> Soul was confined to the persons of Christ and those baptized in his name . . . Animals were bereft of psyche, and children, even when baptized, did not have the full reality of souls. Both modern science as it was then being formed and modern Christianity as it was then being reformed, required that subjectivities be purged from everywhere and everything except the authorized place of persons: the *rational* Christian adult [italics added].[10]

This tenet, that animals have no souls, was understood in the hierarchy of being outlined in the Ignatian Exercises, where they were accorded "consciousness". However, even those beings with souls, human beings, were again graded. Those with baptized souls ranked above the unbaptized. A friend of mine told me that when her eldest son was born, just twenty-three years ago, the nuns would not allow her to bring him into the local convent before he was baptized. This may be dismissed as superstitious nonsense, but in fact those nuns were being consistent. Traditional views of baptism see its opening rite of exorcism as releasing the infant soul from possession by evil forces, into whose power it has fallen through Adam's sin. It is "dead" until reborn in Christ as a son of God.

The implications of this for Christian views of the "unbaptized" are far-reaching. They show once again how hierarchies work as mechanisms for exclusion and separation.

First of all, humanity is divided into baptized and unbaptized *souls*. The consequences of this for Christianity's relationships with other races, religions and cultures have been mentioned in various ecological contexts already.

It is enlightening here to read the reasons Simone Weil gave for resisting pressure to be baptized. She said that this pressure had become a practical problem for her, by forcing her to face the kind of questions we are posing. Christianity, she says, should be catholic, containing all vocations without exception. But it is catholic by assumption and not by fact, since so many things are outside it, so many things she loves and does not want to give up, so many things that God loves, otherwise they would not be in existence. All the immense stretches of past centuries except the last twenty are among them; all the countries inhabited by coloured races; all secular life in the white people's countries; in the history of these countries, all the traditions banned as heretical.

She concludes that it is as well that a few sheep should remain outside the fold in order to bear witness that the love of Christ is essentially something different.[11]

Secondly, the baptized human is separated from the unbaptized world. Therefore she/he is licensed to behave towards it in a detached, scientific manner, one different from behaviour towards God and other "souls".

Though he is not thinking in these categories, the Jewish mystic and scholar Martin Buber is scathing about the kind of religious schizophrenia they entail. People speak, he says, of the "religious man" as one who can dispense with all relationships to the world and its beings. But one cannot divide one's life between an actual relationship to God and an inactual I-It relationship to the world – praying to God in truth and utilizing the world. Whoever knows the world as something to be utilized knows God the same way:

> Whoever steps across nothingness and before the countenance has soared way beyond duty and obligation – but not because he has moved away from the world; rather because he has come truly close to it. Duties and obligations one has only towards the stranger: towards one's intimates one is kind and loving. When a man steps before the countenance, the world becomes wholly present to him for the first time in the fullness of the presence, illuminated by eternity, and he can say You in one word to the being of all beings. There is no longer any tension between world and God, but only the one actuality.[12]

This is a religious vision of a healed rather than a split consciousness with its legitimized utilitarianism. Buber is saying, and ecofeminists agree with him, that a false notion of transcendence limited to a divine "up there" cannot be upheld. It seems to call for a different kind of response from God and from us to certain objects supposedly set aside as "not God". Schweitzer denounced the same kind of split consciousness when he called for an ethical relationship with the world, entailing reverence for all life – not just certain forms of it.

This reverence calls for an attitude of utmost respect for the complexity of Nature, as if it were an end in itself. It fosters the capacity to personify things we are tempted to destroy by considering them as objects, as mere instruments. The best example of something that cannot be regarded as a mere instrument is the human person: another "You". The capacity or desire to personify the non-human world is usually dismissed in Christianity as "animism". But what is "animism" if not the result of a tendency to "personify" the universe which should now be looked at as dispassionately as the tendency to "depersonalize". This latter destroys the universe just as surely as the former conserves it.

Buber (on my reading) is asking that we relate to things *as if* they are sacred or ends in themselves. Of course they are not human persons. But to start thinking of them as persons resists the tendency within us not only to divide human beings into good and bad, men and women, but also to divide beings into *things* and *persons*. Insofar as this division takes over the human mind, everything that is done with "things" is justified by science, or rather in its name. The division can only be healed by regaining *respect* for things we have downgraded as mere means. "That can be done naturally and spontaneously, which is the only real, effective way, only when we 'personify' them, only when we perceive the *analogy* between their processes and our own".[13]

This analogy follows naturally through the use of an ecological paradigm, in which all the circuits represented by individuals and all the systems to which we belong are seen to be integrated into society in all their richness and risk as circuits and systems. The theological basis for this perceived integration is that ultimately, both God's will-to-create and God's will-to-love characterize the one God. All creation is simultaneously being loved and created by God, or else none of it is.

Reintegrating Transcendence and Creation

The practical demands of integrating our relationships with the divine, human and non-human world were illustrated for

Charlene Spretnak by a friend who once lived in a seminary overlooking Lake Erie and said he spent two years contemplating the sufferings of Christ without ever noticing that the lake was dying. Dorothee Soelle had a similar reaction to a group of students who prepared a session on Francis of Assisi. They read aloud from his "Canticle of Brother Sun", and followed this by a pious commentary. Finally she interrupted them and asked: "If you really love Sister Water, can you then talk in a timeless language as if nothing had happened to her? If you really love Brother Wind today, can you then forget pollution? Can you be silent about acid rain in North America? If you love someone who is going to be killed right before your eyes, would you be able to continue talking about the beauty of creation? If you learned anything from St. Francis, can you imagine how he would speak today?"[14] The habit of not situating our relationship to God within the context in which we live must be resisted as unecological, that is, damaging to ourselves and the world. It is the religious form of non-participating consciousness deplored in the first part of this book.

The ecological paradigm outlined there has another pertinent lesson here if it is assumed that *all* beings live in a relationship with God. Therefore our interconnectedness with the non-human world is part of our relationship with God. If the Oneness of God is to mean anything, it must mean that the divine will-to-create and the will-to-love are constant towards *all* creation. If we claim it exclusively for ourselves, then we are claiming that God is exclusively loving towards us, and utilize God's "exclusive" love for us as guarantee of special status; in other words, salvation.

Then God is used as guarantee that the "important" bit of us, our souls (supposedly more important to God than anything else in the world), are secure. The world is used in so far as it helps us save our souls out of it. This joint utilitarianism of God and world pervades most doctrines of fall and redemption.

Instead, if we take transcendence seriously, we acknowledge our interdependence with all the created world related to God in love, and believe that each created being has intrinsic value since it shares a relationship with God in its own way. The heavens have voices which tell of the glory of God, whether we hear them or not. Therefore, in so far as we share in God's transcendence through divine courtesy, so does the rest of the world. And therefore every pathway in it is open to us for exploring our common relationship with the divine. This is a part of Christian tradition we need to re-discover. Nature, according to Tertullian, is God's first teacher. The prophets take second place. We must reverence Nature's law, says Richard Hooker, because, God being the author of Nature, her voice is but his instrument. "By her from him we receive whatsoever in sort we learn".[15]

Today this voice is heard through poets, visionaries, mystics of all religions and some women's groups. It rings loud and clear in the native American Indian tradition. Twylah Nitsch, a Keeper of the Tradition of the Wolf Clan, who are part of the great Iroquois confederation of nations, relates the following story:

> Long before we lost contact with our Nature Brothers and Sisters, all the wingeds, two-leggeds, four-leggeds and the unleggeds gathered to sing of Peace. The "Four Winds" listened and offered to carry these songs around the world for all to hear and enjoy. The South Wind spoke of Faith; the East wind spoke of Inspiration; the North Wind spoke of Wisdom and the West Wind spoke of Inner knowing. Then, when these songs were sung in unison, the harmony healed all those who listened. Today, if we listen within, the same songs can be heard, because they are still popular among those who are in tune with Mother Earth.[16]

Such unbaptized people kept attuned to the harmony between God and Nature. As we grow in awareness of this music, we learn to listen to it and value it for its own sake. We move uncertainly into new ways of resouling the world. We also start to take another Christian tradition seriously, that of the Resurrection of the Body. This emphasizes the dignity of the flesh, of the living tissue we share with the animal and natural world and which is sustained by its living and dying with us.

As these traditions expand our understanding of God and the world, we also discover that, as was hinted in the previous chapter, it is extremely important for Christian women that Jesus was a man. He broke all models of exclusivity for God's love. He broke all the models of patriarchal religious behaviour in his inclusion of women as apostles. He revealed himself to a heretic Samaritan woman and she became the first apostle after John the Baptist.[17] He offered her the Spirit, the water of life, just as she was. She did not require baptism, or conversion to Judaism.

He told her that God is Spirit, and will be worshipped not in temples made with hands on Gerizim or in Jerusalem, but everywhere – among women and in the natural world. This inclusive quality in his life and love is what Simone Weil found essentially different from the exclusivism of the Church.

He did not confine his service of others to the "sacred" zone in synagogue or Temple building. His inclusive, *ad hoc* Eucharists were celebrated in "polluted" places such as a publican's house, on a grassy plain or by the shore. He took whatever was offered from whoever offered it, whether leavened bread at Passover time, oil from a sinful woman or fish from a disciple who had betrayed him. He made no distinctions between sacred and profane, the quality of one bread rather than another, and drew attention to the all-encompassing care of the Creator for the sparrow as for each hair on a human head.

Drawing attention to the oneness of this love, Jesus mediates a vision of being part of a world which acknowledges the relationship between each part and its Creator. If we want to call the ground of that relationship having a soul, or being a person, then that is the sort of language we must be prepared to use in a healing way, just as, until now, it has only been used in a destructive or excluding way. The consequences of re-souling the world then become evident in how we think and how we act. Buber calls it moving from an inactual to an actual relationship with the world. It is what we might call here putting the soul back into *animal*.

We might make some surprising discoveries if we do so. Gregory Bateson tells us that on the whole, it is not the crudest, the simplest, the most animalistic and primitive aspects of the human species that we find reflected in the natural phenomena. It is, rather, the more complex, the aesthetic, the intricate, and the elegant aspects of people. It is not greed, purposiveness, so-called "animal", so-called instincts, and so forth that we recognize on the other side of that mirror, over there in Nature. Rather, we see there the roots of human symmetry, beauty and ugliness, aesthetics, the human being's very aliveness and little bits of wisdom. Our wisdom, bodily grace and even our habit of making beautiful objects are just as "animal" as our cruelty. After all, the very word "animal" means endowed with mind or spirit (*animus*).[18]

We also recognize our capacity to praise, to rejoice, to exult:

Let the heavens rejoice and earth be glad,
let the sea and all within it thunder praise,
let the land and all it bears rejoice,
all the trees of the wood sing for joy (Ps. 96).

Some go farther by recognizing that Nature not only has its own relationships, its own innate values but also its intrinsic rights. Nearly forty years ago, the late U.S. Supreme Court Justice William O. Douglas wrote a Bill of Rights for wilderness which affirmed the "rights" of wild places to exist for their own sake. One of those who argues for them today, and does so in court, is a Californian lawyer called Christopher Stone. He sees rights for the non-human world in a continuum which throughout history has seen the results of hierarchical thinking (without ever explicitly labelling it as such), and has dealt with them by gradually extending legal rights to those groups automatically deprived of them within a hierarchy:

> Throughout legal history, each successive extension of rights to some new entity has been, theretofore, a bit unthinkable. We are inclined to suppose the rightlessness of rightless "things" to be a decree of Nature, not a legal convention acting in support of some status quo.[19]

Stone goes on to give examples of previous rulings which deprived blacks of their rights on the grounds that they were a subordinate and inferior race of beings; the Chinese because they were marked by Nature as incapable of intellectual development beyond a certain point; and Jews were treated as "men *ferae naturae*" in thirteenth century law, wild as the forest or the deer. It took until this century for women and children to be promoted to full human rights. He concludes:

> The fact is, that each time there is a movement to confer rights onto some new "entity", the proposal is bound to sound odd or frightening or laughable. This is partly because until the rightless thing receives its rights, we cannot see it as anything but a *thing* for the use of "us" – those who are holding rights at the time.[20]

All of Stone's arguments apply to Christian hierarchical thinking as much as to the legal kind. But there is an added dimension to the former. Whereas courts interpret hierarchies with their attendant "inferiorities" as man-made, and therefore capable of being changed by future rulings, Christians believe them to be decreed by God. And where the civil law bases its arguments on who does and does not have rights according to Nature, Christianity argues that some do not have souls according to their nature, and therefore have no rights.

At this stage in the history of ideas, it is something to have found a movement in the world which is openly recognizing some of the problems caused by hierarchical thinking and addressing them by daring to think differently. No matter that it has a minority voice. The things it is saying cannot be unsaid. No matter that it is greeted with scorn. Schweitzer's call for reverence for all life was derided in his lifetime as a sort of perverted love for mosquitoes. But eighty years on, it is being revived as a spiritual insight of profound importance.

Ecofeminism's awareness of the logic of de-personifying and its consequences for attitudes to the world is supported and enhanced by the thinking and actions of men like Stone. Having won some sort of recognition for themselves in the civil courts with the help of such courageous men, women are all too aware of why it was withheld for so long. So they have no illusions about the difficulties of having the intrinsic rights of non-human creation recognized.

The Christian ecofeminist has an even harder task, since her voice has not yet been heard in its own right, silenced as it is by exclusive male traditions which deny her authority to speak from God's point of view. But religious utilitarianism toward Nature will prevail until her voice is heard. Until then, the supposed "soullessness" of creation will be generally assumed. Until then, the Spirit's voice in creation will groan in vain for release from human oppression. But what if it were heard? What if there were no hierarchy of being? What if the limits of male monopoly on Christian divine imagery were shattered?

One positive result would be the release of the human capacity to perceive beauty in a purposeless, non-utilitarian way. This is what we call aesthetics, the perception of something as good and beautiful in itself. When the doors of perception are cleansed, the distorting lens of a constricting paradigm broken, we see the created world differently. Simply *observing* is no longer enough. The being of the world is revealed in its fundamental beauty, and arouses wonder, praise and joy. It no longer appears as disposable dead stuff but as a vital growing organism. It is not subjected to examination but questions me about my capacity to receive insight. A relationship is established in which I grasp the unfolding of a capacity in things to become visible to me. This unfolding is usually called incarnation. It is the place of encounter with the divine.

Chapter 8

Metaphor and Context

The previous chapter left us at the doors of perception through which we see or do not see the world as a whole. The capacity in things to become visible to us requires a related capacity in us to be responsive to a whole visual field, experienced all at once and marvellously integrated. Their "openness" to us calls for a corresponding openness in us, and the exchange between us may or may not be conveyed to others, depending on our abilities.

An attempt to convey a particular perception of the world in words is the motivating force behind all poetic language. Aimé Césaire says:

> I want to rediscover the secret of great speech and of great burning . . . As frenetic blood rolls on the slow current of the eye, I want to roll words like maddened horses like new children like clotted milk like curfew like traces of a temple like precious stones buried deep enough to daunt all miners.[1]

Poets and visionaries have always found ways of speaking about the relationships they perceive to exist between God and creation, ways which continue to disclose to others further mysteries of the divine love they have themselves discerned. One such way is to use a form of language known as metaphor, which juxtaposes images from different contexts in order to give more insight into our at-one-ment with God.

A striking example is recorded in the Hebrew scriptures, in chapter 6 of the book of Isaiah. The prophet opens the chapter by saying that he saw the Lord sitting upon a throne, high and lifted up, and his train filled the temple. Above it stood the seraphim, each with six wings: with two each covered his face; with two each covered his feet; and with two each flew. And one cried to the other: "Holy, holy, holy is the Lord of hosts: the whole earth is filled with his glory!" The doorposts shook at the sound of these voices, and the house was filled with smoke.

Isaiah absorbs this vision in its wholeness and particularity. Then he responds to it with a cry of woe for his own unworthiness to behold it or speak about it. "Woe is me! for I am undone; because I am a man of unclean lips, and I dwell among people of unclean lips: because my eyes have seen the King, the Lord of hosts."

In response to his cry, one of the seraphim flies to Isaiah bearing in his hand a live coal taken from the altar. He lays it on Isaiah's lips and says: "Lo, this has touched your lips; your iniquity is taken away and your sin purged."

Then Isaiah hears the Lord ask: "Whom shall I send, and who will go for us?" Isaiah replies: "Here I am. Send me!" And the Lord says: "Go and speak to this people" (Isa. 6:1-9).

It is possible to select only some features of this text for comment here, notably that it can be read as precursor to Denys' vision of the celestial hierarchy. The narrative sequence is important, as it charts the movement from vision to speech. The prophet sees God surrounded by acclaiming angels and is inspired with a terrifying sense of his own unworthiness and inadequacy; with an almost desperate realization of the impossibility of conveying the vision through his unclean lips to a community similarly hampered. His awareness of human incapacity to speak of the reality of God opens him to the power from within the vision itself to do so. Césaire's desired secret of great speech and of great burning are given him, together with the confidence to use it and communicate the vision to his people.

He does not invent a new speech to do this. He takes images with which his people are familiar in other contexts to suggest the majesty of God. He mentions temple, chants and altar to suggest the holiness of God. He talks of burning coals to remind them that their God is a refining fire who will purge them of sin. He juxtaposes the images of earthly courts with those of Israel's recorded religious experience (smoke and fire in the Genesis narrative, for instance) to suggest the presence and activity of God.

It is of major importance for us that the chant he records of the heavenly choir: "the whole earth is filled with the glory of God!" is a most powerful affirmation of earth. It echoes still through the daily prayer of Judaism (Kedusha) as well as the Eucharistic celebrations of Christianity.

Of greatest interest in this chapter is the way in which Isaiah uses metaphor to make the transition from religious vision to language. Before looking at that in particular however, we need to consider metaphor within the broader context of our general use of imagery.

The Grammar of Metaphor

Metaphor relates two entities to each other in a way which affects our perception of one of them in particular. It says in effect: "this is that". The metaphoric relationship between "this" entity and "that" entity applies some ideas from one to the other. As a figure of speech, metaphor uses images transposed into words which juxtapose the ideas in order to express the relationship. This attracts attention and tells us more about the entities than if we thought of them singly. So if we were to say of a woman: "She is an English rose," we would be saying a lot more about her than that she was born in Britain, and more about roses than that they have petals.

There is a process prior to the figure of speech which takes us back to the ecological paradigm. This directed attention to the fact that our exchanges with other systems and the input from them pass through territory which is not always known consciously. Even if one were to make a map of this or any other territory, that map is not the territory. So if, under hypnosis, we retrace our steps through experiences and emotions which are not present to conscious recollection, that journey will still only take us on those pathways chosen by the hypnotist out of many possible routes. We always mean more than we can say in words. The words stop but the meaning goes on.

Bearing this in mind, let us take a closer look at how the metaphor above, by bringing together a woman and a rose, tells us more about her. We do not have the woman or the rose actually in our brain. What we do have is their transformation into images – a coding between them which transfers them from their living contexts, from actual women and roses, into mental images of them. The brain carries over as much as possible into the images of what the woman and the rose mean to us, but we know that the actual woman and the rose seen in the garden mean more in themselves and to us than do their images. These are pictorial patterns that abide in our mental structures.

Furthermore, when we use the words "she" and "rose" we mean more by these words than they can convey to other people who may never have seen either this woman or roses in an English garden. There is a shift of meaning at two stages of the process: when the actual woman and rose are transferred into images or words by the speaker and then when these are transferred into images and words by the hearer.

Our brains form the images. The bringing them together (the spoken metaphor or the metaphoric depiction) is usually a conscious act, a choice from among possible images. In the processes of making and choosing the images and juxtaposing them there is a whole range of presuppositions at work which are built into the metaphor. So it is reasonable to suppose that when we choose an image of a rose to say something about a woman we are not allergic to rose scent, or colour blind. Or if we are, and this is known, then we are saying something different about her.

The words used in the above account of how metaphors are generated are all "carrying-over" words: trans-fer, trans-form, etc. The "*trans*" is the Latin translation of the Greek word "*meta*", and meta-phor literally means "carry across". The actual entity (woman or rose) is trans-formed into an image and that image is then trans-ferred into words, or translated or trans-coded or whatever trans-action is required. In Isaiah's vision, the reality of God is transformed into an image of a lord on his throne in the midst of creation.

These imaginative patterns may never come to words, and may instead be used to create a painting or design. In Kabbalistic art, for instance, the context of the juxtaposed images will determine whether a painted tree is a metaphor of God's creative powers, or of the world, or of humankind, or of life, or of death, or of knowledge: or indeed of all these at the same time. This is the "openness" of artistic images. Behind the creation of the metaphor lies a trans-contextualizing which takes trees from one context and God, world, life, etc, from others, and carries them across into a meta-context: the artist's beliefs and creative abilities. This influences the choice of images and puts them in turn into a relationship with each other. This pattern of relationship between the tree and other entities, when translated into the context of the viewer, will, depending on whether or not she shares or at least understands the beliefs of the artist, evoke the same metaphors in her.

The internal pattern of relationship in a metaphor depends upon the two images being different. They have come from different contexts, out of one into the other. So they bring messages from their own context into the other. The tree brings messages to the artist about growth and decay, about the need for water and roots, about strength of form, about living structures poised between earth and sky. In the personal context of the believer, these may be juxtaposed with messages about God, about the world, about one's physical structure, about the thirst for knowledge and its slaking. As the conscious and unconscious mind receives these messages they are perceived as messages of difference. The tree is not God, or life, or knowledge, or a human person. But even as this difference is perceived it evokes new perceptions of God, etc, which otherwise might be lost. The perception is grasped in the metacontext of difference: difference of context, of entity, of image, of word.

At the same time, within the personal context of the artist or the public context of the viewer, the two images share an identity – what Paul Ricoeur calls an *identity-in-difference*. But the identity cannot be allowed to absorb the difference. Otherwise there is no new perception. In front of me I have a drawing by Truda Lane of a courtyard which opens on to a landscape of trees and fields. This is her personal context. In the centre of the courtyard she has drawn a group of white doves fluttering round each other in a harmonious spiralling dance. Sitting on a window sill to the right of the picture is a cat, just looking on. Truda gives the images their public identity by naming the picture "A Celebration of Peace". But it would cease to be a metaphor for peace if there were no warlike differences between doves and cats in their usual contexts of prey and hunter.

It takes at least two things from different contexts to produce news of difference conveying new insight. This is what is called the *cognitive gain* of metaphor. The two things, whether real or imagined, must be such that the differences between them can be understood in ways which stimulate us into new thought. We receive simultaneous messages: "this is that", and because of the differences between them: "this is *not* that". The characteristic relationship of enmity between doves and cats remains, however much their images are juxtaposed to express peace.

Metaphor relies on dissimilarity for information, a dissimilarity respected as enrichment for thought. In hierarchical thinking, this is viewed with suspicion and may be rejected in favour of a literalness which latches on to either the "is" or "is not" and so resists ambiguity. The inability to cope with this ambiguity leads to an insistence by Fundamentalists on the literal inerrancy of the Bible.

From the perspective of linguistic philosophy, Paul Ricoeur makes a counter-claim for the necessity of breaking out of literalness. Therefore he concentrates on the imprecision of metaphor. Indeed, he urges this on us. Taking the pertinent metaphor "Nature is a temple", he says that there is a tension between the literal and metaphorical interpretations of the verb "to be" in such a metaphorical statement. He calls this tension between *is/is not* the *semantic clash*. It is this clash which keeps the metaphor alive, so that it can include new information and say something new about reality. He warns us to guard our awareness that metaphorical language is indirect, figurative and not objective in the sense of direct correlation between an object and a word. We must continually remind ourselves that the "is like" implies an "is not like".[2]

So when Isaiah describes God enthroned among the seraphim, his hearers know that he is not sitting on a throne as Solomon did, and that if one of its legs broke off, God would not end up in a heap on the floor. But the figure of a throne conveys something of the awe and majesty of God which produced in Isaiah an abject sense of his own unworthiness. God "is" and "is not" sitting on a throne. When Isaiah describes the angel taking the live coal from the altar and carrying it to him in his hand, both he and his audience know that angels do not have hands (on his own authority, they have wings.), or if they do, that angelic hands are completely different from human ones, since they can carry live coals. This difference gives simultaneous messages about the activity of angels: they live around God and around us; they can help our relationship with God by their angelic powers; they come to us from within creation as they recognize the glory of God fully present there; they praise God unceasingly in words which we can use for the same purpose, so our praise and theirs is mysteriously united in the oneness of God's glory throughout heaven and earth.

One of the attributes of metaphor is now becoming obvious. The messages it delivers in an imaginative shorthand take a much longer time to convey in any other way. (This is a fundamental difference between poetry and prose.) Also, the

openness of the patterns of relationship between the images give
an open-endedness to their translation into the context of the
user and their transfer into that of the receiver which justifies
the word "gain". The Israelites who heard Isaiah preach gained
a new awareness of the reality of God in a time when that God's
relationship with creation was taken for granted. For ecological
Christians today, the image of a glory-filled earth will open up
new relationships with it and with God. Glory becomes
associated with the material, with the ground we walk on. So
we tread reverently and softly upon it.

The Context of Metaphor

We use contextual patterns of relationship in order to bring
images of things together. As we do this, we find that our
perception of each has been enriched. My own perception of
trees has been enlarged by my slight knowledge of Kabbalah.
Nevertheless, each living tree in my garden has its own
configurations which differentiate it from any other. Therefore
any information I receive about God, or life, or my own person
in a Kabbalistic context of common patterns of "treeness" always
remains open to revision in the presence of this differentiation.
A drooping cherry tree in front of our home, seen up to now in
the context of a memorial gift from my husband's parents, may
acquire yet another dimension if I attend a lecture on the use of
cherry tree imagery in Oriental art.

This contextual patterning is highly relevant when thinking
about the genre of apocalypse with its use of striking metaphors.
Through the centuries, these have had an abundance of possible
meanings which were contextually labelled. What happens to
them when they are narrowed down into one guaranteed
interpretation by Fundamentalism? They lose their potency if
we deny the complexity of the processes which created them
and keep them potent and discard the ambiguity in favour of
literalness. Then they become stereotypes, that is, fixed conven-
tionalized representations rather than a dynamic interplay of
images. The Bride, the Wife of the Lamb (Rev. 19:7) and the
Woman with child (Rev. 21:1) have become such stereotypes:
the former is taken by some as identical with the Church and
the latter as Mary the mother of Jesus.[3]

Such literalist readings fail to grasp the *"is not"* implicit in
female or male images used metaphorically.

Therefore, the circumstance that patriarchal images of God will naturally arise in the Christian patriarchal metacontext has been taken as a divinely ordained limitation on language about God. Then that limitation has been narrowed still further by sacrificing the openness and cognitive gain even of sanctioned metaphors. These have been frozen into those of literal relationship with God as father, judge, lord, creator, king, saviour, pantocrator or warrior. The Christian community has lost the ability to remain aware of these juxtaposed images of God and patriarchal figures *as metaphor*, that is, as a figure of speech which while it identifies God with a king, demands our understanding that God is essentially *different* from a king. God is and *is not* a father, judge, lord, etc. This metaphoric truth is lost, the dynamic ferment of the imagination is lost, the transcendence of God is lost.

The question posed in the previous chapter was whether or not we can shatter the contextual limitations of Christian images in order to let the truth about God emerge into consciousness. If so, then the way opens for speaking about women and Nature in the context of the divine. It now becomes clear that one way to break through those limitations is by a rigorous application of metaphoric rules to those exclusive images now used which have inhibited the Christian community's relationship with woman and Nature. These images have become a representational system which encodes the female body, as woman or as earth, in a context of alienation from the transcendence of God.

Christian contextual freezing or stereotyping has happened not only to metaphors for God but also to metaphors for the earth. Just as the basic metaphor for God has become atrophied to "God is Father" so also has the basic one for earth been taken literally as "the earth is mother".

In both instances "hard-programming" has taken over and the transformations and differences implicit in metaphoric communication are forgotten or ignored. The simultaneous awareness that God *is not* father and the earth *is not* mother has been lost. One part of the metaphor (the assertion of equivalence) is taken for the whole. The identity has absorbed the difference.

One reason for this state of affairs is that a sin/salvation interpretation of the Genesis narrative has been used as the contextual setting for most metaphors about God and the earth. At the same time the closed-off nature of this Christian consciousness rejects as secular or pagan any metaphor coming from outside this narrow tradition: for example, energy–centred ones in process thought, biocentric ones in scientific ecology, and relational ones within Goddess religions.[4]

A good example of this hard-programmed Christian conscious- ness is found in Zaehner's book on mysticism mentioned in the previous chapter. In his conclusions he reflects on the Genesis story in which, he says, Adam's body was formed "from the slime of the earth" and his spirit was infused into him by God. According to a Zoroastrian catechism, he tells us, God is man's father and the earth is his mother. Zaehner accepts this as a valid interpretation of the account in Genesis 2 of man's creation. Consequently, he holds, Original Sin appears as the prototype and archetype of the Oedipus complex itself: Adam rejects the heavenly Father in favour of Mother Nature, the Earth, from whom his body derived. Original Sin, he concludes, is to mistake the lesser good for goodness itself, to mistake created beauty for the uncreated Godhead:

> It is, as Jung rightly points out, a recession to childhood and beyond, for by falling in love with Mother Nature Adam would have thereby refused to accept the moral and social duties that marriage and the propagation of children brought with them.[5]

The remarkable thing about this interpretation is Zaehner's harmonizing of so many religious traditions, disciplines and cultures with the "given" Christian notion of Original Sin. He assumes that they all use the metaphor "Earth is Mother" in a non-metaphorical, literal and closed way. There is never a hint of ambiguity, of the Earth not being Mother, or that in another context we might be told that it is a shell which housed the Supreme Being, or a dream grasped by our father.[6]

Zaehner's reading is stereotyped by his taking the Genesis story and its manifold interpretations as a story about Original Sin, that is, about Fall and Redemption. This context enables him to set up constellations of images and ideas which oppose Adam and the earth, God and the earth, Adam and God, slime and body, female and male, mother and father, breath and spirit. The context "sin" then determines the patterns of relationships between the images in the following implicit and explicit metaphoric interactions:

Adam's body is formed from the slime of the earth, his mother, by his father God. Juxtaposing his "parents", the immanent slimy earth and the transcendent immaterial God, the information is conveyed that Adam "is" a mixture of the immanent and the transcendent, of the earthly and the heavenly, of the material and the spiritual.

His spirit is given to him directly by his father God. It does not come from the earth. It belongs to the territory of transcendence. It belongs to God and his body belongs to the earth, to "not-God". Adam "is" a mixture of God and not-God.

Adam rejects the heavenly father God in favour of Mother Earth. Even today theologians and ecologists often feel obliged to reject one or the other, though they would not agree on which rejection is to be called "sin". For some theologians, sin "is" to mistake the "lesser" good, created earth, for the greatest good, uncreated God. To fall in love with Mother Earth is to fall out of love with Father God.

Most of this has a familiar ring, for it has been coming up in different ways in previous chapters. What is interesting in Zaehner's account is that it shows how widespread the sin/ salvation interpretation of the Creation story is. It has been forced deep into the Western psyche and so forms the basis of much contemporary philosophical, religious and psychological thinking, practice and therapy. Some of these uses will be discussed in the concluding part of this book. Here the interest lies in its destruction of metaphorical power in Christian imagery and practice, and the replacement of that power with the use of stereotypes.

Staying with the use of metaphor in Zaehner's interpretation, it is possible to show from it that the context he takes for granted (the connection between Nature, the female and sin), has helped to trap Christian language into patriarchal patterns of speech. These establish only the assertions about the Fatherhood of God (associated with all that is good) and the Motherhood of Nature (associated with all that is evil and seductive). They ignore the complexity and centrality of differentiation implicit in metaphor.

Sometimes this failure is implicit, sometimes it is expressed. Expressly, God is Father, Earth is Mother. The "metaphors" for Adam are implied. He "is" an earthly body, a created being along with the rest of the animal world. He "is" a spiritual being, created differently from the rest of the world by a special act of

God (breathing into him a living spirit) which gives him a share in uncreated Godhead. Therefore:

> Adam is of earth, attached to his Mother, in his body. He is of spirit, attached to his Father, in his spirit. His Mother is attached to earth. His Father is not. If he attaches himself to earth, he attaches himself to the Mother, the female. If he attaches himself to the spirit, he is attaching himself to the Father, the male.

> The earth is created. Therefore it is lesser than the spirit, the uncreated. The lesser on this scale of values is the Mother, the female, the passive clay of earth, inert matter which cannot shape itself but needs an active spiritual agency to give it form.

> To choose the feminine earth rather than the masculine spirit is to sin.

Now suppose we treat these metaphors properly, restoring the ambiguity and the discernment of differentiation at the different levels of transformation. The results would be something like this:

> God *is/is not* Father. The earth *is/is not* Mother. Adam *is/is not* body. Adam *is/is not* spirit. The earth *is/is not* passive matter.

Now suppose we raise another great "What if?" question. What if sin is not the right context for reading this story?

Now the metaphors really begin to open up. Their contextually hardened relationships start to disintegrate: of earth opposed to God, body opposed to spirit, Mother opposed to Father, masculine opposed to feminine, lesser earth opposed to uncreated good (shades of Plato.). No longer is our imagination kept bunkered inside conceptually gridlocked traps of hierarchy, patriarchy and dualism. If the sinfulness of the earth no longer shapes our pattern of relationships with it, then we are open to other relationships with it of reverence and love. If the earth is not identified with fallenness, then Mother Nature's intrinsic worth as God's good creation can be affirmed and her own relationship with God respected and celebrated with joy. Our language about God becomes inclusive of the natural world, and constellations of metaphors which bring together Nature and the divine begin to emerge from our opened consciousness. This recontextualizing is the agenda of the last chapters of this book.

The Gathering and Diffusion of Metaphors

We saw when considering Zaehner's use of metaphor that one metaphor never comes alone but calls for others and together they remain alive because of their mutual tension and the power of each to evoke the whole network. In this way certain metaphors arise which *gather* several other metaphors borrowed from different fields of experience and provide them with a kind of equilibrium. These are *root* metaphors, which not only impinge on us but also provoke us into creating further metaphors from our own experience. They have a particular capability to engender an unlimited number of potential interpretations at a more conceptual level. Thus they both *gather* and *diffuse*. They *gather* subordinate metaphors and *diffuse* new streams of thought.

The hard-programming of male imagery into Christianity follows from the gathering and diffusion of metaphors in the context of the root metaphor: "God is male". This network of context and metaphor holds together the fabric of Christian interconnectedness in thought, language and practical hierarchy.

A Jewish scholar, Rita Gross, draws attention to the links between this God concept in Judaism, its exclusively male God language and an androcentric model of humanity which eclipsed women and Nature. So long as the prevailing male-centred definition and model seemed adequate and accurate such linguistic conventions did not raise questions. It is only very recently that Jewish women theologians are raising the great "What if" questions about it.[7]

This Christian inheritance from Judaism was re-invested in a narrow Platonic Christocentricity which equated only the man Jesus with divinity. In a Christianity conditioned by its textuality, by the words written down in a patriarchal culture about the revelation of God, canonizing them has mesmerized us into thinking that the literal tenor of these words contains the comprehensive and "literally" true expression of God's reality. Therefore because Moses praised God as "a man of war", or Jesus prayed to God as "father", such images are seen as the authorized ones for a Christian to use.

Associated with these sanctified biblical metaphors are the writings of the church "Fathers", continually scavenged for spiritual sustenance. In their time they expanded on the male biblical models for God such as king, priest, judge, shepherd and prophet which ensured their perpetuation and the loss of other conceptions. This continued the canonizing process of such metaphors, carried on to this day in official church pronouncements about our relationship with God and Christian engagement in the world.

A typical example is a World Council of Churches working paper on the integrity of creation and a Christian approach to it. In it Douglas Hall identifies three metaphors inherent in the tradition of Jerusalem which can provide insight into the nature of the human "office" in sustaining the integrity of creation: the Christian "is" the steward, the priest and the poet. Hall proposes to gather these male metaphors and then diffuse them into subordinate ones for all Christians engaged in ecology. He "gathers" that of steward from "the ancient biblical office and metaphor", that of priest from "the paradigmatic enactment of this role by Jesus Christ in the Garden of Gethsemane", that of poet, not, he hastens to assure us, from some "extra-biblical" source, but from the office of poet in Israel inspired by the "muse of God", by the divine Spirit.[8]

This gathering and diffusion of male metaphors by appeal to biblical sources and the life of Jesus is endemic in Christianity. On this grid is erected any ground plan or initiative for Christian action. How can women respond in this context except by giving up their most valuable asset in ecology, their identification with femininity in Nature, and forcing themselves to be token men? An increasing number who find this intolerable both on their own and Nature's behalf take their experience of nothingness to its existential conclusion and absent themselves from church programmes.

If this seems too extreme a reaction, imagine the reception that a standard Christian congregation would give to a lecture or sermon which proposed that they adopt and implement three female metaphors for the nature of the human office in sustaining the integrity of creation. To lessen the shock, let us stay with biblical models. Mother, priestess, poetess, prophetess are all biblical paradigmatic roles. But would the same preachers and theologians who propose male metaphors to women present mother, priestess and poetess as role models to men? How many women dare to speak publicly of the Christian role in creation as that of a mother? Yet with numbing repetitiveness women are presented with metaphors of stewardship, trusteeship, kingship and priesthood. Miriam and Deborah gave us two of the greatest poems in the Jewish Scriptures (Exodus 15; Judges 5.), but "poetess of creation" would fare no better than "priestess" of creation. How many educated Christians could use these metaphors without mentally adding the dismissive label "pagan"? Or, to take the favourite model, how many could see themselves as "stewardesses" other than in the context of ships' cabins or airlines?

This unrelenting maleness right at the heart of Christian religious thought and language, with the conditioned acceptance of the male as the theological norm, sustains and reinforces the controlling modern vision of ourselves and the world which authorizes and endorses the supremacy of the Christian *rational* (i.e. male) adult. As long as this holds firm, the possibility of women's metaphors and experience being accepted as authentically Christian is minimal. The marginalization of women from the territory of transcendence is an important factor in the failure of Christian theology to articulate new metaphors for the ecological task. Efforts to do so will fail unless accompanied by a positive shift in Christian theology towards inclusivism at sublingual as well as linguistic levels. If it is considered daring, degrading or alienating to speak of God in female or natural imagery, that indicates something about the way women and Nature are valued in Christianity. Their degradation will continue until some find the courage to say: God *is/is not* woman, God *is/is not* man, God *is/is not* Nature. Is the world forced to wait for the new word to be spoken? The only route to the new words is down through our own common life together, letting go our logic, our authority, our control, our pride and our use of one another.[9]

It cannot surprise us then that within a hierarchical value system, the only place in the Christian language game where the *is not* of metaphors for the divine has been consistently applied is in regard to the female and the natural. The root metaphor has been distorted and has withered into "God is *man/is not* woman". It is time to apply the metaphoric rules and say: God *is/is not* man, God *is/is not* woman. Then we may find ourselves able to say: God *is/is not* Nature. With these as root metaphors, we may learn a new and wholesome kind of interconnectedness in how we think and talk about the non-human world and how we relate to it.

There is one objection to this analysis and conclusion which would be vociferously raised by Fundamentalists, but which operates at a subconscious level in most Christians. This is the argument that biblical and theological words are sacred, i.e., they exist in a timeless and holy vacuum untouched by the conventions of ordinary speech. So what Ricoeur, Bateson, Wren, McFague, Frye or Morton say about metaphor may be all very well for poets, literary critics or feminist theologians to acknowledge, but traditional theologians work in the rarefied atmosphere of the canonized safe deposit of language.

Making their presence felt here are the dualisms mentioned in the opening chapters of this book, so inimical to authentic Christian ecology. The accepted Fundamentalist dichotomy between the "sacred" words of the Bible and the "profane" words of everyday speech is a strategic classification of the contents of human experience into opposed categories, with the underlying notion that one is good and the other bad. It also implies that religious language exists within a *cordon sanitaire*, protected by God from the pollution of everyday life.

But this world and its language are all we have in which to express our relationship with God. This means that the words we have in Christian theology are subject to the same strains and stresses, the same *lacunae* and imprecision as any others. They must also be subject to the same correctives and analyses. So as long as patriarchy reigns supreme in Christian Godtalk, even though it is seen as discriminatory by the "secular" world, Christians ought to feel uneasy. How can their language about God rely on a linguistic freezing which does not follow the spirit of common language in consciously becoming more linguistically open? Why not use the disciplines its Christian metaphors require? Is it afraid to share its images of God with the whole world?

Women's Experience of Christian Metaphor

The degradation of feminine and natural imagery within Christianity has practical consequences. When Carol Christ was one of the only two women in close on one hundred graduate theology students at Yale, she talked in a seminar about the spiritual experiences that gave rise to her interest in theology – her connection to Nature, the oneness with the universe she experienced while swimming in the ocean or hiking in the woods. She was told that such experiences were "aesthetic", "poetic", "emotional", or "confused" and not worthy of theological discourse. (This tallies with Schumacher's memories of his education. See again chapter 6, note 8.)

This opposition of irrational/female to rational/theological exemplifies again the dualism in Christian language which excludes reflection on feminine experience. Therefore it excludes the relational language which would articulate such reflection. "Female" Nature remains pagan, unspiritual, alternately alluring and terrifying in its unpredictability. To qualify Ricoeur's metaphor slightly, Nature is a *pagan* temple for Christianity, to be ignored if not destroyed by all who enter or preach in a Christian church. It is subordinated to a "male" God who "lords" it over creation, "orders" the stars in their courses, brings "order" out of chaos with his creative power, and "orders" man to subdue the earth. His Lordship defines his relationship with Nature and with us.

I remember some years ago being at a seminar in Tübingen led by the eminent biblical scholar and theologian Ernst Käsemann. A couple of women students argued with him about his insistence on the primacy of the "lordship" of Christ. They told him that this was a relationship with Christ in which they could not participate, since it was one of domination. He asked them what would be their chosen model, and they said it would have to be that of love. He responded to this with a joking remark about marriage and male subordination, but it was clear that for him (and for mainstream Christian theology), the biblical affirmation "Jesus is Lord!" would never lose its theological dominance. They, and we, must wait a long time to hear the acclamation in church: "Jesus is Lover!"

The experience of those students is common to many women. Some cope with the problem by trying to change the paradigm formally, as they were doing by their open academic debate. Others concentrate on preserving their personal vision intact. The artist mystic Meinrad Craighead writes of how, through half a lifetime of Christian worship, her secret worship of God the Mother has been the sure ground of her spirituality. The participation in that Mother's body, in the natural symbols and rhythms of all organic life and the actualization of these symbols in her life as an artist have been "a steadfast protection against the negative patriarchal values of Christianity, the faith I still profess".[10]

Both approaches, of public commitment and personal growth in insight, are needed from all who are aware of the problem. Then a new inclusive Christian language generated by the proper use of metaphor can begin to remedy the inimical effects of a hierarchical ordering of reality. It has been accepted until now for many reasons, not least because in an attempt to grapple with the mystery of God's relationship with the world, we have settled for expressing it by something apparently more easy to grasp. To say "God is man" brings the totally unknowable God within human ken. The image of man is juxtaposed with an image of God, bringing together realities which can never be fully expressed. The metaphor relates the reality we call "God" to another reality, man. God is not summed up in the expression, and the religious discipline known as *apophaticism* (an attempt to know God by asserting that God is not, in fact, any of the things God is called) has always stressed this. Similarly, the borderline between philosophy and psychology is littered with inadequate attempts to encompass the reality of being man, ranging from Aristotle's epistemological definitions of the human knower to modern psychological attempts to define the self or the ego.

But the "visibility" of God in Jesus has obscured the fact that in common Christian usage, the gap between the words "God", "man" and the realities inferred by them has suffered chronically from shrinkage. All the complexities of the metaphoric process are telescoped into one assertion of identity. The problem specifically addressed here is that these two words, with their own gaps in meaning necessarily still in place, are used to close the gap between God and humankind. Furthermore, they are so connected in Christian metaphor as to exclude practically any possibility of pointing to other realities than the human male when referring to God.

Women's Response to Christian Metaphor

The opening up of context and metaphor argued for by women is not just an option in an ecological Christianity. It is not just a matter of justice for women. It is not just a matter of justice towards the non-human world. It is all these, certainly, but above all it is a way of doing justice to the mystery of transcendence and immanence we call God.

It is the way forward to an inclusivism which accepts the psychic presence of other beings in the world, reverences them and loves them as they are, in their own relationship with the divine. If the dark and excluding nature of sexism in Christianity is frankly acknowledged, then a new vision of Nature is possible which does not move away from it in disdain but relates to it positively in thought, language and deed.

This inclusivism is subsumed under the word "integrity" in the World Council of Churches JPIC programme. The participant in the programme mentioned already, the theologian Douglas Hall, isolates some of its nuances. Firstly, integrity can refer to truth, and especially to the correlation between "appearance" and "reality". Applying this to the Christian tradition, he says that it has theological implications in Christianity's insistence upon (a) the reality of the created order, which refuses to locate the "real" *beyond* the material world and (b) the still more radical claim that the quest for *truth*, whether scientific or theological, must always relate in a positive manner to the actuality of what is there in the world, and not simply impose upon reality theories and formulas, images and world-views which do not submit themselves to the tests that are set by the created order itself.[11]

An ecofeminist response to this would have to point out that as regards Christianity's insistence upon the reality of the created order, and its supposed refusal to locate the "real" beyond the material world, verbal insistence there may be, but Christian action upon the "real" world is severely hampered by locating its *value* elsewhere. As long as that value is inextricably bound to the advance or retardation of the "eternal" salvation of the human race, the integrity of non-human species is expendable.

Again, to say that the quest for truth, whether scientific or theological, must always relate in a positive manner to the actuality of what is there in the world merits a resounding cheer. But the cheer rings more hollowly when we are told that integrity demands, not the imposition of theories and formulae, images and world views but submission to the tests set by the created order itself. Speaking from within and on behalf of that created order, women can only testify to Christianity's stern refusal to do any other than impose a patriarchal world-view and male images of divinity on the rest of creation.

The most severe criticism however, must be that nowhere in his own exposition of biblical models, alluded to earlier in this chapter, does Hall mention the work and presence of the Spirit of God. We are back with the Christocentricity which makes Jesus God without remainder, and the doctrine of the Trinity redundant. Yet it is only through the gift and power of the Spirit that the relationship between God and the actuality of what is there in the world is made possible. It is only through the creative power of the Spirit from within that we are able to communicate a vision of that relationship.

In the matter addressed in this chapter, how that relationship may be expressed in metaphoric images, the interaction between that Spirit and the spirit of the poet and artist remains our best guide. The "aesthetics" despised by rational male stereotypes in theology must be valued as an open pathway to the beauty of God made visible from within the world, a concept too much ignored in favour of those redolent of power over it.

In one of Piero della Francesca's masterpieces, *Madonna del Parto*, he places the image of a pregnant woman against the backdrop of a tent. Its draped sides are held back by two angels to reveal her in all her physicality, serenity and radiant confidence. For Piero and all those who saw this mural behind the altar of their funerary chapel, this woman was the Mother of God, impregnated by the Spirit with the new being of her Son. The angels who reveal her to them and to us belong to the same company as the one who told her that the Spirit would possess her and her body would bear fruit. They use their hands to hold back the veils concealing vision as the angel in Isaiah held a live coal to burn open the prophet's lips. They keep open the tent around her, symbol of God's presence and protection, the tent of meeting between heaven and earth. This woman is the new Ark of the Covenant between God and creation, the bearer of the ratified relationship between them. The colours of the tent and of the angels' clothes and wings are those of the Tuscan earth – brown, olive, red, ochre, umber and green. She alone wears blue, the colour of divinity. Her left hand rests on her hip. The right one lies protectively over her swollen belly on a white opening in her blue dress. Humanity and divinity enclose and disclose, protect and reveal each other. Their identity and their difference shock us into wonder and delight; into new ways of relating to, thinking of and speaking about God, woman and Nature. God *is/is not* man, God *is/is not* woman, body *is/is not* spirit, earth *is/is not* mother, matter *is/is not* divine, transcendence *is/is not* immanence, God *is/is not* the fruit of the womb.

Chapter 9

Ecofeminism and Canon

The two previous chapters argued for the inclusion of feminine
and natural imagery in the Christian tradition, and for women's
right to participate in the making of that tradition. Interpretation
of the Bible plays a crucial part in any decision made about the
exclusion or inclusion of women. Up to now, it has worked
against them by canonizing the perpetuation of patriarchy and
by making male metaphors for God absolute. A new perception
of what is involved in the process of canonizing may help open
up the tradition to include women's experience as an integral
part of it.

What is the Canon?

An interplay between Bible, tradition and interpretation was the
dominant force in Christianity's development in self-
understanding. This development is reflected in the process
usually called the formation of the *canon*: the process by which
certain historical records of the religious past were chosen as
authoritative. This canon was defined in the fifth century as:
"that which has been believed everywhere, always and by all".[1]
The process is a living one, and its development has rested on
the acceptance by believers that the choice of record made in
canonization (the Bible as we have it today, with or without
certain writings of the church Fathers and conciliar pronouncements) was inspired by the Spirit. Furthermore, it presupposes
that the interpretation of these records is definitively pro-
pounded through the authority of the Spirit handed on (*traditio*)
from one generation to the next. The exclusion of some books
from the Protestant canon and their inclusion by the Catholic
hierarchy does not affect the notion of canon itself. Rather, it
emphasizes it, since both actions were intended to be seen as
claims to the authority to define what it means to be Christian.
Outside ecclesiastical government circles, the ordinary believer
generally accepts that the books of the Bible as printed constitute
the basic written record of the revelation of God given to the
Church.

This is true even of the Roman Catholic Church, which until the Second Vatican Council would have taught that there were two distinct sources of revelation, Scripture and Tradition (the recorded authorized interpretations). In 1965, in the document on revelation, the Council devoted its two opening chapters to revelation and its transmission without explicitly distinguishing them as separate sources. Four of the six chapters in the document deal expressly with the Bible. In it, the document says, God revealed himself to men, spoke to men out of the abundance of his love and invited them into fellowship with himself. By this revelation the deepest truth about God and the Salvation of man is made clear to us in Christ. After speaking in many places and various ways through the prophets, God last of all has spoken to us by his Son, the Word made flesh, sent as "a man to men".[2]

The Protestant position in regard to the revelation of God was stated briefly by Barth when he described Holy Scripture as an entity which stands superior in order to the church, temporal like it, yet different from it. This is because it is the canon of the church, that is, the regulation, the pattern, what is fixed in the church as authoritative. From the fourth century on, he says, the word "canon" has developed into the list of books in the Bible recognized in the church as authoritative, because recognized as apostolic.[3]

The complex process of the formation of the canon is a study in its own right, and it is impossible to give an adequate outline of its development here. What I want to focus on is simply the fact that such a thing as the canon exists, and then to follow up some questions raised by its existence and by the way in which it came to exist. Whether it is ever formally invoked or not, it is taken by ordinary Christians to mean that the Bible is the foundation stone upon which is built the security of faith and practice which comes from having God's will for the world made explicit. Its authenticity is seen as guaranteed by the authority of those to whom Christ handed on his own unique perception of that will, the apostles. The Catholic and Protestant positions come together here by making the apostles the link between the handing on of the truth of God in Christ ("the Word made flesh, sent as a man to men") and the authoritative reading of the Bible in churches today.

Questions Raised by the Canon

The first question raised by the existence of the canon is its dependence on the hierarchical paradigm of Christianity. The power to interpret what is contained in it is assumed to be given "from above", from the Spirit handed on by Jesus to certain men who have the power to delegate it to others. The authority to interpret the Scriptures definitively is attributed to the "highest" level of church government, from which and on which all others depend.

The corollary to this is that the Spirit is confined to hierarchical relationships within this structure, both between the Father and Son and between them and the church. The Spirit is boxed in between Father and Son, Son and apostles, apostles and church. The personal role of the Spirit within the life of the Trinity is confined to empowering the love between Father and Son, or the mission of the Father and Son to the world through the church. The hierarchical church thus makes itself the cause of grace in the world and the means of dispensing the Spirit, rather than simply being the occasion and context where these may take place. The freedom of the Spirit to act as and when and where it pleases, intimated by the image of the wind used for it by Jesus, is lost in the superimposed image of it as a possession of men, handed on, literally, to other men, through the laying-on of hands.

Then there is the question of those who heard, proclaimed, recorded or wrote the texts as they now appear. Neither they, nor today's readers and proclaimers, can isolate themselves and their personal contexts from the interpretative process. They are part of it, not least by the questions they pose and the answers they expect. Their attitudes to women and Nature cannot be isolated from their enquiries into the complex life systems presented to us in the Bible and other canonical sources. This fact will be taken particularly into account in the re-reading of Genesis 1–3 in the final part of this book.

There is the further question of how balanced a view of the world we can expect to find in the records. The Bible and the interpretations of it which came from a patriarchal church necessarily failed to integrate the contribution women could have made to the canon. Male dominance permeates it. To recognize this is difficult and painful: our personal stories are involved, our deepest identity called into question. For male readers it is especially difficult, and one man, a biblical scholar, accepted the analysis, but said it made him feel as if he were being asked to accept castration.[4] How do women feel?

On the basis of these and allied questions, ecofeminists refuse to take the canonical record of male relationship with God and the world, centred on one small group of people in a particular time and culture, as normative for the whole of humanity. They refuse to accept as God's will the continuance of the patriarchal power structures enshrined within this record. These have ensured that women's voices have been omitted from the ongoing interpretative process and that a particular attitude to Nature has been canonized. Therefore ecofeminist theologians claim the right from now on to include women's experience as part of that process which keeps the canon alive as a source of inspiration and strength within the Church.

Therefore they seek contemporary meaning within the texts in a dialogical relationship between them and the primary system of the world we live in. The dialogue is always open-ended, for the meaning emerges in the act of struggling for it in a relational rather than an oppositional way. Therefore it is constantly open to revision through fresh input, for example from the data of scientific ecology.

Starting from these premises, ecofeminist theology challenges the present assumptions behind the canonicity of Scripture. Why these texts and not others? What texts were omitted when it was decided that these were the only revealed truth about God's dealings with the world? Who made the decisions? What effects has this partiality had on Christianity's relationship with the world?

In raising the first question, why these texts and not others, we note that the Hebrew scriptures come from sources removed both hierarchically and demographically from the lives of most Israelites. This is hardly surprising, since in a largely pre-literate or illiterate society, the possibility of keeping records was necessarily confined to certain classes. Those parts of the canon most concerned with human relationships with the land (the Pentateuch) are by the large the product of a priestly, all-male, hereditary group with its leadership based on the Temple, located in the capital city, Jerusalem. Virtually all of the historical writings – the so-called Deuteronomic history, which runs from

Joshua through to Kings and constitutes the core of the Hebrew Bible – were probably based on court records or traditions circulating in royal circles. The post-exilic chronicles were compiled at the behest of governors like Ezra and Nehemiah. (The point at issue here is the common acceptance of this attribution, and not its truth, falsity or the possibility of exceptions to it within the Wisdom tradition.) This attribution to official ruling classes, whether royal, priestly or gubernatorial, excluded most men and the vast majority of Israelite women. The governing establishment was unrepresentative of the population as a whole. Yet the experience of this male part of the nation Israel, even today, has been taken as representing the whole history of God's relationship with this people.[5]

This is equally true of those texts written after the death of Jesus. Paul's education and the evangelists' literary skills were important factors in the acceptance of their writings as normative. Paul was a city person. The city breathes through his language. When he constructs a metaphor of olive trees or gardens, the Greek is fluent and evokes schoolroom more than farm; he seems at home with the clichés of Greek rhetoric, drawn from gymnasium, stadium or workshop. He depended on the city for his livelihood, supporting himself as an artisan in distinction both from the workers of the farms, both slave and free, and from the few whose wealth and status depended on their agricultural estates. When Paul rhetorically catalogues the places where he has suffered danger, he divides the world into city, wilderness, and sea (2 Cor. 11:26). His world does not include the *chora*, the productive countryside; outside the city there is nothing – *eremia*. Since his world consisted, practically speaking, only of the cities of the Roman Empire, he makes the extraordinary claim that from Jerusalem and as far round as Illyricum, he has fully preached the Gospel of Christ, so that he no longer has work in these regions. What he had actually done was to plant small cells of Christians in scattered households in some of the strategically located cities of the north-east Mediterranean basin.[6]

The authors of the Gospel records may or may not have included a countryman. Popular attribution ascribes them to a physician (Luke), a philosopher theologian (John), a Hellenistic catechist (Matthew) and a disciple of Peter's who made his way to Rome and became recorder of the community there (Mark).

Whoever they were, their accounts concentrate almost exclusively on what is commonly called the "public" life of Jesus, centred on town and city, and on his debates with the ruling classes in the context of his trial and death at the hands of spiritual and imperial elites.

The Pauline Epistles and Acts record Paul's own battles with these as well as with the male ruling council of the emerging church. Attribution to him was enough for the so-called "Pastoral" letters to the churches to be taken as authoritative, especially where they lay down rules for the "normative" relationships within church hierarchies which, for example, exclude women from spiritual authority. The pseudo-Pauline letter to Timothy gives an inaccurate gloss of Genesis in its attempt to justify the male right to exclude (cf. 1 Cor. 11:3, 5; 14:34f; 2 Tim. 2:11-14). This appeal to a flawed male hermeneutic of Genesis was to have lasting consequences for the role of women and Nature within Christianity.

This process within the canonized Bible of using interpretations of existing Scriptures to reinforce certain religious and cultural assumptions must be seen for what it is, a literary and interpretative device. Then the internal dialogue in the New Testament between the Jewish scriptures and the nascent Christian community after the death of Jesus will be seen as aspects of this system of reinforcing the authority to interpret. They are not master codes possessing the ability to bring about the truth. Seen like this, the Pauline emphasis on Jesus as Lord is respected as no more than that, a vital personal relationship and not a universal one to be given dominance over all others.

The Partiality of the Canon

From an ecofeminist theological viewpoint, priests, prophets, kings, officers, bureaucrats and apostles are seen to be small élite groups within masses of population, both male and female, all of whom have a relationship with their creator God. The biblical concentration on these élites, to the exclusion of the rest, has necessarily given us a partial picture of our religious origins which has taken such groups out of their metacontexts and raised them to the status of the whole. This goes some way towards answering the question about which records were kept and which discarded. However small in number these groups were, they had enormous power and influence, not least because of their ability to articulate the meaning of their relationship with God and the world around them.

So their ideologies, in the sense of their religious understanding of events and ideas, came to be considered as normative by everyone. Not only that, but they also became the apparent divine norm, and certain social and religious structures (notably monarchy and ecclesiastical hierarchy) were established on this basis. Not only must we acknowledge the relative status of these writings. We also need to analyze the positions of power which underlay their circulation.

We must also keep in mind the group of theologians (the church Fathers) who up to and since the fourth century have kept certain interpretations of these writings in a position of dominance over the Christian imagination. They shared a Greek culture and transmitted their teaching through the concepts and categories of Greek philosophy. They also shared the reverence for Scriptural authority manifest in the Christian records written after Jesus' death. So when Denys, the author of *The Celestial Hierarchy* wanted to give his vision authority, he wrote under the pseudonym "Denys the Areopagite". Denys was the first of Paul's converts in Athens, and Athens meant philosophy, and more precisely, Plato. Denys the Athenian convert stands at the point where Christ and Plato meet. The pseudonym expressed the author's belief that the truths that Plato grasped belong to Christ, and are not abandoned by embracing faith in Christ.[7] This view was shared, as we have seen, by some of the most influential shapers of the Christian tradition.

Returning to the Israelite stage of the tradition for the moment, those who shaped it were not only exclusive in number and education. They were separated from most of their fellow Israelites in that as residents of Jerusalem or of other major cities, they participated in an urban pattern of life. This is of more than passing consequence for assessing the effects of those texts included or excluded. For a start, most people lived in the non-urban settings under-represented in the Bible. Its androcentric bias and also its urban, élite orientation mean that even the information it does contain about agrarian life may be a distortion or misrepresentation. So the highly stylized Leviticus texts, for instance, cannot be taken as universally applicable norms in respect to women and Nature.[8] Indeed, even within the Christian canon there is a notable outburst attributed to God, no less, against such stereotyping when Peter is reminded forcibly that no creature created by God can be classified as unclean (Acts 10).

Such partiality toward urban society, its relationships with and its distancing from the land, has been hard-programmed into the Christian interpretation of the biblical sources in all sorts of covert ways. Until recently, biblical archaeology concentrated disproportionately on the urban sites most likely to provide verification or illumination of the political history recorded in the Bible. Consequently the sites chosen tended to be major cities assumed to have been cultic and administrative centres. Archaeologists concentrated on fortification systems, palaces, villas, and public buildings. In doing so, they chose features of urban life related to the military, to the governing elite, and to the cultic establishment. This contributed further to the lack of visibility of the middle and lower echelons of society, and of all those whose realm of activity was oriented to private or domestic affairs. Insofar as women's lives were typically confined to the domestic realm, biblical archaeology has offered virtually nothing that could be used to reconstruct the social or religious role of women or anyone else belonging to the non-urban, non-élite or non-specialist segment of the population.[9] In short, almost nothing was done up to now to recover a balanced understanding of early Israelite society or the "ordinary" person's relationship with God.

The same invisibility cloaks the life of the early Christian communities, but is often compensated for by haggling over visible sites associated with the life and death of Jesus. In the Christian Diaspora imperial basilicas are studied to provide ground plans and scale maps for Christian worship. By the late second century, the episcopal model of leadership had developed into an urban hierarchy in which the bishop became the presiding pastor at the major congregation of the city and supervised others. The pattern of episcopal hierarchy expanded in the next two centuries into provincial and imperial forms by which the presiding bishops at major sees supervised bishops and elders under them. Gradually, the church began to duplicate the political structures of the late Roman Empire and to evolve an ecclesiastical counterpart to the Roman system of urban and provincial governors.[10]

In such ways, the very notion of church became identified with visible structures designed and built by men, and church membership appeared synonymous with attendance in them. Churchgoers, that is, those who went out of the home to worship, were counted as "the Church".

Effects of the Canon on Women and Nature

One obvious effect of this split in religious consciousness was that the home, woman-centred in its rituals of bringing forth and nourishing life, became desacralized. Instead of ritualizing natural birth through the water and blood of the mother, baptism in church became the religious rite by which one rejects one's natural life, derived from and nourished by the waters of the mother's womb, and undergoes a "rebirth" through "holy" water blessed by men hierarchically chosen to possess the Spirit. Women's experience of life-giving was alienated from the sacred and excluded from canonical authority.

If it were included, it would integrate the mother and child into a community representing the whole of human relationality. The experience of naturally giving birth is intrinsically linked with the nourishment and sustaining of life through food. Women's continuous experience of lifegiving centres on the nurture and growth of bodies through food shared at meals. This is the central symbolic act of Christianity known as Eucharist. Yet it has been most radically alienated from its natural setting by being literally taken out of women's hands and transferred to a church sanctuary. There the symbolic act of blessing and giving food and drink has been "elevated" into a symbol of the power to control divine or redeeming life, a power that the clergy claim to possess in a way that is beyond the access of "natural" human beings.[11]

This tendency to reserve Eucharistic actions to those males in churches seen as sole possessors of the Spirit has contributed much to the desacralizing of our attitudes to "ordinary" food and the acceptance of "consumerism" instead. In Chapter 12 the theological and ecological implications of this will be discussed at some length. An ecological Christianity would seek to heal the division between Eucharist and home by restoring a sense of the sacred to every meal, and by re-valuing women's role in bearing the Spirit of a God who continually sustains us through eating.

This bias toward church buildings in the city incorporated an important shift not only in the perception of home but also of

Nature. Certain man-made edifices became isolated sanctuaries, holy places dotted about a natural, profane world. The sacred was sequestered within the walls of a public building made with hands. Human activities were classified as "holy" according to whether or not they took place within a "consecrated" place. Implicitly, therefore, one stepped outside such a place into a world that was not sacred. The accepted reason for the "profanity" of Nature was that it became corrupted through Adam's Sin.[12] But whereas humanity was redeemed within these buildings through baptism into Christ the second Adam, outside them Nature remained unredeemed.

In such ways the foundations were laid for a dualistic modelling of Christian society into two kinds of activity, the private and the public, which came to be seen as corresponding to the profane and the sacred. The private domestic sphere revolved around home and field and the reproductive processes centred on women and the natural world. While not explicitly excluded from the realm of the sacred, it was definitely not its primary locus either. The public sphere was everything outside the home environment: collective rituals, legal or judicial regulation of supradomestic matters, and official worship.

Theologically as well as culturally then, female identity was linked with the domestic and male identity with the public. Women were associated with the "natural" functions taking place in the domestic contexts, and men more closely identified with public functions.[13] Consciously and unconsciously, the female natural habitat, whether of humankind or beast, was linked with the profane, and the male public sphere was the area of encounter with the sacred. In regard to the non-human world, any possibility of locating the divine there was repudiated.

Today it is official Christian teaching that Nature is desacralized, "fallen".[14] Yet hardly a day goes by without someone reminding us that unless we recover a sense of reverence for Nature, we are not going to win the battle for its and our survival. How is this sense to be recovered in a tradition which has consistently denied Nature the possibility of its own relationship with the divine and the right to reverence for its own sake?[15]

A start must be made by acknowledging the endemic partiality of Christianity. This runs right through its canonical tradition. It is based in texts which make small sections of the community representative of the whole and it allows that community to believe itself to be the isolated recipient of the whole of God's revelation to the whole of creation. That self-perception turns all too easily into one which knowingly displaces the rest of creation, whether women, non-Christians, non-human species or inert matter, into a desacralized zone. This continues as long as Christian assertions are made (for example, that no one comes to the Father except through the Son, or that no one is saved outside the church), in ways which seemingly accept that God has created the whole world in order to save a very small number of baptized human beings out of it.

So far this book has given a glimpse of some of the covert and overt effects on women and Nature wherever it is assumed that the male part of humanity's experience of God can be taken for the whole. It has left us with a few further questions here: who decided which part of the tradition should be so taken? Why these records and not others? The recent discovery of so much "non-canonical", inter-testamental and preChristian literature, such as the Nag Hammadi texts and the Qumran scrolls, poses the question with renewed force.

The Canon and the Spirit

The Christian canonization of Scripture, ·begun in the second century C.E., assigned authority to certain writings chosen out of those circulating among Christians at the time. The men who chose these and rejected others claimed absolute authority for themselves to decide which books were authoritative. They based their claim on their possession of the Spirit. In all Christian churches, including the non-episcopal ones, this claim to possession of the Spirit in order to choose and interpret the essential books of the Bible continues to constitute that church's claim to be a Christian church, and guarantees its members' belonging to Christ's Body. In episcopal churches, the claim is made that the Holy Spirit is passed on to ordained ministers through the bishop, the successor of the apostles. An up-to-date statement of this claim is found in the Vatican II Dogmatic Constitution on the Church, *Lumen Gentium*, 24–8.[16]

This claim on behalf of one section of the community gradually absorbed (or eroded) any counter-claim to possession of the Spirit. Traditional theology held that the spiritual phenomena of the early times had disappeared because they were no longer needed. The strength of the church made them unnecessary for confirming the faith of the people. The liberation theologian José Comblin asks: "Was it not rather the opposite; that the (human) strength of the churches closed the doors on the Spirit and its gifts?"[17]

The closure is exemplified in the first centuries of the Church by the exclusion of Christian women from spiritual authority. This was justified by a "canonized" interpretation of the Genesis narratives (cf. the reference from 2 Tim. 2) which blamed the daughters of Eve for the fall of man. This interpretation was legalized in the twelfth century canons of Gratian (*Corpus iuris Canonici*, Pt. II. C.33. q.5, c.12, 13, 17, 18).

With this interpretation of the fall of man through woman's weakness as its major presupposition, all traditional Christian efforts have been directed at finding a remedy for this fall. The resulting doctrines of salvation have elevated man twice over above women and Nature. They are agents neither of their own damnation nor salvation. It is the fall of Adam that is credited (!) with the corruption of all succeeding generations. In him we are all fallen. Correlatively, it is the second Adam, Jesus Christ, who is credited with the salvation of both man and woman. Only a male can save us from the sin generated by a male. This logic denies women the power to be agents of salvation for themselves or others. They have access to redemption only through men.

This effectively blocks them from any relationship with the Spirit other than through male mediation. It also effectively blocks any relationship with the Spirit other than a utilitarian one, useful for human salvation. Comblin remarks dryly that the domination of the poor of Latin America was accepted for so long because of the traditional view that the clergy hold the keys of the kingdom of heaven, so those who wish to be saved have to accept the whims of the clergy – outwardly at least. But their present experience of liberation through the Spirit is of a new sense of responsibility for themselves, of being capable of acting on their own initiative. So they are now expressing their own opinions about sin, life and death. As are women.[18]

The doctrine of salvation from sin through the power invested in the clergy was seen to be effective for human beings alone. Yet Adam's fall was deemed sufficient cause for Nature's corruption. When he fell, so did the whole natural world.

Augustine adduced postlapsarian thorns and thistles as evidence for this. But when the man Jesus Christ redeemed humanity from that fall, the thorns still flourished and the thistles spread: Nature remained corrupt, condemned to be subdued and exploited by men. There was no recognition of its own relationship with its Creator, nor any effective mediation of salvation through the church offered to it.

Therefore St Francis's preaching to the birds is usually regarded as a pious aberration, and blessings of animals are generally treated as either certifiable or suspicious, on the grounds that they have no souls. The Rogation Day blessing of fields has withered away, and while there are some attempts to revive harvest festivals in a meaningful way, their success is limited in the Northern Hemisphere by the fact that most churchgoers shop for their food, and the festival is set in the context of the Eucharistic celebration with its emphasis on a different sort of food again.

As long as sin/salvation rituals dominate Christian practice, this cutting off of the non-human world from the church's ministry will continue. Its own perception of its role in salvation, as sole mediator between God and the world through its possession of the Spirit, effectively breaks the relationship between the Spirit and the whole of creation.

Therefore it also breaks the bond between the Trinity and creation, a bond traditionally expressed in the doctrine of the "economic" Trinity. This treats of the process of God's self-disclosure addressed to creation in the three-fold aspect of Father, Son and Spirit.

While this notion of economy seems to bear little relation to what is now understood by the word, among its original meanings was the popular understanding of it as distribution, organization and arrangement of a number of factors; in this case, the ordering of right relationships between the whole of creation and different aspects of God recorded in the tradition (Father, Son and Spirit). It is also noteworthy that the earliest reference to the "divine economy" occurs in Ignatius's Epistle to the Ephesians (XVIII, 2), where the words *oikonomia theou* refer to what one might call "God's management of the divine household". The Greek original has the same root (*oikos*: house, home, inhabited world) as ecology and ecumenism. It seems fair to say that the department marked "human salvation" appears not only to have taken over all the others but has effectively closed them down.

Ecofeminist Critique of Canon

Ecofeminism calls for their re-opening as a matter of priority. It asks that human beings positively assert their relationship with Nature, and their common relationship with God, in particular under the aspect of the Spirit. What if we spoke of the Spirit of God the housekeeper? What would happen then to Christian attitudes to home and garden, to meals and housework?

Such a shift in perception can happen only if we integrate women's lives into the living canon of Christianity. We must reject the common demotion of women, their bodies, work and habitat, to all that is not divine. In company with the figure of Wisdom in the Jewish scriptures, women must again raise their voices to recount their role in the fashioning, in the sustaining of the world.

How can they be heard in a church which includes 2 Timothy in its canon? The violence with which Quaker women were treated in the seventeenth century (from whippings to hangings and burnings) when they dared raise their voices to interpret scripture is evidence of how well this male prohibition had worked until then. Is it so different now? The physical violence may appear to have gone, but psychological and pseudo-theological barriers remain firmly in place. So unless women's interpretations of the book of Genesis are given authority, rather than the biassed views of a pseudo-Pauline author or an Augustine, their desacralization together with that of Nature will continue under the name of Christian orthodoxy. So too will Christian theology continue to be obsessed with fall/redemption doctrines which start from the premise that Nature is condemned to live in fear and dread of humanity because of its complicity in that fall.

The inclusion in the canon of women's experience of the Spirit takes account of the fact that the scriptures evolved through a process kept going by the tension between different points of view, different cultures, different theologies and the attempt to include them in some fashion. A re-valuing of this process will be based on the knowledge that the Spirit gives a diversity of gifts, to women and men alike, and that a new manifestation of the Spirit's power from within Christianity is found in women's speech. Their silence within the tradition was a commonplace. They talked elsewhere, in the home, in the fields, in the shops, and latterly in offices and civil institutions. But in the presence of church authority, they were silent.

Now, however, the Spirit sustains them in their access to God. The Spirit enables them to say worthwhile things of themselves and of Nature. The Spirit enlightens them in their study of the formation of the canon. They become aware that what it testifies to *directly* is not the religion of the whole of Israel or of Christianity, but of individuals and groups attempting, with varying degrees of success, to make their vision emerge in the wider society. What it testifies to *indirectly*, especially in the legislation, the historical narratives and prophetic denunciations, is that the whole relationship between God and Israel, God and Christianity, was something quite different. It becomes clear that the canon does not contain its own self-justification, especially in its hierarchical patterning, but rather directs our attention to the living tradition which it mediates partially.[19]

Without this tradition, partial as it is, there is for Christians no shared memory, no metacontext for our religious metaphor and no believing community in which to express our relationship with God. Without this tradition there is no structure against which the prophetic Spirit can react. Without it, the process does not continue whereby we are led as an ecological community to the truth about the world, the truth about God and the truth about ourselves; the economic, ecochristian truth. Without it, once its partiality has been recognized, there is no clear task of reconstruction in the light of the present.

Part of that task today is a re-interpretation of the Genesis texts as a decisive event in the life of the tradition, as the basis for a sustainable theology. Such a theology sustains hope in the face of ecological apocalypse, sustains life in the face of decomposition and death. It is sustainable also because it remains open to the hard data of science, to feminine imaginative consciousness and to the vision of thinkers and doers in other disciplines. It unites us all in a common purpose: to work with the divine economy of creation and sustain the life of the earth.

PART FOUR
Genesis Now

Chapter 10

Hierarchical and Ecological Power

Anyone wishing to use an ecological paradigm in theology cannot escape the influence of the prevailing hierarchical one. Basic to both ecology and feminism is an attempt to think through and re-think one's own history in the context of this paradigm so as to free one's thought from its silent preconceptions and enable one to think differently. Extending this ecofeminist discipline into one's theology introduces an epistemology that is foreign to it. Therefore traditional theological presuppositions are challenged as one asks what happens if they are seen from a systemic, i.e. non-hierarchical point of view.

The truth of this becomes evident as soon as a traditional theologian ventures into the foreign pathway of ecology. It seems to bring Christians up against a closed door marked "truth". This door hinges on the question of which pathway is the right one to lead us to God. Then one realizes that the question itself could only be raised in a hierarchical framework, because such a structure presupposes that one system ranks above another in relation to the knowledge of God, and that pathways to God different from the one sanctioned by tradition are of no value.

But this devaluing is not only unecological. It begs the deeper question of how any human system of thought could be anything other than an approximation to what is always, in principle, a transcendent truth. On this evaluation, the ecological system is no different from any other, and good theological practice recognizes its approximate nature. It acknowledges that diverse expressions of faith express diverse relations to transcendent reality, and that the principle governing them all is that they are time-bound and culture specific.[1] Neo-Platonism and Aristotelianism had their day. Why not ecological expressions now of relationship with God?

An Ecological Way of Doing Theology

They are certainly appropriate as the culture-specific framework of ecology opens directly into the contemporary context in which

195

theology must now make its approximations. Both hierarchy's ladder and ecology's open systems can lead us to ultimate truth, though never to its ultimate formulation. But the modern context and metacontext, of constant proof of the interconnectedness of ecosystems and of scientific perception of the systemic interaction of matter at the sub-atomic level, requires that we leave behind hierarchical approximations masquerading as "certainties". In contrast, ecological approximations do not claim to be anything other than approximate, since they always remain open to further exchanges of information. For them, hierarchical certainty is displaced by Heisenbergian uncertainty.

There are other criteria of suitability. Hierarchical consciousness formally excludes women's consciousness and consciousness of the intrinsic value of all creation. There are also signs of the times, ranging from the global politics of co-operation ushered in by various summit conferences to the ecological apocalypses delivered from environmental bodies almost daily. Therefore it appears to be a question not of whether theology ought to become ecological, but of how quickly it might do so. If not now, when?

Striving to express the reality of God revealed in Jesus is Christian theology's contribution to re-thinking human relationships with the planet. The Spirit of this God is that Spirit active in the Genesis event: all-awakening, all-resurrecting, irrupting and encompassing power from within creation. To believe in such a God is to complete the Copernican revolution which taught us that the sun does not revolve around the earth. Now we are all learning the painful lesson that the earth does not revolve around humankind. Christians are being given the further lesson that our relationship with the world does not revolve around the salvation of the human being.

This new self-perception brings a change in attitude for women and men alike. We learn that we are all responsible for a world in which man, woman, God and earth revolve around each other in cycles of life, death and resurrection.

Christians who remember only what they learnt about God's transcendence vis-à-vis the world must now re-discover what they also believe about the reality of the body of Jesus embedded in the systemic creature earth. The doctrine of his incarnation means that he was, as much as we are, an organism in a particular environment. He lived, as we live, in interaction with all the religious, cultural and societal systems surrounding his primary one. He reacted against them, as we do, from within them.

Ethical Issues From an Ecological Perspective

For anyone thinking about and re-thinking theology through the grid of ecology and feminism, the problematic nature of Christian ethics in regard to women and Nature forces itself on our attention within a hierarchical culture which has created and sustained these ethics. The ethics were not formulated for or addressed to women, even though generally they subjected women to extremely strict constraints. Nor did they take account of human relationships with the earth other than in terms of male property rights over its resources. They were and are an ethics for men, thought out, written down, taught by and addressed to free men. Women have figured in them only as objects, or at best, as partners to train, educate and watch over when in one's power, but to stay away from when under someone else's power, whether father, husband or guardian. Similarly, Nature and its resources have figured in them only as the dumb objects of human conquest, exploitation or ownership. They are mentioned only when the male rights inherent in such activities come into dispute between those in possession.

This has been brought home forcibly to me while observing the conduct of the current crisis in the Gulf. All the decisions about property, invasion, rights and the movement of people are being taken by men: whether in the United Nations or in the United States and Iraqi governments; in the constant meetings between heads of state and various defence committees.

It is also the case that, in the Christian countries allied against Iraq, male bishops and churchmen are seen to be arbiters of Christian attitudes to the war.

The male ethics our culture has inherited did not try, until very recently, to define a field of conduct and a domain of valid rules for the two sexes which took notice either of their differences or of what they have in common. They were an elaboration of masculine conduct worked out from the viewpoint of men in order to give form to their behaviour. Moreover, they spoke of precisely that conduct in which they were called upon to exercise their duties, their rights, their power, their authority and their liberty. Important basic foundational moral conditions of modern life were formulated, interpreted and imposed by socially élite men in the church and judiciary. The impulse to change may be recognized formally now in some legislation, but it remains no more than an impulse to date, as some celebrated, or rather notorious judgments in rape cases clearly show.

The biblical basis of Christian ethics, the Ten Commandments, are addressed to men who were chosen to proclaim the name of God and to keep it from profanation; who could destroy graven images made by pagans; who went to war and could kill each other; who could commit adultery with another man's wife; who were eligible to bear public witness in civil and religious courts; who were tempted to covet their neighbour's wife and/or their neighbour's goods.

These ethics related to areas of everyday male experience: man's religious duties, his family obligations, his public role, his relationships with neighbouring families. They invoked a code of morality, a set of values and rules of action recommended to individuals through the prescriptive agency of religion. They were also a rule of conduct, that is, a way of measuring conduct and also a measure of the way in which one ought to conduct oneself. Not only could the individual male's behaviour be measured against these norms, but the individual could measure himself against them as an ethical subject and recognize himself as bound to put them into practice.[2]

Hierarchical Principles and Ethics

The hierarchical principles embedded in these ethics, that is, in male control of the household and of public order, have had an impact on the individual Christian's experience of God. Divinity has been envisaged and experienced in terms of the dynamics of relating to fathers, husbands, patriarchs, kings, lords, stewards, popes and bishops. The discussion in chapter 8 mentioned the unquestioning primacy given to the lordship of Jesus as a category of relationship with him. A glance at a Christian service book gives many instances in which he is addressed as king, even though he is reported to have literally fled from the crowd who wanted to make him one.

This totalitarian view of our relationship with God permeates our perception of power. It is conceived of as power over those lower than oneself on whatever scale of being is in question. It makes no difference that this power is supposedly invoked for our or their good. A friend of mine told me the jolt he received when he heard himself joining fervently in the response: "Great is his love, love without end!" to such verses as: "He smote the first-born of the Egyptian! He cast Pharaoh and his host into the sea!"

What matters in these subliminal messages about God is that those who wield power and those who are the objects of it use this relationship to define their relationship with God and with those placed over them in hierarchical groupings. The Hebrew Scriptures document how unacceptable the idea of a king was in the early days of Israel's existence as an alliance of tribes (1 Sam. 8:4f.). But gradually the desire for a visible representative of God's power prevailed and Saul was anointed king. It may indeed be the case, as some scholars would argue, that the overall process of intensification of agriculture involved a complex interweaving of demographic and economic needs which were best balanced by a shift to monarchic government in order to provide centralizing mechanisms to organize labour, spread the risks of highland agriculture and secure additional territorial or market resources.[3] But the way in which the ideological battle was fought out between the anti-monarchical Samuel and the tribes of Israel was on the grounds of the supremacy of Yahweh's kingship. This theocratic ideal was then invoked to validate the institution of monarchy. In the service of morning prayer in the Church of England the following prayer is still made: "Almighty and Everlasting God, King of Kings, Lord of Lords, the only Ruler of Princes, Who dost from Thy Throne behold all the dwellers upon Earth, most heartily we beseech Thee with Thy Favour to behold our sovereign lady Elizabeth the Queen and all the Royal family."

Even in republics, the most basic Christian image of the world is that it is a spiritual monarchy, a system of order imposed by spiritual power from above. At each level of government, that spiritual power is invoked in interlocking roles of authority and submission, of president and council, of ministers and civil servants, of directors and directed, of managers and managed, with lasting effects on the self-perception of both parties. They become defined by relationships which give authority to one and security to the other: which assign responsibility to one and dependence to the other. Both roles can be equally destructive

of a healthy interaction and a proper self-image, since to govern
or be governed places one in a relationship where the intrinsic
value of either person may be seen as of no account. This takes
us back to the theme of self-esteem associated with theologies
of liberation which re-define both oppressor and oppressed in
terms of their value before God, thereby freeing them both to
be themselves. Who can tell an Emperor he has no clothes? He
shivers in ridiculous isolation until a child sees him as a naked
man and not as one with power over her.

In our interaction with Nature, this image of God-given power
over those "below" us on the scale of being is fundamental to
and apparently ineradicable in Christian self-perception. I had
an interesting example of this in discussion with a male
theologian who had heard me speak on the differences between
the hierarchical and ecological points of view. He told me that
he found what I said interesting and provocative, but untenable
because "ultimately human beings are in control over Nature.
It's just a question of changing the type of control to the right
one."

When I pointed out that the evidence is against him, since
global warming for instance is now seen to be beyond our control,
he agreed that such is the case, but was confident that that only
meant we had to try harder to find the proper way to handle
her (Nature). In this God–appointed role of dominance over the
natural world, men have supposedly "ruled" the waves and
"conquered" the mountains by divine right, and confidently
expect to continue to do so – Canute and global warming
notwithstanding.

The history of this moral totalitarianism which has become
part of a Christian ethical response to the natural world has to
be thought through in the context of the rules and values of the
hierarchical and therefore patriarchal societies which formulated
and perpetuated it. These had as a common feature the accepted
subordination of women and of Nature. They took account of
male conduct as a relationship of superiority to women and of
ownership to Nature. Both were subsumed under man's
relationship with God.

This subservience of women and Nature to man was assumed
in the covenants made between God, Abraham and his male
"seed forever". Seed was imagined to contain within itself the
essence of patriarchal continuity, and took on a symbolic value

for the male writers of scripture which had little to do with its relative biological significance. Sophisticated theological and philosophical reasoning, therefore, was based upon that most vulnerable aspect of male psyche, the male seed itself. According to some of this reasoning, it contained the essence of life. Women could contribute the matter of the body, but as philosophers from Aristotle onward have claimed, only the male seed could "ensoul" or "enspirit" the base matter.

Concern for the preservation of the male seed, which stood for preservation of the certainty of God's covenant promise to his people, brought about some tortuous reasoning in the field of morality. The sin of Onan, the wasting of the seed, was singled out as specially heinous. Intercourse during menstruation was forbidden lest the precious seed be lost in the flow of blood. In Christianity, priests delved into the secrets of the marriage bed in an attempt to see how, and under what conditions, the male seed might go astray. Whenever sexual intercourse took place, it was imperative that the male seed be allowed to reach its destination, the womb, and its destiny, fruition, without interference: even at the cost of the woman's life.[4]

An interesting modern secular relic of this exaggerated reverence for the male seed appears in the very reluctant and late acceptance by the scientific community that sperm can be responsible when something goes wrong with reproduction. Working on the causes of handicap in children, researcher Margaret Wynn and her husband Arthur documented all they could find to account for it. Their first work about women, *The Prevention of Handicap and the Health of Women*, attracted mostly favourable attention. It was when they turned their attention to men and the possible link between sperm damage and handicap that it became harder for them to find publishers for their papers. It took the discovery of a link between men working in the nuclear plant at Sellafield and subsequent leukemia in their children to make the scientific establishment reappraise its position. As the Wynns point out, the last three surveys on perinatal mortality asked pages of questions about the health of mothers, but the only questions addressed to fathers concerned their social class and whether or not they were living with the mother of their child.[5]

The presumption enshrined in these religious moral codes and this scientific practice is that the seed sown by man is destined for fruition, whether in a woman's body or in the earth. The spiritual power of God is wielded in sowing the seed and bringing it to fruition regardless of the intentionality of the body sown, if indeed such intentionality is even attributable to that body.

As part of the covenant which promised Abraham heirs as numerous as the sands on the seashore, those heirs were given the land with access to all its fertility (Gen. 17:6–8; 28:3–4; 35:11). This was then interpreted as divine intentionality which placed the fecundity of women and Nature under the control of men. Men sowed, men reaped, and God gave the increase. Women and earth were the raw material supplied by God to be impregnated by men, and were taken for granted as means to the end of fulfilling God's promises to them. A concept of divine power over fertility allotted women and Nature their place in the scheme of things.

It is true to say that those who hold these views in the churches today seldom appeal to Abraham or Jacob as father of their bill of men's rights. Nor would my theologian friend have asserted his control over his wife sitting beside him as confidently or as unthinkingly as his claim to control over Nature. But the whole nexus of such feelings and reactions to the question of control over female fertility can ultimately be traced back to the invocation of some form of divine power over it. Scientific utilitarianism invokes other gods, but they too are based on male expectations of the potency of seed which must do its job of reproduction unhampered by female recalcitrance.

Women and men alike today resist this view of their bodies in ways ranging from private decisions to remain single to joint decisions with their partners not to have children. The added fact of overpopulation of the world outweighs for many of them the assumptions about marriage, fertility and procreation which still rule Western culture and are reappearing to great acclaim in bio-reproductive technologies.

Hierarchy and Genesis

The whole question of divine intentionality in female fertility is now raised for all of us against the background of the refusal or inability of Nature to accept her allotted role. Her barrenness has effectively destroyed the plot, the *muthos* which placed men, women, plants, animals and God on stage in Genesis and brought them to a heavenly apotheosis in Apocalypse. This desertion of her role by Nature (desertification), this impending environmentally apocalyptic ending to the plot, sends us back to read the script again from the beginning: back to the opening chapters of Genesis. A particular reading of this foundational text has given Western culture the fundamental idea that the universe is a hierarchy: a system of order imposed by spiritual power from above, an order to which we owe obedience. The acceptance of this system entails a complex of ideas and sub-ideas which have been implicit in discussions in previous chapters. It is now time to make them explicit.

There is the idea that the physical world is an artefact, made or constructed by God out of inert matter. It had no intelligible shape or particular structure until worked over by the external power of God. God's spiritual energy formed the world: unintelligent brute matter was formed into things by intelligent active spirit. Whenever we affirm belief in God as "Maker of the universe" we are referring to this image, and reinforcing the claim to have and to exercise "spiritual power" over matter, to form and de-form it as we will, whether our "material bodies" or those of others. So we say that we are made of body and spirit, with the idea of spirit as a separate instrument of control.

But ecologically, we must acknowledge that we are not "made of" body and spirit: we *are* body and spirit: that a tree is not made of wood, but that a tree *is* wood: that a mountain is not made of rock, but rather that a mountain *is* rock. So we cannot talk about our birthday as the day we "came into the world", which assumes that before the parts were, so to speak, "put together" to make us, we were not in the world. A little reflection shows that we did not come *into* the world but came *out* of it, out of the systems which sustained our parents and theirs before them.

The Genesis account does not only give us a perception of the world as "made". God forms each thing "according to its kind", so that trees grow in one way and mountains rise in another. This gives us the sub-idea that the different ways in which a tree is one thing and a mountain another are governed by laws operating in obedience to the design of God their maker. This classification "according to their kind" goes back to the Genesis three-fold scheme in which creation is divided between the earth, the waters and the firmament, and creatures live in one or other of the three elements of earth, water, or air.

This classification according to kind and element is accepted as a divine principle in other biblical narratives which distinguish between "clean" and "unclean", "pure" and "polluted". The presupposition is that "clean" animals conform fully to their class and behave properly according to their element. Those species are "unclean" whose members do not fully conform, or whose class itself confounds the general scheme. So those animals who do not hop, jump or walk, but creep, crawl or "swarm" upon the earth, are unclean. In the Genesis narrative, the serpent is the archetype of this class, "cursed" to crawl on the earth on its belly and to lie beneath the heel of the woman. This graded classification of animals can also be seen as the basis for the holiness codes in the book of Leviticus. To be "holy" is to be "whole", to have integrity, perfection of the individual, of the kind and of the behaviour.[6]

This sub-idea lies behind the hierarchical grading of animals and people according to a perceived norm discussed in chapter 5. Those people and animals who do not behave "according to their kind", whether religiously, sexually or physically, are devalued on the assumption that there is a divine principle which requires them to conform to class and environment.

Furthermore, the inference of laws of behaviour, whether attributed to Genesis or genetics, can and are used to legitimize our control over the processes of Nature, since we assume that we are the only species divinely inspired, or smart enough, to work out these laws for ourselves.

Genesis and Ecology

In spite of the religious and cultural overload attached to the language and translations of the Genesis narrative, reflection on the Hebrew wording of Genesis 2:7 helps restore some balance by the way in which it stresses our oneness with the earth. The Revised Standard Version translates this as follows:

> Then the Lord God formed man of dust from the ground and breathed into his nostrils the breath of life and man became a living being.

In order to capture the flavour and meaning of the original text, the words *'adamah* and *'adam* must be translated in ways which communicate the integral connection of humanity with its earthly matrix. So the text should be rendered something like:

> Then God Yahweh formed an *earthling* of clods from the *earth* and breathed into its nostril the breath of life; and the *earthling* became a living being. (Meyers)

> Then God Yahweh formed a *human* from clods of the *humus* and breathed into its nostrils the breath of life, and the *human* became a living being. (Meyers)

> IHVH God formed the *grounding,* soil of
> the *ground*
> He blew into its nostrils the blast of life
> and the *groundling* became a living soul. (Korsak)

> then Yahweh God formed *the earth creature*
> dust from the *earth*
> and breathed into its nostrils the breath of life,
> and *the earth creature* became a living *nephesh.*
> (Trible)

Carol Meyers points out that to translate *'adam* as "man" is to imply a priority for male existence and also to ignore a magnificent Hebrew wordplay. The word for the stuff from which the first human being is formed is *'adamah,* usually translated as "ground" or "earth". The words for "human" and for "ground" are thus connected phonetically and perhaps etymologically. The English word "human" is not the combination of *hu* with *man,* but rather is derived from a theoretical Indo-European root (*ghum*) meaning "earth" or "ground" from which comes Latin *humus* (earth) and Old English *guma* (man).

She also points out that names or substantives were not simply labels; they were indicators of the very essence of the thing or creature designated. The term *'adam* tells us that the essence of human life is not its eventual classification into gendered categories but rather its organic connection to the earth. And the earth in this case is not general, vague, unspecified soil or ground but rather *'adamah,* that reddish brown substance that is capable of absorbing water, being cultivated and supporting life. A friend of mine who is a Kabbalist scholar translates *'adamah* as a mixture of "blood and breath". At the very outset then, human existence is thus portrayed as intimately related to that which makes life possible: land, water, blood and air. It is inextricably caught up with concern for sustenance. This image rings very true today in a world where we are relearning our relationship with *'adamah*.[7]

However, even when proper translations of the Hebrew are taken into account, the notion may linger that we are "made out of" separate parts, spirit and body, and that the body comes out of the earth but the spirit does not. It is put in us directly by God from somewhere outside this world. (This goes back to the Platonic concept of the soul "falling" into the world and materiality.)

But in all the translations given, the fusion of earth and breath creates life: that is the moment when there is a "living being", a *nephesh*. There is no breath, no spirit without life. There is no life without earth to sustain it. The hard data of science leaves us in no doubt of the intimate interaction between them.

Such readings of the text do not allow us to assume, on the basis of a false asceticism, that with enough effort we can separate out the component parts of body and spirit in ourselves. Neither do they allow the false assumption that spirit comes from God and body does not, and that therefore spirit can apparently rank above body in value and power. There is no suggestion either that the spirit (rationality) of human beings ought to control the body of the world, and that their salvation ought to take precedence over that of the world.

In an ecological view of ourselves, the fusion of earth, blood, breath and life *is/is not* body, *is/is not* spirit. We are bodies of interacting spirit, intelligence and matter. We are not put into the world as subjects of a king, or victims of a series of laws. We are not put into the world at all. We *are* it. The world is not controlled by a God outside it or men who are not part of it. Every individual being is an intrinsic part of it and responsible for what it is becoming. An ecological view of the self would not identify us in the usual terms of race, colour, class, sex or occupation, but as an earth creature who is/is not body; is/is not spirit.

An ecological vision of the God presented in the Genesis text is not received in the context of a concept of transcendent divine power over the world which makes God external to it. Therefore the earth really is filled with the glory of God. Therefore the behaviour of individual characters in the Genesis account may appear rather differently. The manner in which they obey or resist an interdiction or a prescription, the manner in which they respect or disregard a set of rules may then be seen as initiatives towards personal integrity and identity. Eve is the role model for this. The fact that she has until now played her part to a tragic end says much about the audience's preconceptions of the plot and their expectations of her.

Genesis Read Non-Hierarchically

The fact remains that it is well-nigh impossible to read or hear the Genesis text other than in the hierarchical framework in which one first encountered it. Nevertheless, the attempt must and will be made in the following way. Firstly, as neutral a rendering as possible of the text will be given, merely recounting what is there. Then a familiar interpretation of it will be given which pinpoints some of the ideas taken as axiomatic in such interpretations, and made axiomatic by them. These are not usually, or at any rate consciously, adverted to when this story is told.

The story usually begins with the first account of the creation of man and woman on the sixth day (Gen. 1:24-31), when they alone out of all creation are made in the image and likeness of God, without reference to any natural context or substance. They are blessed with fertility, dominion over the earth and food from every plant and tree. It has been suggested that this first narrative arose in the context of a pre-huntergatherer, vegetarian society, in contrast to the narrative in Genesis 9 which states that every moving thing that lives shall be food for the sons of Noah.

Wherever it arose, the idyllic picture of Genesis 1, in which the culmination of God's creative work is the creation of Adam and Eve, serves as prologue to the second scene: creation followed by decisive action. (Gen. 2:7 – 3:24.)[8] This time their creation is ordered differently, with man created before woman. (Some feminist readers would argue that this order, on the basis of the first account when both are created last and then given superiority over what had already been created, establishes woman's superiority over man. But this, of course, is simply to fall into the hierarchical trap of assuming that someone has to be superior). Creation is described as a process, not a *fait accompli*. God is a potter, shaping the earth creature with dust from the earth. God is the one who breathes into this creature to animate it, the gardener who plants a special garden in a special place

where this creature may live in delight. There is never a hint
that this creature could live other than in this setting of growing
plants and trees. There is never a hint, either, that God could
live elsewhere.

Some of the trees are named: the tree of life and the tree of
the knowledge of good and evil. The garden is watered by a
river flowing out of Eden (delight) and dividing into four.[9] It is
a place where waters flow continuously, in which there is no
fear of drought. The trees are pleasant to see and good to eat.
God commands the earth creature to eat from all the trees but
one. Then God gives him company: beasts and birds which he
names. He still lacks a helper like himself until God causes him
to sleep, and while he does, takes one of his ribs and from it
builds him a helper. She is brought to him and named "woman".
They are united in one flesh. Sexuality re-unites what has been
differentiated.

In the following scenes, the attention is focussed on a single
decision and a single action. The serpent is introduced, described
as the shrewdest creature in the animal world. Its dialogue with
the woman, the first recorded conversation in the text, brings
together on stage the animal, divine, human and plant worlds.
Human life and human death are defined as not-eating and
eating. Knowledge of good and evil also is defined in these terms.

The woman takes, eats and gives to the man who is with her.
Their eyes are opened as the serpent said, but they do not die
as God said. They are evicted from the garden and judgment is
passed on them and the serpent. It is cursed, with a peculiar
posture and food, and with perpetual enmity between its seed
and that of the woman. The woman is to suffer the consequences
of her deed through giving birth in pain to the seed which will
crush the serpent, and through unsatisfied yearning for man
who will rule over her. Finally, man is not cursed himself, but
through him the earth is cursed. In toil and sweat he must now
struggle to obtain food from it.

Then God makes robes for the two of them and clothes them.
He says that now man is like "one of us, knowing good and
evil. Let him not put out his hand and take from the tree of life
also and eat and live for ever!".

In the final scene, God sends man away from the garden of
Eden, with the command "to serve the ground from which he
was taken". After his departure, God makes the Cherubim to

dwell East of the garden, and the scorching, turning sword to bar the road to the tree of life.

Those who reflect upon the deeper relationships between the characters and their worlds link the curse upon the earth caused by man with the curse upon the serpent. It must eat dust from the earth all the days of its life. He must eat of the earth in pain until he returns to the dust eaten by the serpent, the same dust from which he himself was formed.

Those who sum up the action focus on the judgments following on the woman's dialogue with the serpent. The good earth is cursed; plants give way to thorns and thistles; fulfilling work has become alienating labour; power over animals has deteriorated into enmity with their representative, the serpent; sexuality (for woman) has splintered into unfulfilled longing and subordination. The fruit that is eaten has become a symbol of the knowledge of good and evil. The fruit that is not eaten is the ability to live forever.

In the dialogue between the woman and the serpent, man stands silently by and God is offstage. He only appears after they have acted, to question their actions and to pass judgment on them. After he has done so the man speaks and calls his woman Eve, "because she is the mother of all the living".

Common Perceptions of the Genesis Story

It is now possible to bring to the surface some of the presuppositions which usually colour our reception of this text. This story of relationships between God, humankind and the plant and animal worlds takes their interconnectedness for granted. This interconnectedness is presented in a sequence in which the relationships are changed irrevocably. It is usually assumed that they have changed for the worse as the result of human actions, and so the story is received as a tragedy, in which the interconnectedness established by God is shattered by woman, man and Nature.

It has also been received as an account of origins, told from the point of view of a witness there from the beginning who recorded the events more or less accurately as they occurred. The events themselves then appear to take us from a beginning in nothingness or chaos through to the dénouement, a shattered world. The Creator remains the same throughout: directing events before the decisive action by Eve as well as after it.

Reading the story as an account of origins has had the effect of treating the characters and actions in it as prototypes, not archetypes. To grasp the difference, we must appreciate that the characters present the *essential* (archetypal) features of human life at the time the story was recorded, and are not the *first* (prototypical) humans in a historical sense. The features depicted of their life are those thought by the story-teller to be shared by all humanity.[10]

The classification of their actions as prototypes, by Augustine and others (first man and woman, first parents, first sin), has reinforced the linear concept of time which leads us to assume that this is a story of origins and that it parallels chronologically the life of the earth and the life of the human race.

The God who is there before this "first" pair, who sees them act and judges their actions, is implicitly understood to be the raconteur. Who else could it be? According to the story itself (the prologue) human beings did not appear until the penultimate day.

The unconscious attribution of divine authorship or inspiration, even by those who would reject the label Fundamentalist, has had another effect on how the tale is told and received. If it is God's point of view, so to speak, of the world and all the relationships between the different species in it, then we cannot tamper with the text. From God's point of view, we were meant to live in a certain relationship both with God and the natural world, but that was spoiled by our forebears at the beginning of the relationship and so we live in disharmony with Nature and isolation from God.

The basic assumption on which the others depend is that this is a story of sin, of the fall of humankind through Eve's initiative. Her punishment, to bear children in pain, is judged as a more severe punishment than man's struggles with the soil. Therefore her sin is assumed to be greater than man's. Her desire for her husband is seen as God's way of keeping her subordinate and submissive to him. Therefore God is seen to judge that man should be in control over woman, with power over the earth cursed because of him.

God's actions and words are read through a hierarchical grid in some of the following ways. He is male. Also, he creates man first. Both of these features of the story are taken to mean that man is superior to woman. God punishes them both because they reject his power over them: the power to tell them what to do and what not to do, which is ultimately his power over their life and death. In this theocracy, God does not only exercise this power over them. He has absolute power over the plant and animal worlds also, and therefore can decide to punish them too: not for what they have done themselves in regard to the fruit of the trees, but for what the woman and man have done. Even though the earth has played no part in their actions, and the serpent only an indirect one, the former is cursed because of man and the serpent's issue placed under the woman's heel. They are to live under human control, a control delegated by God in a theocratic world.

Because God is said to have placed the man and woman in a garden of delights, it is presumed that that is where God wanted them to stay. But God could not keep them there because his will for them was a certain course of action which they refused to follow. His will ranks above his desire for their happiness, and his will has been disobeyed. It takes precedence, so even though God wanted them to be happy, even more did he desire their obedience. Our relationship with God is then defined as one of submission to his will. This submission can be made either directly to him or through those to whom he has delegated power over us.

God does not want humanity to suffer, and so placed the man and woman in a setting which by its very name precludes the notion of suffering. They did not obey and were banished from the delights of the garden. It was their fault. If we do not obey God, then we too suffer: but what we endure is also our own fault. Suffering now is inevitable for all of us, since through Eve's disobedience, women must suffer the pain of bearing men's seed while filled with unsatisfied yearning for its possessor. The animal world is locked in enmity with that seed, and must bear the pain of subjection to it. Men must toil in pain to find the means of sustaining life from the soil that is cursed through association with them.

Furthermore, the inclination to disobey and its consequence, pain, are now part of our nature. Our will to obey has been disordered since our ancestors refused to obey God's order. We continue to disobey and therefore know for ourselves what it is to suffer God's judgments. If we accept suffering properly, that is, acknowledge it to be punishment for sin and a result of our flawed character, then God may re-admit us to Paradise after our death.

The Rise and Growth of these Perceptions

Most if not all of these interpretations were current during and after the fourth century, during and after Augustine's writing and preaching on the Genesis narrative, though, as we shall see, they did not go unchallenged. He inherited attitudes from Greek culture, the Roman Empire and the Hebrew patriarchal worldview which were absorbed into the Christian tradition and handed on through the writing and preaching of the sub-apostolic church Fathers and bishops. They can be found in the New Testament in such passages as 1 Tim. 2:13-14: "For Adam was formed first, then Eve; and Adam was not deceived, but the woman was deceived and became a transgressor". By the early centuries of the Christian era, instances of such attitudes toward Eve were commonplace in religious literature. The association of Eve and sin with temptation, sexuality and lust is expanded in both Christian and Jewish post-biblical sources, with the serpent playing an increasingly satanic and phallic role. And of course the more Eve is identified as the source of sin, the more urgent becomes the need to control, subdue and dominate her.

These interpretations were exacerbated by translations of the Hebrew which subtly changed and distorted the meaning. The patriarchal views of Jerome, for example, coloured his extremely influential translation of the Hebrew Bible into Latin, a version used by Augustine. He translated the passage in which God addresses Eve after eating the fruit (Gen. 3:16), as:

> I will multiply your toils and your conceptions; in grief you will bear children, and you will be under the power of your husband, and he will rule over you.

The Hebrew for "rule" is given an absolutism by Jerome lacking in the original by an interpretation of it as being under the husband's power. This notion of power over a woman's body resonated with certain strands in the Christian tradition which Jerome received. In the writings and life of Cyprian of Carthage, we get the picture of an embattled male community, the "tight bond of brotherhood" of the Christian church. This was drawn up in battle array against the *saeculum*, the world of Roman society behind whose brutal face Cyprian sensed the abiding presence of the devil and his angels. Christians were "in the fighting line" of the devil's war against the human race. The view of the human body that Cyprian bequeathed, with decisive effect, to Ambrose, Jerome and Augustine was determined by this overriding preoccupation. The "flesh" of the Christian was a bulwark against the world. This flesh might be dedicated to Christ in virginity by men and women in order to preserve its integrity. But "flesh" remained a point of perpetual danger, an outpost of the self tensed to receive the myriad blows of the world. The body of the Christian was a microcosm of the threatened state of the church, which itself was a compact body, held in firm restraint by the unshakeable, God-given will of its head and guiding mind, the bishop.

Ambrose was just such a bishop, Augustine another. For Ambrose, human sexual feeling stood out in dark silhouette against the blaze of Christ's untouched body. The transformation from one into the other was that brought about by conversion and baptism in the Catholic Church. Through this, human bodies "scarred" by sexuality, could be redeemed by a body whose virgin birth had been exempt from sexual desire. Baptism was an intimate participation in this perfect flesh of Christ. Such a contrast between the birth of Christ and the birth of ordinary human beings would provide Augustine with what he took to be irrefutable support of his own views on the intimate relation between the act of intercourse and the transmission of "original sin".[11]

These themes of a battle to retain power over the world, sexuality and flesh, which became standard terminology for much of Christian spirituality, had another outlet once Constantine adopted the Cross as a symbol of victory in the battles of the Roman Empire. The marching columns of the imperial army became a model of the Christian battle against the pagan world so vividly portrayed by Cyprian. Violence in the name of the perfect flesh of Christ against the flesh of the unbaptized and the pagan was sanctified. After all, even before Cyprian, Tertullian had made the momentous choice of the word *sacramentum* for the baptismal vow, a term used of the oath of allegiance to the Emperor taken upon entry into the Roman Army. Military metaphors still abound today in baptismal services and hymns associated with incorporation into the body of Christ.

It is, therefore, important to realize that Augustine's interpretation of the Genesis account of creation, which was to become the standard one, arose within the context of conventional hierarchical Roman society, where Emperors commanded their subjects to live or die in a particular manner. Landowners controlled peasants by flogging and worked their lands by the sweated labour of those peasants. Male heads of households had absolute authority over wives, children and slaves. Augustine concurred with these prescriptive agencies to the extent that in C. E. 405 he accepted that the Roman state could bring to bear the force of its own laws so as forcibly to "reunite" Donatist congregations with the Catholic church. In doing so he upheld the view that the hierarchical structures of authority that gave cohesion to society might be called upon to support the Catholic Church.[12]

This link between Christianity and physical violence forged in the name of church expansion or spiritual good is one of the ugliest manifestations of its hierarchical character and its perception of power. It sanctioned military, domestic and economic violence of the cruellest kind. Rape and pillage are the inseparable companions of war, and religious wars have been no exception.[13] In a matter with direct bearing on the theme of this book, the witch trials and burnings carried out by Christian authorities both in Europe and in America were sanctioned on the grounds that the dark side of woman, that is, her lust and wanton sexuality, were associated with unruly Nature. The blame for the bodily corruption of the male was attributed directly to temptation by the female after the example of Eve. The supposed disorder wrought by lusty women was portrayed in hundreds of paintings and graphics on witchcraft produced from the end of the fifteenth century until the close of the seventeenth.

These, together with the Dominican tract which articulated church doctrine against witches, the *Malleus Maleficarum* (popularly known as the "Hammer of Witches"), were the basis of the witch trials. Not only were women the majority of the accused (some authorities give figures of one hundred to one), but they were primarily in the lowest social orders, the bulk of them illiterate. Religious, social and sexual attitudes towards women and Nature played a significant part in delineating the victims. This tract stated that woman conspired constantly against spiritual good, having insatiable lust by nature. Because of this, she consorts with devils and is especially prone to the crime of witchcraft, from which men have been preserved by the maleness of Christ.[14]

The point I want to focus on here is one that was made earlier. Through the extensive use of battle imagery both for the individual Christian's relationship with the body of Christ, the church of baptized Christians, and for the external manifestation of this in religious wars and the persecution of witches, the notion of divine power was linked to the image of government through force. Relationship to divinity became defined in terms of the dynamics of hierarchical relationships of power, in which one either exerted power and chastisement over one's own body: or a group of men with physical and spiritual power exerted it over others, all in the name of God. Those under control were taught to see salvation in terms of absolute submission to this power.[15]

Julian wrote her wonderful exemplary story of our relationship with God as that of a lord and his servant waiting to do his will while she was living under the ecclesiastical jurisdiction of the "martial bishop" Henry Despenser. He executed the peasants sent to ask for the king's pardon after the revolt of 1369. He also led a crusade to the Continent on behalf of Urban VI in the great Schism of 1377. Her picture of God as lord is an idealized and transformed version of an instantly recognizable relationship to authority in her own context.

Luther's major commentary on Genesis, incorporating earlier interpretations, was written when Emperors and Electors controlled armies, fathers had absolute authority in households, husbands absolute control in marriage. In his own household he rebuked his son for disobeying him on the grounds that doing so was offensive to God's majesty. He also lived through a peasants' revolt, savagely put down by an alliance of princes and bishops. On the day when Bishop Conrad rode in triumph into Würzburg, the event was celebrated with the execution of sixty-four citizens and peasants, after which the bishop made a tour of his diocese accompanied by his executioner.

In both revolts mentioned here, the peasants toiled to meet the demands of their overlords either by handing over produce from the land or exchanging it for money to pay taxes. When either the crop failed or the taxes rose, they were unable to pay and saw their families starve and their holdings seized. The presuppositions built into the Augustinian interpretation, that such oppressive conditions of life were the result of and punishment for sin, were in part responses to the enigma of suffering in everyday experience and became self-reinforcing. The "explanation" of how things became the way they are functioned as a sanction for the present order. It helped people answer the perennial questions about conditions in the natural and social worlds, and also helped them accept the answers. When it came to interpreting the Genesis narrative, there were no competing images to place against that of God as a despotic parent demanding total obedience to his will, under pain of death, from the creatures of a world under his power. Nor was it a cause for wonder that such a God should be presumed to have punished this sinful flouting of his will by suffering inflicted on those who had sinned and all their descendants. The flaming sword set against Adam and Eve was a powerful reminder of those seen raised against the declared enemies of church and state.

Wider Implications of Hierarchy

The wider implications of such hierarchical relationships, especially the suffering, wilfulness and violence which pervaded them, was the catastrophe which Augustine set out to explain. He did so systematically by seeing the present state of affairs, in which cruelty and coercion were built into the structures of society, as evidence of the distortion of the human will through Adam's fall. The original, God-given bonds of control in human society – friendship, marriage, and paternal command – had given way to sickening shocks of wilfulness which strained those bonds, broke them and changed their nature. Adam and Eve had originally enjoyed a harmonious unity of body and soul which no longer existed on any level.

For this reason, death always remained for Augustine the most bitter sign of human frailty. For death frustrated the soul's deepest wish, which was to live at peace with its beloved, the body. Death was an "unnatural" occurrence.

He connected with this the disjunction between conscious will and sexual feeling which seemed to betray a dislocation of the human person quite as shocking as was the obscene anomaly of death. For Augustine, sexual intercourse was, in itself, a miniature shadow of death. Like death, the onset and culmination of sexual sensation mocked the will. Its random movements spoke of a primal dislocation, an abiding principle of discord lodged in the human person since the fall. It had not been so in Paradise, where will and sexual delight had run together in perfect accord for Adam and Eve. Their married intercourse, if it had occurred before the fall, would have been an object lesson in the balanced rapture with which all human beings might have used the physical joys showered upon them by their Creator. Only in the virgin birth of Christ had Mary recaptured Eve's first harmony.

The important psychological and physiological move here was that sexuality was effectively taken from its physical context and made to mirror an abiding, unhealed fissure in the soul. (Compare this with a different view of it proposed in Chapter 3.) The uncontrollable elements in sexual desire revealed, for Augustine, the working within the human person of a permanent flaw in the soul that tilted it irrevocably towards the flesh. This *flesh* was not simply the body: it was all that led the self to prefer its own will to that of God. With Adam's fall, the soul lost the ability to summon up all of itself, in an undivided act of will, to love and praise God in all created things. This incapacity was the sign of a human race condemned, by the justice of God, to endure, in their bodies and their minds, the permanent presence of a reciprocal punishment. This echoed in the body the unalterable consequences of mankind's first sin. As Peter Brown writes:

> Only by baptism and by incorporation into the Catholic Church, a church whose basilicas were now plainly visible in every city of the Roman world, and whose hierarchy embraced and disciplined all forms of Christian life, would human beings be enabled to join the one city of which *glorious things* might be spoken: the Heavenly Jerusalem, the City of God. Only in a city at the end of time, and in no city of the Western Empire in its last century, would the ache of discord, so faithfully mirrored in the flesh by sexuality, give way to a *pax plena*, to a fullness of peace.[16]

Such a powerful systematic exposition by Augustine of the connection between the Genesis narrative and the world of his day, in conjunction with the ideas dependent upon the image of God as King and Maker, had, not surprisingly, certain enduring and notable effects on Christianity. The cruelty and coercion evident in relationships between human beings and between them and Nature was explained by their condemnation to this state through the justice of God on account of sin. Christian notions of human creation, death and sexuality tended to prise the human person loose from the physical world. Rather than seeing humanity as a systemic link with the fertility of Nature and in dependence on the natural elements, the individual person was seen in relation to a distortion of the human will, a break in harmony between what God intended us to be and what we are. Augustine himself saw the restoration of that harmony in social terms, as a redemption of society. But the point at issue here is that by detaching us from Nature other than as necessary for the sustenance of life, it too was seen as an object of control by the will.

This type of control has become lethal with modern technologies. But the unquestioned assumption of the right to control was established with the primacy of the spirit and will over the body. The indissoluble connection between sexuality, sin and female fertility served only to strengthen the determination to master both woman and Nature.

The human body was not encouraged to share with the animal world pleasures which made it realize its solidarity with the things of earth, but rather to aspire to the glorious things of heaven. Human prayer to the one God, offered by those who strove to control the flesh by the will, replaced the natural cosmic praise which linked the exuberant earth with the transcendent God. In church buildings, sermons were given which kept alight the great hope of future transformation at the end of time, when Paradise would be regained. Birth alone did not guarantee salvation. By insisting on celibacy for its hierarchy, as a way of life uncontaminated by sexuality, the Catholic Church made plain that it enjoyed a supernatural guarantee of patriarchal continuity based on baptism administered by men who did not beget children themselves. The genetic covenant with Abraham was replaced with a new umbilical cord: apostolic succession.[17]

These historic phenomena created a climate in which control over Nature was taken for granted. The development of baptism into a form of re-birth eschewing natural birth denied any creature born through natural processes alone its natural relationship with the divine. All creatures other than baptized human beings were relegated to the zone of the profane, of the unsacred and irreverenced. The results of this dualism have been mentioned many times.

In the context of this chapter, where we have been looking at hierarchies functioning as theocracies of divine power over creation, it is true to say that there is now a slow change in consciousness in regard to women. Sexism, now that it has been defined as injustice by the secular world, cannot publicly be claimed as a mark of the true church. But in so far as hierarchies were and are ecclesiastical structures which arrogate relationship with divinity to the male of the human species, and through him to women, sexism in the name of God still holds sway in the churches. Jerome's translation of Genesis is still part of the Christian rationale for its exercise of power over women.

However, the presuppositions of a theocracy about the place of man and Nature remain unchanged. Nature is still perceived as existing for man's sake, *by divine decree*. In a culture in which mastery is the realm of men, the male self comes to be identified with all that represents control, spirit, transcendence of Nature. This skewed self-perception needs a new consciousness of Adam's connection with the earth, with the *humus*, with the body, its feelings, vulnerability and mortality. In Christianity, maleness needs to be reconnected with being grounded in the natural world. The Jesus who was nurtured in the waters of his mother's womb did not need baptism to be a child of God. He accepted it as incorporation into the living tradition of his shared community, at the hands of one bound to him by ties of flesh and in the natural waters of a river vital to the sustenance of his family.

Ecological Reflections on Power

Christian women and men together need to address themselves to the major theme of this chapter in regard to hierarchy: the concept and practice of "power-over". For all of us, power-over shapes every institution of our society. It is linked to domination and control. It comes from the Christian and Western scientific consciousness which distances itself from the world and atomizes it into non-living, mechanically interacting parts, not valued for their own sakes but only in relation to their usefulness to humanity.

For Christians, it has been a consciousness modelled on the image of a God who stands "over" the world, above it and beyond it: a God outside Nature whose will must be obeyed under pain of death; a God uninvolved with the messy business of being human. This God rules over the world with a panoply of weapons ranging from fear of damnation to hope of salvation. This God punishes through suffering and toil in this world those who disobey his will. Those who inhabit the earth have no inherent worth; that was forfeited when Adam and Eve sinned. Now they rely on grace "bestowed from above" to redeem them from the state of sin (unworthiness) in which they live. The guarantee of that grace is baptism, which gives them power over their bodies to live a life in the spirit that will be rewarded by salvation.

The ramifications of this concept of power are of theological concern today in that it sanctions violence against the natural world. Its violent overtones build up strategies of destruction against that world. It trains us to see spirit as something severed from the material world and from the world of political, economic and environmental action.

Ecology has different models of power: power-from-within and power-with. It reunites spirit and body, humanity and Nature, God and world, in the name of immanent value. When matter is sacred, inherently valuable, it is seen to be empowered by the spirit which awakens all to new life and brings that life to fullness and death. This attitude is exemplified in the *Chipko* movement.

Power-from-within is the power we sense in a seed, in the growth of a child, in writing, working, making choices, recovering health. It has to do with the root meaning of the word power, from the late Latin root word *posse* (to be able). It is the power from within the earth community which is present as connectedness, sustenance, healing, creating.

Our own exercise of it stems from a consciousness of the world as a living being, made up of interacting systems interrelated in patterns too complex to be ever more than partially described. We are conscious of ourselves *as* the world: not above it, outside it or made out of it. We are living being as it is.

Power-from-within is more than a feeling, more than a flash

of individual enlightenment or insight. It involves our sense of connection with others, our knowledge of the impact we have on others. It is the power that comes from the willingness to spend ourselves, to be there for others at the price of risk and effort.

Therefore it is the power which creates and sustains ecological community. It enables us to exercise power-with: the power to cooperate, to share, to change. It also embodies a particular kind of consciousness: it is conscious of the world as a pattern of relationships between men, women and Nature which can be shaped and shifted. It values beings, forces and people according to their effects on others and the appropriateness of their actions. It takes account of the effects of its own actions in relation to the largest number of systems possible.

This is a caring form of power. It is power aligned with love. It is the combination of both power and love which makes a community workable and sustainable. It is the combination of power and love which Christians call the Spirit, and which empowers us to shape our common future for the good of all.[18]

Chapter 11

Uncommon Perceptions of Genesis

Following on from the previous chapter in which well-known and accepted interpretations of the first three chapters of Genesis were compared with what is actually in the text, the next discovery to be made is that certain canonized words and concepts are simply not found there. The word "apple" does not occur. More pertinently, neither does the word or idea of "fall". The use of this term is a good example of an interpretive concept which has been so hard-programmed into Christianity that it is assumed to derive from the text itself. The image of a "fall" associated with the creation of humanity, comes from the *Phaedrus*, where Plato describes heavenly perfections shedding their wings and *falling* to earth to be implanted and born as humans. The previous chapter showed that the application of this concept to the Genesis text distorts the Hebrew meaning, particularly when applied to the description of God fashioning the earth creatures from the earth and their becoming living souls. It is also misleading if one stays with the Platonic text, where the fall is associated with the creation of human beings and not with their subsequent actions.

Christian interpreters did not use Platonic imagery in order to mislead. As we saw with Denys, they used it in an attempt to show the goodness of what God did in creating us; to safeguard the belief that everything that God did was good because everything that God is, is good. In the Platonic tradition the ideal form of unity, the idea of the One, which has had so supreme a role in the world of ideas, is a unity without parts, a unity without differentiation or division of any kind. It is a unity of this absolute sort that the church Fathers claimed to be characteristic of God. "God is simple uncompounded being", according to Irenaeus; "no parts are to be ascribed to God, for the One is indivisible", says Clement of Alexandria; "God is one and altogether simple", says Origen.[1]

Common Perceptions of Genesis 1–3

Faced, therefore, with the reality of suffering, cruelty and wilfulness, Christian interpreters took the Platonic notion of creation as "fall" and applied it to the actions of those created "first". This action then affected all subsequent creation of human life *by humans*, that is, through procreation. Birth, they argued, was the result of a sexual act flawed because it was not under the perfect control of the will. This will itself was "fallen", that is, was not in control because it had been irrevocably damaged by the wilful disobedience of the "first" (prototypical) woman and man.

This concept of "fall" applied to the Genesis story is inextricably bound to another concept: that of "sin". Once again the word itself is not found in the first three chapters of Genesis, even though this is commonly taken to be a narrative about the beginnings of sin in the world. None of the Hebrew words for sin and transgression are used in the story. When God pronounces judgment on the specific act which leads to the couple's eviction from the garden, only the act itself is given as the reason. Interpreters may label this act as disobedient. Exegetes may study it in the context of other passages about sin. But in the text no such label is attached nor is any such connection made or attributed to *God*. Nor does the Hebrew Bible ever associate any of the many sins later perpetrated by the children of Israel with the behaviour in the garden. Even the prophets, continually haranguing the Israelites about their sinful behaviour, never mention the couple. In their evident concern about sin, judgment, punishment and banishment, the prophets threw the book at erring kings and idolatrous peoples – with the notable exception of these first three chapters.[2]

The word "sin" first appears in the Hebrew text in Chapter 4 of Genesis. There God warns Cain before he kills Abel that "sin is crouching at the door". The masculine Hebrew noun (*hatta'th*) used for "sin" is said by one scholar to represent a demonic being, and the image conveyed is of Cain's attention being drawn to this figure waiting for him to make a choice: a choice between doing the right thing or not, a choice which will either deliver him from sin or into its grasp.[3]

Yet commenting on the narrative in Genesis 3, the same scholar states that its author shows "with absolutely convincing simplicity, which a child could understand, how sin happens, what it is, and what it leads to". He then points out how remarkable it is that the usual technical Hebrew concepts for sin, all of which he has enumerated, are all lacking in this text. His next sentence reads: "The reader is only aware that this is a story about sin". Not content with that bald assertion, he quarrels in a footnote with another scholar who would say that this view was first taken by the Deuteronomists. Contradicting him, he states categorically: "The Israelite author (of Genesis 3) knew, as well as all his readers, that sin is the main point of the story."[4]

Reading the story later through a particular interpretative lens, people may indeed think they know this. But if it was so evident to the author, why didn't he say so as clearly as he does in the following chapter, when he paints such a vivid picture of God warning Cain of sin? May it not simply be the case that at any point in history murder is clearly a sin but eating a piece of fruit is not? Or are we being asked to believe in a God who considers them equally grave?

The author of Genesis also fails to make another connection so obvious to traditional Christian scholars. The horrendous deed by Cain, the offspring of Adam and Eve, is not linked with the parental act of disobedience. There is no intrinsic identification made between the acts in Eden and those sinful acts perpetrated outside it, nor between them and the human proclivity for sin.

This brings us to yet another curious fact. Apart from these early chapters of Genesis, there is in the Hebrew Bible no further mention of Eve, the figure made to bear the sins of the world in later Christian interpretations. She reappears (though not by name) in extant literature written in Greek in the second century B.C.E. in the Book of Ecclesiasticus. This book is part of the canon in Catholic Bibles but not in Hebrew or Protestant ones. There is an apparent allusion to her when the author, Ben Sira, says: "From a woman was the beginning of sin, and because of her we all died" (Eccl. 24:25). In associating the origins of sin with a woman, Ben Sira was in a minority. His contemporaries tended to ascribe it to Adam or, on the basis of Genesis 6:1-4, to the fall of evil angels and their cohabitation with women. Nevertheless, as the first known author to state that sin and death are the negative results of a woman's act, this early sage provided one of the most extraordinarily tenacious interpretations of the Genesis narrative. Its tenacity, as we saw in the previous chapter, had much to do with its systematic elaboration by Christian exegetes before and after Augustine, not least in its reiteration in such passages as 1 Timothy 2:13-14.

Interpretations from the Text

Looking at the Genesis narrative carefully, God's warning to Cain gives the reason against killing: it is not good. In the dialogue with the earth creatures, the consequence for them of eating the fruit is also given: if they do, they die. The serpent tells them another consequence: they become like God, having knowledge of good and evil. God has told them, as the woman reminds the serpent, that if they do eat, they will die. They are not told this in terms of whether or not it is good to eat, or bad to die: they are simply told what will happen. The woman sees that the fruit is good to eat "to get insight from", and takes it and eats. She gives it to the man, and he does the same. Then their eyes are opened.

The possible results of their action are told them by God, but the decision is theirs. God does not say: "If you do one or the other, you are behaving in a good way or a bad way", or "You will please/displease me". God simply says: "you will die". The serpent says: "You will become like God, knowing good and evil". Both describe consequences, not divine wishes. If certain actions are taken, certain consequences follow. It is worth noticing too that the serpent tells the truth, but God does not. The woman and man do not die, but live on in conditions recognizable to any Palestinian at the beginning of Israel's national life in the early Iron Age.[5]

Yet in the Christian tradition generally, it is assumed that not eating (with its consequence of not knowing good from evil) is good. The further assumption is made that God did not want them to eat, to die or to have knowledge of good and evil. But compare this with another well-known story in the Hebrew Scriptures. When Solomon married and brought his bride to Jerusalem, the Lord appeared to him in a dream and asked him what he wanted. Solomon replied that because God had made him king in place of his father David, and given him a great multitude of people to govern, therefore he would ask God to give him an understanding mind, "that I may discern between good and evil" (1 Kings 3:9). God is pleased that Solomon asked for this rather than for "long life or riches or the life of your enemies": so pleased that he grants him these as well. Note also that the same Ben Sira who castigates woman for the beginning of sin and for bringing death into the world personifies Wisdom as a female who cries out to Israel: "Come to me, you who desire me, and eat your fill of my fruit!" (Ecclus. 24:19).

It is Eve in the Genesis narrative who perceives the desirability of procuring wisdom, in dialogue with the wisest of animals, the serpent. It found in the woman that intense thirst for knowledge that the simple pleasures of picking flowers and talking with Adam did not satisfy.[6] Its wisdom is recommended to us by Jesus (Matt. 10:16).

Such attention to the text should make us wary when it is assumed that God did not want the woman and man to know good from evil. What a very infantile stupid pair they would have remained! Exegetes reading the story assume that they themselves have the faculties required to make judgments about the goodness or evil of the actions recorded there and to label some of them "sin". Would they consider themselves fully human without these faculties? Would they forego them in order to keep God happy? Do they believe in a God who would need to deprive us of knowledge in order to protect his divinity?

Even if we ignore some of the logical consequences for us of taking the outcome of actions as intimations of whether or not they were desired by God, Ben Sira leaves us with a further discrepancy based on the cause-and-effect relationship between sin and punishment presumed to govern the Genesis story. He says bluntly that sin and death came into the world through woman. This premise, when applied to Eve, loses sight of the fact that in the narrative in Genesis, *after* she has taken the fruit and eaten it, the woman is given the name "Eve". This, literally translated in the text itself lest its significance be lost, means "the mother of all the living". How then can Ben Sira make her the mother of death? Yet the connection made by Ben Sira between sin, death and woman has been so accepted into Christian consciousness that it has been assumed that as God did not want her to eat (sin), neither did God want her to die. It was her own fault that she did both. This leads to the further assumption that God never intended us to die either.[7]

Augustine and Julian of Eclanum

This assumption was made by Augustine, and in his own lifetime was hotly contested by Julian of Eclanum. He replied to Augustine that mortality is not the result of sin but of nature. Why does Genesis not say that because Adam sinned he would return to dust? His return to the earth is not linked to sin. Instead, Julian argues, the author says that because he came from the earth, he would return to it. Because of our nature, our intrinsic connection with the systemic creature earth, we die and our bodies disintegrate back into their organic elements. As we have seen, the final instruction given to Adam is "to serve the ground from which he was taken".

Also, argues Julian, God created and blessed human fertility even before Eve's taking the fruit (Gen. 1:28). In the normal course of events, human beings were to replenish the earth depleted by mortality. The command to increase and fill the earth supposes that there will be room for that increase, and if everyone were to survive then the earth would not be filled but choked. This fourth century criticism of Augustine is pertinent to our modern attitudes to death, which evade the problems of increasing life-expectancy, overpopulation and overtaxing the earth's resources. The modern technological development of cryonics, which deep-freezes the bodies of the rich so that they can be resuscitated at a later date when the disease from which they died has become "curable", does not invoke sin as death's cause. But the refusal to accept death as part of our nature betrays the same unwarranted assumption that we ought to be able to prolong life indefinitely.

For more than twelve years Augustine and Julian debated the nature of human nature, of sexual desire and death. After Augustine's death, and after considerable controversy, the church of the fifth century accepted Augustine's views and rejected Julian's as heretical.[8] Of most interest to us are the connections Augustine made and Julian rejected between the centrality of human sin and the non-human world. Augustine held that because of and after original sin, not only humanity but the natural world as well became subject to disorder. Julian argued that God created fully innocent natures, capable of virtue according to their will, not only in Paradise but now as well. Human nature – mortal, sexual and vulnerable as it is – participates in the wholeness and goodness of the original creation. Augustine assumed that frustrated desire is universal, infinite and all-consuming. Julian held that sexual desire is innocent, divinely blessed, and, once satisfied, entirely finite. It offers us the opportunity to exercise our capacity for moral choice. (He himself was happily married.) Augustine concludes that we are as helpless in the face of death as we are defenceless against sexual passion, because we are punished for sin. (He became a celibate after illicit and guilt-provoking experience of sexual pleasure.) Julian says this is to confuse physiology with morality. Death is not a punishment for sin but a natural process, like sexual arousal and childbirth – natural, necessary and universal for all living species. It is *spiritual* death that is a matter of choice.

This clash between two world views 1600 years ago resounds again today between those who hold an ecological world-view and those with a hierarchical one. Julian preempts the Copernican revolution ecological thinking seeks to complete. Man, in the person of Adam, is not the centre around which the whole of creation revolves. Because we suffer, die, inflict suffering and make wrong moral choices does not mean that one man's actions flawed our natures irrevocably. Even less does it mean that the whole structure of the universe is transformed for the worse. Rather, instead of making Adam the pivot on which the balance of the world stays or falls, we must dislodge him from there and place him within the systemic world in which he is an archetypal member of one species among others. Women's consciousness has alerted us to the dangers of elevating the generic male in Adam above the rest of humanity. Ecological humility helps counteract the impulse to elevate the human above all other species.

Yet the canonized interpretation of the Genesis text still keeps Christianity confined in the conceptual trap of a traditional fall/ sin theology. That has been taken and is authoritatively upheld as the only true and valid account of why and how we relate to each other, to the world and to God, in spite of textual, moral or ecological difficulties. The rehabilitation of Julian as an orthodox theologian is not, as far as I know, on the official Christian theological agenda, though his views continue to fuel academic debate. I became a follower of his the day I realized that the beautiful little baby girl being baptized in our church was first to be exorcized of the demon which had supposedly possessed her since the moment of birth. Or was it at conception she was supposedly "enslaved to Satan"?

If questioned, such rituals are explained by an Augustinian interpretation in which God is presented as the one who is disobeyed, Adam and Eve as the ones who sinned and handed us over to the power of Satan, and we are exhorted not to repeat their mistake. Any attempt to question the thinking behind such practices is ultimately treated as Julian's was: as a rebellion against the hierarchical authority we are told is placed over us by God and from which comes the only remedy we have against the flawed nature of our own judgment. In this way Augustinian assumptions and self-perceptions are endlessly recycled until the Catch 22 is complete. Rebellion against them is the symptom which proves the illness. This argument, as we saw (chapter 5, note 18), was used against women by Luther as a warning against any complaint about their subordination to men.

Even those who would never dream of taking the Genesis stories secondhand from Augustine, and who indeed would be anxious to point to such textual errors in his exegesis as his mistranslation of the passage in Paul which he renders as: "death spread to all men because of (Adam) *in whom* all sinned", rather than "in that [i.e. because] all sinned" (Rom. 5:12), usually accept without question his fundamental assumption that human nature and this world as we now experience it are totally other than what God intended them to be. We were not intended to know good from evil, we were not meant to sin, we were not meant to suffer, we were not meant to die. The fact that we do do all these things (which God never intended and we find abhorrent) is explained on the grounds of a flawed human decision by our "first" parents to eat an apple expressly forbidden to them.

We saw these assumptions at work earlier in the discussion of the Hebrew vocabulary for the concept of sin. Likewise, even a scholar like Phyllis Trible, who has done so much work on the Hebrew Text, can conclude her exegesis of the story by saying that:

> Life has lost to Death, harmony to hostility, unity and fulfilment to fragmentation and dispersion. The divine, human, animal and plant worlds are all adversely affected. Indeed, the image of God male and female has participated in a tragedy of disobedience. Estranged from each other, the man and the woman are banished from the garden and barred forever from the tree of life. Truly, a love story has gone awry.[9]

The situation is summed up perceptively by Elaine Pagels, who remarks that if any of us could come to our own culture as a foreign anthropologist and observe traditional Christian attitudes toward sexuality, and how human nature is viewed in relation to politics, philosophy and psychology, we might well be astonished at attitudes that we take for granted, many of them derived from the story of Adam and Eve. Even those who think of this only as literature, and those who are not Christian, live in a culture indelibly shaped by interpretations of it. This echoes James Hillman's remark that the psychological history of the male-female relationship in our civilization may be seen as a series of footnotes to the tale of Adam and Eve.[10]

Can Common Perceptions be Changed?

The traditional interpretation analyzed here is based on the premise that sin is the paramount interpretative category for this story. If one accepts that assumption, then attitudes to women, men and Nature which are clearly seen to be unacceptable ecologically will inevitably continue to be sanctioned. The interpretation and its conclusions have prevailed for over two millennia. Is it possible to change them now?

Before we can begin to answer the question about the possibility of change we have to ask why it hasn't happened before in any significant way. One answer is implicit in the process of canonization of the tradition mentioned in chapter 9. As it took control, the Church Fathers' images and arguments became the authorized, that is, orthodox, Christian approximation to the ultimate reality of God. Their images came from the Graeco-Roman world to which they belonged and to which they were concerned to speak. The pioneering days of Greek philosophy were over but the influence of its great schools continued diffusely in the general intellectual climate of early Christianity. Maurice Wiles sums up the situation neatly:

> The Fathers were the scholars of the Church, and both halves of the definition are important. They were scholars, seeking to express the faith in as intelligent and coherent a form as they could devise. But they were not working in a vacuum, nor in the setting of a modern secular institution. They were scholars of the Church, continually in touch with the day-to-day worshipping life of the Church.[11]

Their scholarly authority was invoked against individuals until the intellectual ferment that had characterized the great theological debates of the early centuries of the church settled down into received dogma.

It was a lengthy and complex process by which Graeco-Roman concepts and imagery were filtered through an Augustinian interpretation and became absorbed into theology and church life (baptismal ceremonies and creeds, for example). This is not evidence of a conspiracy theory of Christian doctrine taken over by Greek and Latin scholars. It is rather an acknowledgement of their own particular and magnificent attempt to express the ultimate reality of God in ways which were intelligible to their contemporaries. Every such achievement is necessarily a time-bound and culture-specific approximation.

What gave theirs an enduring place was the fact that, as Wiles mentioned, they were *Fathers*, male heirs to the divinely sanctioned authority of Christ *in the church*. Their works were studied by generations of churchmen in preaching and pastoral roles, and became part of the devotional reading in the daily Office of monks and clerics. As the generations passed and the thought-world of the Fathers became more remote, more and more time was spent on recapturing it and amplifying and qualifying their images and concepts. Theology gradually took these over as its own language and proper study, and so concepts like "Incarnation", "Trinity", "Redemption", "Fall", and "Original Sin" became standard terms and subjects, accepted ways of summing up the mystery of our interaction with God, with each other and with the world.

The question that arises for the church today is whether or not they are relevant or appropriate within the current ecological context. Do they help Christians to find meaning in their lives and work? Does not taking original sin as an interpretative concept for our relationship with creation make us perceive the very worst side of human life as inescapable, rather than giving us grounds for hope in our natural relationship with it? Does it make sense to prise man loose from creation in a post-Einsteinian world?

Another factor is implicit in Wiles' statement. There were no Christian *Mothers* in the Church. Therefore in the interpretation of the Genesis texts, the one which prevailed was a male construct, bound by and acceptable to the preconceptions of a

patriarchal culture and specific to a time when male consciousness was taken as the norm. The inherent contradictions in the
story and the inferiorization of women presumed in its exegesis
were handed on in ways which sustained the process of
inferiorization of women and Nature, and at times, as in the
persecution of witches, their terrorization. Had women had
access to formal theological education and to spiritual authority,
the canonized interpretations might have been exposed in their
bias and illogicality long before now, and women and men alike
would have benefited.

So when the question is raised today about a different
interpretation, it comes at a time when, with the rise in women's
consciousness and the beginnings of their acceptance as theologians, there is an unprecedented opportunity for a fresh and
balanced view of these foundational texts and consequently for
their fruitful incorporation into a Christian ecological vision.
Turning a metaphoric sword into a ploughshare, so to speak,
we could rephrase the ruling of the American Tract Society that:
"She who was first in the transgression must yet be the principal
earthly instrument in the restoration," and say rather that she
who was first transgressed against must yet be the principal
earthly instrument in the restoration of the earth.

How will this come about? What difference does it make to
all of us today if we do not read the Genesis story of creation
through the interpretative grid of Original sin?

Some of the possibilities have been appearing in earlier
chapters and in the present discussion of the text. This
groundwork enables me to propose some uncommon perceptions of the characters in the story and then to ask how they
contribute to an ecological Christian vision.

Uncommon Perceptions of the Genesis Text

First, *an uncommon perception of man*. Instead of the hierarchical
male of the standard interpretation, placed in power over his
female dependents and over the earth, man shares with them
the common clay and the spirit of all living being. There is no
reason to believe that his will, his intellect or his body is by
nature at the mercy of disordered sexual desire. He is not seduced
by woman from a proper relationship with God. His sexuality
is an intrinsic part of that relationship, and of his interaction
with other living beings. He is not set apart from them in his

spirit or in his body, in his life or in his death, but forms with them and with God the world in which each is created mortal by nature. He gives names to all the other living beings, and woman he names as mother of all the living. He toils to bring food out of the earth, and his final and most solemn instruction from God is that he is to serve the earth, not the earth him. When he dies, he returns to that earth from which he came.

Second, *an uncommon perception of woman*. There is no suggestion of inferiority to the man in the way she behaves. She opens the conversation with the serpent on behalf of both of them, judges for herself that the fruit is good to eat, to get insight from, and takes the initiative in eating it. She receives insight into the nature of good and evil, shares it with man, and he accepts it from her. Are the consequences of this so terrible for them? God admits that after eating the fruit all that differentiates him from them is eternal existence. According to the prologue, similarity to God was bestowed on male and female from the beginning. In the garden story it is won from God through the woman's action. The human race has won self-awareness and the ability to exercize judgment and discretion. It has leaped irreversibly into maturity and independence. Female fertility is named by man as the source of all life in the world and this life is sustained through eating the products of man's interaction with the earth's fertility.

Third, *an uncommon perception of the serpent*. The serpent, representative of the animal world, is a symbol of wisdom offered to humankind in interaction with that world. This is the wisdom subjected to scrutiny in other books of the Bible like Job, Ecclesiastes and certain psalms, which deal with the meaning of the paradoxes and harsh facts of life. The serpent exposes, in all its complexity, the problem of keeping rules of conduct, imposed norms of behaviour. At the interpersonal level, there is always a tension between growth in personal identity and integrity on the one hand, and social intolerance and acceptance on the other. But any rules which operate as rules of helplessness must be resisted. These invoke penalties for self-reliance, competence, effectiveness. Even supposedly divine codes must be called into question. Religious prohibitions placed on knowledge or learning foster dependence on hierarchical structures for making decisions about relationships with the world. The complexity of relationship with the natural world is also presented by the serpent. The woman articulates both the consequence and result of that relationship. Do we take the insight the world of Nature offers as a pathway to a relationship with each other and with God? Where else do we expect to find this insight?

Fourth, *an uncommon perception of God*. God appears as a rather benevolent, albeit tyrannical male parent, kind enough to give his children life, a cosy existence and suitable playmates. In return he demands total obedience from them, under constant supervision. They are denied basic human liberties: the knowledge of good and evil and freedom of choice. God secures their obedience by threats. Any normal child responds to this by rebelling, thus risking, even inviting separation from the parent, with loss of physical and emotional comfort. This is the price of growing up. Liberation from law, even religious law, is a central factor in religious maturity.[12]

To those who object to bringing God down, as it were, to the level of a parent, honesty compels the answer that the real objection is that he is imaged here as a parent no human father or mother would want to adopt as a role model. He uses a classical "double-bind" method – a combination of favours and threats, sticks and carrots – in order to tie his offspring to him. He even lies to bind them to him.

There is an extremely important perception of God at stake here, one which makes us want to reject this image of God out of hand as "anthropomorphic", without facing up to the fact that we use such images all the time. The problem with this one is that it represents a *bad* human parent. God is a father, certainly. But God couldn't be a *bad* father! God is a mother, certainly. But surely not a *bad* mother!

One of the cornerstones of the original sin hypothesis, as we saw, was the urge to keep the goodness of God intact. In pursuit of this, any action less than perfect, or rather any so perceived, must be attributed to the serpent, the woman or the man. It is axiomatic that whatever God does in the story is good. His actions are consistently read through rose-coloured spectacles. By contrast, human and animal actions are read through sin-coloured spectacles in an attempt to explain why it is that we suffer, inflict suffering and die in pain. In this way "sin" is projected on to all the other characters in the drama but God. His actions are assumed to be beyond reproach even when patently they are not. The best analogy for this is that Christians who read the text in this way become inhabitants of Hilton's lost valley, where everyone is blind. Those who enter must, if they wish to remain there, give up the gift of sight.

Or else, develop *an uncommon perception of sin*. The Cain story presents it as a choice to be made in favour of or in rejection of one's fellow earth-creatures. It is a choice made within one's own ecosystem and in interaction with those of others and their common relationship to God. It is no accident that the "occasion" of the sin is the possession of certain products of the earth's fertility and their offering to God: an offering whose "acceptance" would ensure continued fertility.

So I have not invented a new sin when with the theologians of the poor of this earth I talk about sinful structures or structural sin. I am not attributing a specific sin, properly applicable only to an individual, Cain, to abstract, impersonal agricultural systems. The central problem then, and now, is the creation and maintenance of structures and powercentres, whether in the city or the country, which are bound to block all effective forms of loving our fellow earth-creatures either in public, in our church practices, or in our homes. By and large, these structures prevent the recognition and growth of diversity, and foster an us-versus-them categorizing tendency that remains the very essence of sin. In Cain, it prevented him, a herdsman, from recognizing, literally, the gifts of the farmer. In the context of our worship of God, the same drive to exclusiveness has fostered hatred, division and war. In the context of our relationship with non-human species, it has led us to deny the intrinsic worth of the rest of creation.

The second step towards an uncommon perception of sin is to recognize that these structures have power on a global scale to enslave human beings, to make them useless and to kill them. From this perspective, Abel was the first victim of an eco-war. The tally today reads, as we have seen, in millions, whether in Bhopal, Latin America or the Ethiopian desert.

This step demands that we consider the mechanisms which turn us into unwitting co-authors of this sin. It is not just *outside* us, we are part of it: we are its accomplices. This is one clear fact which emerges time and time again from ecological studies of environmental problems with their quota of death, destruction and suffering. One of the mechanisms is the relationship between us and hierarchical law, including religious law. There is an inertia involved in living under the rule of law, in which sins are by omission, by going along with policies of exploitation against "them". Women know this only too well. Hierarchical government sanctions the rule of "power-over" at the cost of power-from-within. It sanctions sins against the Spirit, devaluing and destroying diversity which creates ecological community and fills the earth with glory.[13]

What God do we see now in the Genesis story? What happens if we do not take the goodness of God for granted, if we accept that in some mysterious way the oneness of the earth's systems and the oneness of God challenge us to think about God in the context of the structural sin of those systems?

The first thing that happens is that we have to decide whether or not we really believe in the oneness of God. Judith Plaskow tackles this question in a discussion of Jewish monotheism. She tries to give voice to a new, inclusive monotheism that embraces and mirrors the diversity that we want to see honoured in the world. In the male monotheism which has shaped our common religious heritage, monotheism is understood as the worship of God as the king of all the earth. This is undoubtedly a male image. Yet Plaskow does not want us to stop at the difficulties created at this level. If we were to call God "Queen of all the earth", it might soften and change the picture slightly (for those who have never heard of Boadicea or Maeve, perhaps). But it does not alter the basic image of God as dominating Other who drowns Egyptians in the sea and enforces obedience on children through a mixture of bribes and punishments. It is not clear that She is any more a God feminists of either sex would want to worship. From the issue of male language we have moved to the particular issue here of the nature of this one God affirmed in monotheism.

Plaskow tackles this head on. She says that one of the things she has most valued about Judaism is its holistic understanding of God in relation to the problem of evil. A number of strands of Judaism have acknowledged that if God is the creator of the world, and the world contains pain, ambiguity, and evil, then these must have their origins in God at the same time that God urges us to choose life and justice. (The book of Job is an exposition of wisdom wrestling with this problem of the relationship between God and evil.) She says, "I do not think that it is God's wrath alone that poses a special problem for feminists, but rather both mercy and wrath when these are meted out by an authoritarian parent trying to get human beings to do his will."[14]

Plaskow's honesty in wrestling with the monotheism of the biblical God of Judaism brings us back to the problems created by the Platonic notion of unity. Wiles puts them succinctly. The Bible, he says, speaks in emphatic terms of God as one. But the concern of the biblical tradition is to declare the falsity of all forms of polytheism and idol-worship. It is the fact that there is one and not many Gods that is taught. This is the fact that Plaskow wrestles with in all its complexity. What does it mean to say that this God knows good and evil? Does God know it in the same way as we do, as inextricably bound up with the fact of being part of this world?

This leads us on to *an uncommon perception of Jesus, of incarnation*. It forbids us to strip Jesus of anything which, from the standpoint of an ideal, could be regarded as weakness, limitation, or concession. The opposite tactic, of attributing everything to him that is divine and transcendent, has been dealt with in earlier chapters. What is required here is a deliberate step in the direction of recovering his total humanity, and with it, the realization that he was, as much as we are, involved in sinful structures. He too was guilty of categorizing: the Jews are "us" and the pagans "them", as he told the Syro-Phoenician woman. He dealt with another "them", the Pharisees, in ways which provoked their enmity, and sharpened and fomented conflicts with them. He derided them as hypocrites, who doing exactly the opposite of the ideal he proclaimed with regard to dealing with one's enemies.

Seen in his authentic historical context, Jesus was polemical or ambiguous because he did not appear isolated from sin.[15]

On the contrary, he was identified with it: "we *know* that this man is a sinner". Therefore, as was said before, he did not die *for* sinners, but *with* sinners. Therefore, in the context of the Genesis story, his perfect flesh did not suffer death because of everyone else's sins but his own.

This perception of Jesus has been operative throughout this book, for as an ecological interpretation of his life, it does not isolate him from his environment or from the living earth systems which sustained him. It leaves open the paradox of the incarnation, of humanity and divinity. One way in which the paradox was grappled with by Christian exegetes was, as we saw, to ignore it. By assuming that God is undifferentiated goodness, however you define it, then all the problems with "badness" in the Genesis narrative were projected on to the other characters in the biblical story, on to human sin and the death of Jesus.

An Ecological Reading of Genesis 1–3

The dynamic tensions within the concept of monotheism will be taken up again in the concluding chapter. The rest of this one will try to answer the question: if sin is not the proper interpretive category for this story, what is? What if we assume instead that this story, like all the others in the Bible, arose in the context of a particular society in which the actions of certain individuals or groups in the story are consistent with the rules and values operative in that society? What if we place it in the context of a particular ecosystem, a set of interacting bodies, self-regulating to a large extent but vulnerable and open to the larger ones around, both natural and human? What if we do not read it as a story of origins, but as a superlatively imaginative account of a particular group's faith in God?

In such an ecological reading, God is not either dictating the script or directing the action to a foregone tragic conclusion. No one doubts whether or not he is onstage. He is there: a mysterious presence intimately related to the other three worlds in the story: animal, plant, and human. He is totally involved with the action, but since he cannot be pointed to and the other characters can, his involvement with them is measured in terms of how well they interact. His will is perceived as a proper order of relationships between them. So for a vegetarian society recounting the story the plants are his gift of food, remembered as such even when the script is written down in a later carnivorous society in which the animals are to be eaten with his blessing.

In this society, men do the naming, the ordering, the ploughing, the sowing, the weeding out of thorns and thistles, the sweaty labour of breaking new ground. Women are subject to their husbands, treated as Abraham's Sarah is treated, a body created to be his companion, to be blamed for his misfortunes, bartered for his survival or used to bear him a son. Such women yearn to be loved for their own sakes and fear barrenness as a hindrance to this. They bear children in pain and anxiety, anxious for their survival in the harsh conditions of an environment where plant, animal and child must vie with each other for water and sustenance.

Rereading the story in its context of early Israelite society, it becomes a revelation of human longing for integrity in its relationships with the world and with God. It also intimates how good life can be when those relationships are properly ordered. Above all, it is a story of what it means to be human, of what human nature is capable of, both positively and negatively.

It is also a story of how we wrestle with the mystery of God, with the notion of the oneness of God. How do we live with a God who creates a world of harmony and happiness but leaves within it the possibility of its destruction? How can we solve the puzzle of God's nature? Is it good or bad, or both at once? Is God responsible for the suffering of those he creates or is he not? Does God give us the necessities for life at some times and withhold them at others, so that sometimes we are offered life and at other times death? Are life and death inextricably bound together, different sides of the same coin? Is God someone who forces obedience on us through a mixture of bribes and punishments? If God is the creator of the world, and the world contains pain, ambiguity and evil, then these must have their origins in God at the same time that God urges us to choose life and justice.

Taken in this way, the story gives expression to an inclusive monotheism that embraces and mirrors the diversity of experience of God in a particular time and place. It presupposes God's responsibility for the whole of creation and therefore God's relationship with each and every part of it. It leaves us with the picture of ourselves embedded in all the other systems that make up the organic whole we call earth.

Once the barrier of later derogatory perceptions of Eve is removed, the way is open to seeing the narrative as it existed in Israel before the emergence of the influential expositions of Jewish and Christian antiquity. With the realization that the ancient biblical texts were both responsive to and reflective of their own late second- or early first- millennium world, and with some knowledge that conditions in that world were different from those in later times, we can discover the Eve that existed before the time of her prototypical linkage with sin and suffering.

This Eve existed in a Palestinian setting where "Eden" was a place where waters flowed continuously, a place in which the constant fear of drought would be lifted from the anxious shoulders of Israelite farmers. Life was not possible, according to Genesis 2:5, without two critical elements: rainfall and human labour. There was no bush nor sprouting grain until Yahweh sent rain upon the land, and there was an earthling to work the earth. Humanity is created (Gen. 2:7) in the middle of two situations: one without rain or workers and hence without food (sprouting grain), and the other (Gen. 2:9) with availability of food established by God. Because the creation of humanity occurs centrally to this arrangement, the whole passage is telling us that human existence is inextricably caught up with concern for sustenance. The Israelite highlanders, confronted with the daily reality of intensive labour, were drawn to the idea that life might be otherwise. Hence the narrative unfolds: it holds up the ephemeral state of Eden for a brief glimpse and then brings humans at last into the real world.

While sustenance alone would be sufficient for animals, recognition of an intrinsic human need for more than mere survival is present in the phrase which tells us that the trees are "pleasing to the eye". The creative sequence nears completion when the earthling finds no helper, a word which in Hebrew can refer to a superior as much as an inferior, notably when applied to God to whom one turns in distress (Ps. 121:1-2). The prepositional phrase in Genesis 2:18 and 20 tells us what kind of helper is meant here. It establishes a non-hierarchical relationship between the two. It means "opposite", "corresponding to", "parallel with" or "on a par with".[16] Yahweh casts the earthling into a comatose state, far closer to original non-existence than ordinary sleep, and the creative sequence is completed with the differentiation of human life when woman, the helper, is formed.

In this context what takes the place of sin, if it is not the basic thematic element of the Eden story? It is in the vocabulary and the word usage that an answer is found. The language that dominates the narrative must be taken to be significant and intentional. The repetition of words and phrases is a characteristic way in which Hebrew literature, especially the biblical narratives, which would have been repeated orally to attentive audiences, provides emphasis for ideas and objects. Verbatim repetition, in particular the reiteration of individual words, is a usual device for stressing motifs in non-literate cultures. This stress usually disappears in the translation into modern language where the idiom is impatient of such repetition.

One such theme word in the Genesis narrative is the verb "eat" and the noun "food", both developed from the same root. This repetition is lost in languages such as English which do not use a cognate noun and verb. The problem already came up in the translation of *'adam*. The Hebrew root word in question here is *'kl*, "to eat". It recurs in one form or another more frequently than any other word in these two chapters except *'adam*. Its appearance at key places in the narrative draws attention to pivotal features of the action. The very first words that a living human being hears in Genesis 2:16 – "And the Lord God commanded the human saying: 'you may eat freely of every tree of the garden'" – concern the existence of a food supply. The striking repetition and placement carry their own message: the beginning of human existence coincides with a search for sustenance. Original human consciousness, as set out in this story, consists of two vital aspects: the human ability to relate to God and understand God's instructions about our relationship with the earth, and the human need to know about the sources of food.[17]

This very simple fact has been forgotten or overlooked in cultures where the means of sustenance is abundant. In our industrialized consumer society, the consumption of food is largely taken for granted. We scarcely notice shelves filled with delicacies and yearn rather for money, power or sexual favours. Small wonder then we read the references to sustenance in this narrative on a full stomach, so to speak. This is a very different experience from hearing it or reading it on an empty one, which was probably quite usual for those who first gave voice to its drama and for those who first heard it. Eating for them was not simply or primarily a vehicle or a literary device for introducing the concept of disobedience, which is the way it is now read or understood. Eating was a central issue in itself, the literally gnawing concern about the availability of sustenance. There is an integral relationship in the story between this sustenance and the difficulties of securing it.

These are recognized in the speeches to the woman and man in Genesis 3:16-19, where the inevitability of that cycle of birth, toil, and death is given the sanction of divine will. They recognize the difficult nature of humanity's intrinsic connection to the ground in the Palestinian highlands, whose inhabitants had to carve cisterns to store winter rain and summer dew out of the bedrock that lay close to the surface of the hilltops where most of the early villages were located. This required monumental expenditures of labour, whether done with bronze or iron tools.

Besides the fluctuating pattern of annual rainfall, the Israelites also faced the constraints imposed on agriculture by mountainous terrain, not the easiest place to plant and grow barley. The scarcity of level ground led to the construction of terraces, and archaeologists have identified a number of systems dating to the period of earliest Israelite settlement. This deceptively simple technological device made all the difference. It allowed the creation of fields, gardens and vineyards on slopes otherwise too rocky or steep for anything but thorns and scrub oak to grow. But extensive terracing required a huge output of human energy, a staggering investment of time and labour. Terraces needed to be maintained against flooding and erosion. A suprafamily collective labour system would have been necessary. For women, the increased labour needs had a double aspect. More work meant more women employed in the back-breaking labour of building and repairing walls, etc. In addition, increased labour needs required a larger work force, which in turn called for larger families. Responsibility for meeting the extraordinary labour requirements of highland dry farming rested ultimately on the shoulders of both women and men and on the reproductive capacity of women.[18] Small wonder then that the river valley environments and the flat stretches of arable land to the East in Mesopotamia provided a picture of Eden.

While I was enjoying Carol Meyers' absorbing account of archaeological digs and analyses of Israelite life at the beginning of the Iron Age (the time which she thinks most likely as setting for the Genesis narrative), I happened to see a programme on agriculture in China which showed canals, terracing, and the intensive manual labour of men and women alike. The reporters gave statistics and information about deaths from famine following on crop failure or flooding. It brought home to me the basic problem we in the developed world have with this text.

We no longer work in order to eat in order to live. Food is only an item in the family budget, often a relatively small one.

Yet the integral relationship between sustenance, the difficulties of securing it and human relationships with the world around us are the interpretive grid through which once again, ecology reminds us, this narrative has become relevant today. The ecological slogan: "There is no such thing as a free lunch", is just another way of reading the judgments of God in Genesis 3: 16f. The way we live keeps us deaf to this message, whether in the Bible or in ecological slogans.

Chapter 12

The Spirit of Genesis

The story of Genesis reminds us of our bond with the earth: we came from it, serve it and will return to it in death. The God of this story creates woman to be man's *ezer neged*, his equal in power with whom he steps into maturity, leaving the security of his parents' home in order to share life with her.[1] The God of this story blesses the fertility of the woman and man in the same way as he blesses that of all species, plant and animal alike. Their fertility is inextricably bound to the mystery of sustenance: the sustenance contained in the earth, toiled for by human beings and which each living being partakes of until it returns to that earth to become part of its fruitfulness for others. Death has its "moment" in the circuit of each life. Acceptance of it, at the right moment, is a source of life for others. The pattern of death and life cannot be closed off from the pattern of fertility and nourishment.

This understanding of death shines through the words of the Jewish resistance fighter Hannah Senesh, written shortly before her execution in November, 1944:

> Blessed is the match that is consumed in kindling
> the flame
> Blessed is the flame that burns in the secret
> fastness of the heart
> Blessed is the heart strong enough to stop
> beating in dignity
> Blessed is the match that is consumed
> in kindling the flame.[2]

The Spirit which inspired this poem and the life from which it springs is that of the God of Genesis: the Spirit of life and death: life handed on and sustained in and through the life and death of some being, whether in seed or body. Hannah's words facing death breathe the Spirit of God the Sustainer of the world: the same Spirit which in the Apocalypse is the source of newness and diversity in whatever is coming into existence (Rev. 21:5).

The concept of one source sustaining us in life and death affirms rather than denies diversity. The fact that creation contains the infinite variety that it obviously does contain, and is energized by one Spirit, leads to the conclusion that the God of this Spirit has a preference for diversity.[3]

The God of the Fall

In contrast to the image of life-sustainer and renewer associated with the God of the Genesis narrative, the God enthroned above the great pillars of the fall and redemption doctrine appears to be one who decrees that death, not life, be transmitted through the fertility of human, animal and plant species: death through sin associated with human fertility, with man's closest possible encounter with female fruitfulness. Augustine's word for the external genital organs, *pudenda*, binds sex and shame irrevocably together. This God who has judged human bodies to be carriers of sin is apparently concerned only with whether or not they obey him.

The recorded decision of Adam and Eve not to do so, if looked at honestly, is inevitable. Otherwise, as we saw, the pair lack notable characteristics of mature human beings. To call their action "sin" is a logical impossibility, because for an action to be labelled "sin", evil and blameworthy, it has to be done from choice, with free will. Otherwise, it is rightly argued, not they but God would be responsible for what they did. But if they do not have knowledge of good and evil, how can they choose between them? You cannot blame them if they choose what we call evil, or making the wrong choice. If God is not responsible for what they choose, he must, in giving them a choice, have made it possible for them to make the right one, i.e. choose good. But by making the object of their choice the means whereby they could choose correctly, then they really had no choice.

This God of the "double-bind" is discernible in both the story of Genesis and the doctrine of the "fall" in Christianity. But in talking about "the fall", no account is taken of whether or not Adam and Eve could have done anything else. In the story, as opposed to the doctrine, their action is not prejudged sinful and blameworthy. In the doctrine, the emphasis is laid on what they "should have" done and didn't do, and what happened to them afterwards is then construed as punishment. The sentencing to exile, toil, pain and death, the domination of earth and woman by man are taken to be proper effects of a self-evident cause. The question about the propriety of the cause is not raised.

If the question of their ability to act in a human way is not raised by traditional Christianity, neither is the question of the type of God who would link such a cause with such an effect: who would create them as human beings and yet expect them to behave like automatons. As we saw, the traditional image of divinity is linked with the assumption that no matter what God does it has to be good. So the question of God's involvement in the débâcle, raised persistently for honest readers of Genesis like Judith Plaskow, is reduced, in the fall/sin hypothesis, to that of a judge of human deeds distanced from him. All of God's actions in the story are emptied of problematic, negative content by stressing the heinousness of the "crime". God is then presumed justified in punishing it horrifically. The projection of horror on to the disobedience of the human pair is balanced by the horror of the punishment. So the goodness of God is preserved intact through stressing the "greatness" of our fall and its effects.

Julian of Norwich and the Fall

The more the greatness of our fall is stressed, the more we feel our inability to do anything about it. Julian of Norwich expresses this most poignantly in the story of the lord and servant already alluded to. The servant stands before the lord, ready and eager to do his will. He is sent to a certain place, and goes dashing off at great speed:

> And soon he falls into a dell and is greatly injured: and then he groans and moans and tosses about and writhes, but he cannot rise or help himself in any way. And of all this, the greatest hurt which I saw him in was lack of consolation, for he could not turn his face to look at his loving lord, who was very close to him, in whom is all consolation; but like a man who was for the time extremely feeble and foolish, he paid heed to his feelings and his continuing distress, in which distress he suffered seven great pains. The first was the severe bruising which he took in his fall, which gave him great pains. The second was the clumsiness of his body. The third was the weakness which followed these two. The fourth was that he was blinded in his reason and perplexed in his mind, so much so that he had almost forgotten his own love. The fifth

was that he could not rise. The sixth was the pain most astonishing to me, and that was that he lay alone. I looked all around and searched, and far and near, high and low, I saw no help for him. The seventh was that the place in which he lay was narrow and comfortless and distressful.[4]

The tenderness and poetry of this account arouse compassion for the servant's great fall. The description of the lord, who sits in state looking on his servant "very lovingly and sweetly" gives a picture of their relationship as one of mutual love and trust. This makes the servant's plight all the more devastating, as Julian makes clear when she says that his greatest hurt was that he could no longer see his lord.

The relationship between the lord and servant (God and Adam, she tells us later) began in trust and harmony, but, for the servant, the fall broke that relationship. Adam could no longer see God. This is one of the hidden assumptions behind the doctrine of the fall which Julian brings to light with her deep prayerful pondering. As Adam and Eve were expelled from Eden, so too they were expelled from the presence of God. They no longer, in the popular phrases, walked with God in the cool of the evening or when morning had broken. Their access to God was now blocked by an angel with a fiery sword.

This gives the further idea buried deep in the Christian psyche that the earth outside Eden to which they were expelled was a "no-God's land", a place "narrow and comfortless and distressed" where they could no longer expect to see God, to hear his voice or speak to him. This place of toil and suffering, this earth cursed by God because of Adam, is outside the territory of transcendence. It is there to be worked, used, raised into a slag heap or hollowed out in cisterns without any reference to God. The relationship with him was grounded in the natural world in Eden, but outside it, that world no longer enjoys God's presence. It is emptied of the value which divine presence would give it.

Furthermore, when Adam was put out of Eden, then not only was he expelled from his relationship with God but the earth he had to work in toil and sweat was cursed because of him. The relationship of guilt by association links them together even as it distances them from God. Great is the fall indeed! . . . And all was for an apple, an apple that he took! . . .

Even as one pursues Adam into the pit in the wilderness of
sin, so to speak, one's attention is drawn back irresistibly to the
figure of the lord. Julian is at pains to tell us how loving, restful
and peaceful he is. She is also at pains to tell us that she could
detect no fault in the servant, nor did the lord impute any kind
of blame to him. And indeed, even though he can no longer see
the lord, the lord looks on him most tenderly, with great
compassion and pity. The lord tells Julian that the beloved
servant has had and accepted harm and injuries for love, and
that therefore it is reasonable that he should be rewarded for
his fright and fear, his hurt and his injuries and all his woe. She
understands this to mean that the great goodness and the
personal honour of the lord require that the servant should be
highly and blessedly rewarded forever, above what he would
have been if he had not fallen. So much so that his falling and
all the woe that he received from it will be turned into high,
surpassing honour and endless bliss.

Julian's reverence for the figure of the lord leads her to impute
no responsibility for the servant's fall to him, even though it
was his errand that the servant ran to execute. It is equally clear
to her that the servant cannot be blamed either. And since there
is no blame, there cannot be punishment. The servant's fall into
terror and weakness is not the result of something he has done.
In refusing to blame the servant for his fall, Julian shows not
only great integrity in her attitude to God and to the servant,
but also considerable courage. She takes the very remarkable
view that it is in fact the result of over-enthusiasm on his part
in carrying out his lord's will. Such departures from the official
teaching of the church appear even more courageous when one
remembers that the martial bishop Despenser was burning
Lollard heretics in a pit close enough to Julian's cell for the stench
to reach her nostrils.

She describes sin therefore as being injured in one's powers
and made most feeble, as being diverted from looking on the
lord, blinded and hindered from knowing his will. She is at pains
to know and to describe how the lord looks on us in our sin.
He is meek and mild to the servant, although the servant himself
is not aware of this:

Our courteous Lord comforts and succours, and always he is
kindly disposed to the soul, loving and longing to bring us

to his bliss . . . The compassion and the pity of the Father were for Adam, who is his most beloved creature.[5]

Julian keeps faith with a God who does not abandon Adam in his fall, nor is their relationship shattered as far as God is concerned. The servant's will to do the lord's bidding is preserved. The lord remains kindly disposed toward the servant. This is reminiscent of the God of the Hebrew Genesis narrative who makes clothes for the couple in Eden after they have eaten the fruit.

The lord continues to love the servant. In a mysterious way, the lord seems to have more regard for him after the fall and its effects. This was shown, says Julian, so as to make it understood how God regards all men and their falling.

Julian wrestled with the meaning of this showing for twenty years, and the fruits of her struggle make wonderful and consoling reading today. The greatness of the fall is conveyed in graphic imagery of wounding and helplessness. The love of the lord grows in greatness and mystery even as the state of the servant becomes more desperate. And, she says, this relationship between human weakness and divine love is true for all of us.

This is indeed consoling doctrine for those taught that wrath and justice were the deciding factors in our relationship with God after Adam's fall. It is also a comfort for all of us who feel our inadequacy and sinfulness pressing hard upon us. And when self-loathing is at its worst, it is reassuring indeed to be reminded of the unconditional steadfast love of God for us whether we find ourselves lovable or not.

But is it unconditional? Julian goes on to describe again the lord sitting in state and the servant standing respectfully before him. Now she sees in the servant a double significance. The servant is both Adam and Jesus Christ, the Son of God. The lord is God the Father. The Holy Spirit is the equal love which was in them both:

> When Adam fell, God's Son fell; because of the true union which was made in heaven, God's Son could not be separated from Adam, for by Adam I understand all mankind. Adam fell from life to death, into the valley of this wretched world, and after that into hell. God's Son fell with Adam, into the womb of the maiden who was the fairest daughter of Adam,

and that was to excuse him from blame in heaven and on earth . . . The strength and the goodness we have is from Jesus Christ, the weakness and blindness we have is from Adam, which two were shown in the servant.

And so has our good Lord Jesus taken upon him all our blame; and therefore our Father may not, does not wish to assign more blame to us than to his own beloved Son Jesus Christ.[6]

This passage brings us to the second pillar of this version of the Christian faith: the greatness of our redemption. It usually supposes that the sorry figure of Adam supports the first pillar (the fall) and the wise and good figure of Jesus supports the second (redemption). Adam fell from life to death. Jesus fell from heaven into the womb of the maiden. The Platonic note struck here is no surprise. Humanity "fell" in both traditions. But Christianity teaches that the humanity which clothes Jesus differs from Adam's in that the latter's is all harm and weakness and that of Jesus is all strength and goodness.

This distinction takes us back to a point made in the previous chapter. In the development of the doctrine of original sin, Ambrose and then Augustine insisted that human bodies, scarred by sexuality, could be redeemed only by a body whose virgin birth had been exempt from sexual desire. It was a heady antithesis, with a long life ahead of it, destined to "inject a powerful and toxic theme into mediaeval theology".[7] To mix metaphors slightly, the thesis of Adam's sin supports one pillar, the antithesis of Jesus' "virgin" body supports the other, and they are joined in a canonized doctrine called redemption. In this structuring of Christian reality, antithetical views of humanity are kept in place by the doctrine of the fall. Any weakness is on the side of human scarred flesh. Any strength is that of the divine virgin flesh of Christ, unscarred by sex and sin.

A different perspective on the flesh of Jesus was offered in the previous chapter. Julian's wonderful exposition of the relationship between Adam and Jesus, if the assumption is not made that they are two separate beings, would then appear rather differently: as a source of hope for all flesh. This is an example of how precious and reassuring this doctrine can be, and how finely balanced the relationship between God's justice and love appears in the hands of such a practical mystic.

Nevertheless, the creativeness of the account must not prevent us from seeing its focus: the servant's fall. Without that, there would be no development of the relationship between lord and servant, between Adam and the Son of God, between the Father God and the Son. The fall establishes the Christian basis for thinking about ourselves in relation to Father and Son; for thinking about them in relation to each other; for thinking about the Spirit only in relation to them, as part of their relationship with each other and with us.

Trinity and Redemption

This brings us back to a point made in chapter 9. Thinking about the relationship between the Trinity and the world on the basis of the fall/redemption hypothesis alone breaks the relationship between the Spirit and the whole of creation by narrowing it down solely to an aspect of the relationship between Father, Son and world. This is an unecological approach to the mystery of personhood in God, since it reduces in value the diversity of relationships enjoyed by each divine person within the Trinity and with the world. Such devaluing of the role of the Spirit leads inexorably to an exclusively Christocentric church, in which the Spirit becomes the exclusive possession of the apostles' successors. Figures of creative power in the Hebrew scriptures which have feminine connotations, such as Wisdom, are subsumed into that of Christ. Women are not seen to have direct access to the Spirit, nor is Nature infused with it.

An ecological doctrine of God opens up such strictures in our thinking by allowing us to relate to each manifestation of the Spirit in scripture, tradition and Nature without fitting it into the cubby-hole of preconceptions about the activities of Father and Son. This creative process in a living canon creates and is created by the response of faith in ecological communities. It forces upon us the task of re-reading the literary sources of our tradition in the light of present knowledge about the world and then asking ourselves what the Spirit of God is saying to the churches in the ecological apocalypse of today. At its simplest, it is saying that there is no room for the sustaining Spirit of all life on earth in traditional doctrines concerned only with the human desire for salvation. At a more profound level, it is asking us to be critically aware of the need for an ecological reading of the Genesis narrative which restores the mystery of divine relationships with Nature: in which incarnation does not mean that Jesus or anyone baptized in his name is defined as the antithesis to Adam.

Unless this is done, the real mystery of God's relationship with sin and suffering in the world, God's transcendence *and* God's total involvement in the good and the bad of human and natural existence is narrowed down to a vision of a Father God working out the best way to redeem mankind from one trivial human act, and being prepared to use his own Son as an instrument towards that end. This closes off the "personality" of God from the dynamic and intangible mysteriousness of the relationship with the world suggested inferentially in the Genesis narrative, where the God of chapter 1 is rational and uninvolved compared with the intimate interaction of divine and human in chapters 2 and 3.

The transcendent and immanent image of divinity in Genesis emerges from the narrative through a number of sources, such as the use of verbs, where God is experienced through action – that which creates, makes things grow, ordains limits, establishes the generative and formative conditions of the world. Then, abstract qualities, such as knowing good and evil and living for ever, are presented as specific attributes which set God apart from the world with objective knowledge and immunity from change. These are the qualities the human couple aspire to in order to be like God, rather than making rain, clothes or animals. Most interestingly, in a concealed metaphor: *"lerûah hayyôm"* (in the breath/spirit/cool of the day), the couple hear the voice of God in a sonorous wind which stirs the leaves in which they hide. God's Spirit is assimilated into the voice of the wind and into the passage of the day. Breeze and evening, unobtrusive, pervasive, gently moving, are images for the dynamic indefinable God suggested and experienced through the diurnal rhythm of Nature's systems. Finally, the words "Behold, the earth creature has become as one of us", remove us from the leafy scene of the garden to the heavenly court where the divine assembly is addressed.[8]

This dialectic between reason and mystery, human and divine, flesh and wind, Nature and God, heaven and earth, transcendence and immanence, clarity and ambiguity, is lost in doctrines which reduce the relationship between God and world to a redemptive transaction between Father and Son, which, as was pointed out earlier, is utilitarianism carried to its uttermost heights or depths, depending on where one sees oneself in relation to God.

The basic unease which one might feel about this is coped with by using a kind of theological "double speak" about the death of Jesus, in which his suffering becomes glory, his pain a crown, his weakness strength and so on. The paradox of the cross is lost, in which strength and weakness, foolishness and wisdom co-exist, opening us up through the shock of their equal presence to the mystery of suffering in God. Instead, "bad" words are exchanged for "good" ones, so that the human suffering Jesus becomes the all-powerful divine Redeemer.

This cloaks the fact that when we use what we consider "good" words about God such as power, wisdom, immortality, justice or goodness, *we don't know what they really mean in respect to God* any more than "bad" ones. All words used for God are metaphorical, bringing images from different contexts together in the attempt to suggest the reality of a God beyond all imagining. We have no other than human images and words, certainly, to use. But the point is that the resistance we feel to using any other than "*good*" words shows that we do, after all, think that these words have some specific relationship to the reality of God not enjoyed by any others.

In practice then, a hierarchy of theological terms has been built up: a ladder of excellence, so to speak, by which all human and negative connotations are withdrawn from talk about God until we arrive at the summit of abstraction from whence we can proclaim all absolutes of value (in our terms) as disclosing the divine nature of Father and Son. So the categories of Goodness, Truth, Beauty, Knowledge, Wisdom and Unity are all judged proper approximations to the nature of divinity. By virtue of the human rational intellect, the scholastics taught, "man" and only "man" ascends from the visible world to the invisible God described in such categories.

But, says the woman reader of Genesis or the honest Christian: what do you do with the contradictory, composite and ambiguous concepts in Genesis, in which God creates everything and says that it is "good", and yet sees that the lonely situation of the earth creature is "not good"? What do you do with the God of the "double-bind" who issues commands about the trees? How do you cope with a God who tells lies? What do you do with the categories of weakness, powerlessness, devaluation and agony attached to death on a cross? What do you say about the depths of God revealed there? Where is Truth, Unity or Power here?

At the very least, these questions open us to the mysteriousness of divinity: make us realize that there is no word, no category, no formula which can capture definitively the reality of God. This is as true of words we invest with "good" values as it is of words we shun for their evocation of "bad" ones. This is as true of rational statements about God as it is of irrational ones. This truth requires that both women and men respect the partiality of their particular vision and imagery, valuing both for bringing diversity into the tradition which enriches us all. It also requires consciously supplementing the male images of Father and Son with new perceptions of the image of the Spirit active in woman and Nature.

Jesus and Death

There is yet another mystery opened up for us by taking the Genesis narrative and the Cross as authentic images of the reality of God. If the fall was not the question answered by the death of Jesus, what was? If his death was not required as expiation by the Father, why did it happen as it did? In the light of Eve's choice to eat the fruit and her expulsion from Eden and death outside it, what choices did Jesus make, as a person in a particular environment, which led to his expulsion from and death outside the holy city Jerusalem?

Some answers to these questions began to emerge in the preceding chapter when we looked at Jesus' life and death in its natural context of first-century Palestine. Within this setting, he was assimilated not only into the human pure and simple (the flesh) of all of us, but also into the human condition *insofar as it is sinful*. This he shared with Adam and Eve and with us. There is a relationship between his life and projects on the one hand and their final deactivation: death.[9]

The debate between Augustine and Julian of Eclanum about the relationship between sin and death reminds us that in the traditional fall/ redemption hypothesis none of us would have suffered death were it not for "original" sin. Gregory of Nyssa claimed that only in the fall did the sinful creatures take on "coats of skin" to hide their original purity (nakedness). These coats represented the devolution of the original spiritual body into a carnal body subject to decay and death.[10]

Therefore if we hold that view, and hold at the same time that Jesus as the divine Redeemer was necessarily free of this sin (God's Son fell into the "immaculate" womb of the maiden), then we might expect that Jesus was not destined for death as every other human being is. His sinlessness ought to fit him for immortality. He alone ought to be entitled to the immunity from death attributed to God and denied to Adam and Eve on account of sin.

But he died. This fact forces users of the traditional logic of redemption to make the crucial connection between sin and death in Jesus' life a matter not of his own sins, but the sins of others. It follows then that his Father allowed him to die horribly for something unconnected with his own life but connected with all other human lives: the sin of Adam.

But what if we don't make that logical move? What if we believe that he was not outside the total human system which includes sin and death, and look at his life as one which was subject to the same strains and stresses as ours, with the same lurking presence of sin as part of it? What if we rightly keep "incarnation" within the circuit of the living organism earth?

The actual moment or mode of Jesus' death is not thereby robbed of its terror or unexpectedness. But neither, as Hannah Senesh believed, and he is recorded to have believed, is it robbed of its significance. On the contrary. It assumes enormous significance for his fellow earth-creatures. If Jesus' death is not given significance as redemption for the sins of everyone else but himself, then we find its significance in the "likeness" Paul sees between the fully human condition of Jesus and that of every *mortal* human being. We have to ask ourselves to what extent he was involved in sin; to what extent his death was due not only to the incomprehension of his disciples and the solid resistance of his adversaries; to the sinful structures of the religion and state to which he belonged; but also to his own actions and reactions to the bodily, social and religious systems within which he lived. If we do not do that, then he is not seen as human, and his death has no intrinsic connection with the life and death of every living being. To believe that it has is the true core of every doctrine of at-one-ment between God and world.

Jesus and Sustenance

One who spoke of himself as a vine and knew Isaiah's parable
of "Israel the vineyard of God" would not have seen his life or
its pruning in death in isolation from that of others. Nor would
he who spoke of his death as that of a seed dying in the earth
claim exemption from our common sustenance by the earth. As
in the Genesis narrative, there was in Jesus' life an apparently
disproportionate amount of attention paid to food and to eating.
He summoned disciples at a meal shared with tax collectors. His
public ministry began, according to John's Gospel, with a
wedding feast at which the drink flowed so freely that it ran out
and he performed his first miracle to make sure it continued to
flow. Further miracles followed in which he multiplied bread
and fish simply because those who followed him had no food
and were very hungry. Even though there was more than
enough, what was left was to be treated with respect. He ordered
that the fragments be gathered up in baskets and saved.

As with the Genesis narrative, it is interesting to read the
account of the miracle of multiplication of food in John 6:11f. in
terms of the repetition of words about food. In verse 11, Jesus
takes the loaves and fishes, gives thanks and distributes them
to those sitting down, as much as they wanted. The next two
verses are taken up with his instructions to gather up the
fragments, the carrying out of his orders and the record of the
grand total of baskets filled. The next verse tells us that when
the people saw the sign which he had done, they said: "This is
indeed the prophet who is to come into the world!" Then, the
narrator says, perceiving that they were coming to take him by
force and make him king, Jesus withdrew again by himself to
the hills.

It is after this miracle, commonly read as John's account of
the institution of the Eucharist, that we hear Jesus insist: "My
body is real food and my blood is real drink". This could be
inverted to say: "Real food is my body, real drink is my blood".
There can be no split between sacred and profane meals, between
Eucharist and picnic. An ecological reading of the text allows no
distinction between fragments of altar bread and those left over
from the breakfast table. To eat in either place is to live by
sustaining the body.

This refusal to make distinctions between what is sacred food
and what is not came up again in Jesus' defence of the disciples

who ate the corn on the sabbath. He cited the example of David who satisfied his hunger with bread set aside for the priests' use only, which it was "not lawful for him to eat" – according to religious law, that is (Mark 2:23f.). Jesus used the symbols of grain, loaf and yeast to teach his disciples about the mystery of God's kingdom, summarized as "the lesson of the loaves".

He and they were a source of scandal not only because of what they ate but also because of how they ate it: with unwashed hands. He defended himself against this charge with one of the harshest responses of his ministry, rejecting a tradition which makes distinctions between the outside of a man and the inside – what is in the heart. "You fools!" he said, "Did not he who made the outside make the inside also?" (Luke 11:37).

He was also a source of scandal because of the people he chose to eat with. After Matthew's account of his own calling we read that many other tax collectors and sinners joined Jesus and his disciples for a meal. The Pharisees, guardians of the religious law, were appalled: tax collectors were traitors, employees of the hated Roman occupation forces, and were notorious for their dishonesty and avarice. Small wonder that they were invariably bracketed with sinners by the ethnically pure, law-abiding Pharisees. To eat in such company was defilement, rendering a man unfit for Temple worship. Therefore the acceptance of these outcasts into table fellowship with Jesus would be understood as according them worth before God by someone revered as a prophet. Not only did Jesus accept these religious outcasts when they turned up, so to speak. In the meal with Zacchaeus it was Jesus who took the initiative and invited himself in to eat, an action which Zacchaeus recognized for what it was, a total flouting of the rules about food.[11]

We are gradually building up a picture of the way in which Jesus made sensitive choices about what he would eat, how he would eat it and with whom. The gravity of those choices is lost to us today. That it could lead to a person being put to death seems unthinkable. This distinguishes us from the world of Jesus as much as from the world of Adam. We in the "First" world no longer realise that food and drink are a matter of life and death. We have lost the *"epikeian"* Spirit which would help us respond sensitively to the multifaceted relationships involved in our eating habits, to the momentous interaction between our greed and others' deaths.

Eve's decision to eat a particular food and share it with Adam, against religious prohibition, was the same kind of ethical choice made by Jesus. In both cultures food was a symbol of life: of life shared and sustained at every level, including our relationship with God. When the imperative to eat and share life is overridden by law, no matter from whence it comes, then, said Jesus, we must be prepared to break the law, and, if necessary, to die for doing so.[12]

Jesus and the Spirit

To believe that Jesus' death has no connection with his own actions robs his body of its intrinsic connection with the Spirit which sustains the whole world: in life and death and resurrection from death. Instead, an exclusive relationship between him and the Spirit is posited to explain his ability to perform works of power, his equal love with the Father and his authority to bestow that Spirit on whom he would. The resurrection of his body through the power of the Spirit is treated as a unique event; guaranteeing the salvation of our souls through the power bestowed on the apostles to forgive sins. For such a traditional view, as I have heard it scornfully expressed, "Easter has nothing to do with daffodils".

But if this were so, then the one Spirit, single source of life, would have nothing to do with the power that through the green fuse drives the flower into light and glory each spring. If this were so, Hannah Senesh's prayer was in vain and her death did not kindle life and hope for others. If this were so, Jesus would not have died like a grain, as he envisaged, resurfacing in something that seemed as radically different as the message of Paul (not even one of the Twelve). Paul's new modes of expression, new concepts, new implications do not include a single significant quote or anecdote of Jesus himself.[13]

Jesus undoubtedly spoke and acted as someone with power, divine power to break purity codes, to heal, to cast out evil spirits and to raise the dead. The power he was so vitally aware of was that power of God to give life which we call Spirit. Jesus' consciousness of the power of the Spirit was of God *already* operative in a decisive way.[14] He was born into the ecosystem of Israel. The waters of his mother's womb were blessed with sustaining power through the Spirit of Israelite mothers with whom she rejoiced in God. The Spirit was already present in the living community into which Simeon welcomed him. For him, it was not so much a case of "Where *I* am there is the kingdom of God" as "Where the *Spirit* is there is the kingdom".

Yet in traditional doctrines of redemption, the focus is on the relationship between the Father and the death of the afflicted Son. Even those theologians who see renewal of faith in the Spirit as part of the integral liberation of Christians, still see it only as a means to know God the Father and his Son Jesus Christ who revealed him.[15] The role of the Spirit is lost except in the process of raising the Son to glory after death and in being handed on to the apostles and their successors as power to preach the good news of Redemption and make it available to Christians through baptism. A utilitarian perception of the Spirit ties its coming to the church in order to carry out its mission in the world. Therefore the debate between Christian theologians remains focussed on whether Christianity began with either the birth or death of Jesus, or with the Easter or Pentecost event. In truth, in so far as it "began" at all, one must say that it was generated through the Spirit of Genesis in the archetypal act of creation.

The Spirit and the World

The attempt to rediscover the role of the Spirit within the whole history of the world gives us an ecological model of the Trinity as a source of life for all creation and re-creation. The relationship between the Spirit of God and all that lives and breathes is recognized as existing in its own right, as power-from-within all creation; not bounded by those systems of belief or thought which acknowledge the Son and the Father as God.

Unless the independence of the Spirit is valued in this way, we are left with a hierarchical model of Trinity which curtails the mystery of God's relationship with the world by subordinating the transforming power of the Spirit to the authority of either the Father, the Son or both together. Jesus' recognition of the Spirit present in the world independently of himself is an example Christians must learn to follow.

When they do, the way is open for discerning the role of the Spirit in the renewal of creation and for their empowerment to create ecological community.

The power of this Spirit-from-within is like the wind, blowing where it will and seen only in its effects. It forced a shepherd like Amos to leave his sheep and become a prophet in Israel. For Ezekiel, it brought dry bones together into an exceedingly great host, the whole house of Israel. It quickened the wombs of Sara, Hannah, Elizabeth and Mary. It drove Jesus out into the desert to pray and sustained him there. In the biblical *Apocalypse* it calls for the thirsty to take the water of life without price.

Within us, it transforms us into agents of liberation for the living communities we belong to. It animates the gift of perception within us, opening our eyes to how things really are. It gives us the gift of *epikeia*, the ability to respond with sensitivity to the presence and reality of other living beings, creating relationships and exchanging energy.

This "homely" appraisal of the Spirit brings us back to the basis of ecology, to the home and food systems Christians share (or do not) with others. The Garden of Eden was nearer to Jesus' home system than it is to mine, but all three share the symbiotic relationship between the fruitfulness of the earth, the command to serve it and each other and our need for sustenance. These are the basic elements in any life, and Jesus' was no exception.[16]

Some global implications of this shift in focus for church hierarchies and their celebration of the Eucharist concern us here. The Christian cultures of the Northern hemisphere are richer and waste more of the world's resources than any other. This is certainly true of food, whether through over-eating or by throwing away leftovers. Recently I heard a mother bemoaning the fact that she did not know what Christian practices she could teach her children. I suggested, on the basis of Jesus' practice in the story of the bread and fish, that collecting litter might be a good exercise to start with. Waste of any sort, whether inside or outside the home, has to be seen in its systemic relationship to the life of the planet. The connection between Nature and waste, whether its generation, or its collection and disposal, is made loud and clear by environmentalists. But what Christian sees our attitude to waste as a spiritual discipline? The connection between sustenance and spiritual life that makes crumbs of bread and fish a matter of moment for Jesus and his disciples is not part of Christian teaching today, with one notable exception: any crumbs from "sacred" bread broken at the altar.

Intellectual perceptions of the wisdom, goodness and power of God break down, as Paul clearly saw, before the weakness and foolishness of the cross. Intellectual perceptions of the nature of God, as Luther clearly saw, neither confer wisdom and goodness on us *nor does their recitation demand them of us*. To be able to speak in abstractions of divine power and wisdom makes us no wiser in the exercise of power. To be able to discourse on the "transubstantiation" of Jesus' body into bread has not, as far as one can judge, had any effect on the way Christians handle bread other than that on the altar. To speak of it alone as the bread of life is to close off the reality of Jesus' life from our own. Taking any piece of bread in one's hands one can say of it: "This is the bread of life, given to me to be broken into fragments for my life's sustenance". In Gary Snyder's beautiful phrase, the bread blesses us before we bless it. This demands that we treat it and its fragments with the same reverence as we would Jesus' body. Then instead of giving thanks (eucharistizing) only in church for the bread of life, we would do it every time we eat.

The distancing of what we say about Jesus from what we do with food is rather more problematic for women. Their constant engagement with food, with the means of sustenance for others, keeps them alive to its many interconnections with life. Their exclusion from patriarchal theology and liturgical power has kept their perceptions of the eucharistic bread more open to its lived meaning. Until recently, they have not had "power-over" a piece of bread to change it into the body of Jesus, or to rationalize the process by which this is said to be done. "Power-over" this body, as over bodies generally, has been a male prerogative.

Those who live "under" power recognize it more quickly than those who exercise it. Women in touch with Nature bring to an ecological Christianity a perception of hierarchical, rational, dominant power not discernible to those who habitually wield it. They bring a different perception to bear on rules and ethical codes, rules which if implemented systematically can bring death to the weak and vulnerable. The women who braved the soldiers and the mob to stand at the cross broke the religious codes of behaviour for "good" women in their desire to be with Jesus. In America the women's affinity groups who went to jail for their part in anti-nuclear demonstrations experienced the controls of their culture directly. "The shapes in our minds that limit our power-from-within are mirrors of the prison, the gun, the guard", said one of them, Starhawk.[17] In *Chipko*, the women and men who hug the trees put their skin between the bark and the saw.

Eve was told that to eat was to die: but she ate. Her breaking of the code was based on the knowledge that not to eat was to live in a way less than human. In so far as one can tell, Jesus knew that to eat with sinners was to leave oneself open to being reckoned one of them. His breaking of the code was based on the knowledge that not to eat with these people was to deny them life and to deny God's involvement in their lives. "I have come that you may have life and may have it more abundantly".

The Spirit of Ecological Community

If that is the driving force behind the life of Jesus, where did he find the courage to make the choices he did about implementing it in his table companionship? Where do we find the courage either to conform or not to the codes of our society or our religion? Where do we find the strength to cope with the mysteries of suffering and death?

We find it and experience it where he did, in a relationship with and recognition of the all-awakening, all-resurrecting, all-sustaining Spirit of God. This Spirit had a relationship with all living beings before humanity came into existence, and it will continue to have it if we disappear. This Spirit enables each species to be what it is intended to be within the ecosystem which surrounds it, and is the source of newness and diversity in each species through the action and interaction of others. This is the basic presupposition of an ecological paradigm of Christianity.

This Spirit liberates us to become fully human in our own time and place, to wrestle with the complexities of existence and the presence of evil and sin. Therefore it is a transforming Spirit, not separate from positive action through which we put ourselves and our certainties at risk, define ourselves and discover the power within ourselves. The call to action ensures that the paradigmatic shift in consciousness is not confined to theory or words alone. Starting to buy low-energy light bulbs, to recycle waste or to say grace before food is as much evidence of transformation in the Spirit as the rise of *Chipko* communities, the growth of women's consciousness-raising groups and the formation of base communities in Latin America. The common experience of the Spirit is that something new is coming about in our midst, reversing our situation and changing us from passive objects to active subjects.[18]

As evidence of this newness, women and men alike find themselves empowered to speak out, to voice the suffering and hope of their community. So for women the process of inferiorization in the churches is being reversed. If what women are saying and doing now were being done by men alone there would be nothing new about it – it would be part of the traditional order. But now women are starting to comment on matters theological and ecclesiastical in ways that have not been heard before. They are writing their own prayers, leading their own services, no longer reciting male formulas. They know that their own words and lives have value before God. They no longer accept that speaking about God, theology, is the exclusive property of the ecclesiastically powerful, those whose hierarchical positions have made them confident with words. The radical element in this is that those who had been made dumb in and through hierarchical structures have spoken. Their experience of the Spirit is experience of the power to speak.

This new speech springs from below: from the root sources of oppression. Women have felt the pain of the stereotyped images of ourselves and of Nature. Our tongues have been loosened now and we have heard ourselves utter a new speech – a new creation: haltingly perhaps, or boldly, but authentically for the first time in our lives. The women's writings quoted extensively by me differ radically from those of the traditional patriarchal interpreter. We have listened and heard one another ask the great "What if?" questions about God, Nature and human nature.[19]

This experience of new speech has not been for ourselves alone. In the journey into the roots of our oppression we find ourselves beside and speaking for all those who suffer from the stereotyping of man and woman into hierarchies of power, gender, norms and value. We find ourselves too beside and speaking for the figure of Nature, banished to a "no-God's land". Instead of looking up, we have learned to look around us and open ourselves to what is there: one flesh, one body, one breath flowing in all beings. Instead of looking for revelation of the divine in human spirit alone, we have opened ourselves to its mystery in the whole of creation.

This experience of the Spirit springs from one single reality: God and creation united. It is experience of God acting on us and on the world at the same time, relating us to the world and the world to us within our own ecosystems. There is no separation between action and prayer, ecological practice and celebration. There is no separation between our love for one another and our concern for the well-being of the ecological community of human and non-human species. There is only the Spirit of commitment to recognizing the diversity of gifts in whatever is coming into existence.

Epilogue

Some ecologists today approach problems through the concept of the end–user. In the production of energy, for example, where formerly attention was placed on the generation of power and how it could be increased, now the emphasis lies on how to manufacture an efficient light bulb.

This has turned out to be an end-user's book. I embarked on it as an end-user of ecology, feminism and Christianity, concerned to bring the three disciplines together and discover interconnections between them rather than explore just one of them in depth. I was convinced of the power and fruitfulness of each for my life and hoped that they could illumine one another so that they would burn more brightly collectively than singly. This proved to be the case, and I pass the book on in the hope that it will cast light on the relationship between the world and a Christian tradition which believes in the power of the Spirit to generate life and resurrect it from death.

The interaction with other disciplines can be and must be part of Christian commitment to the regeneration of life in the context of ecological apocalypse. Just as we need and use the multi-faceted work of Nature to sustain physical life, so do we need the work of other disciplines to articulate and sustain vision. This is not to deny intrinsic worth to either ecology, feminism or Christianity. It is certain that anyone working full-time in one of these disciplines will notice the gap between power-house and light bulb. As a theologian, I have myself made the comment, and heard it from others, that any one chapter could be expanded into a book, and that particular issues should be dealt with at greater length. Abundant references have been given so that fleeting visits made here may be pursued in greater depth elsewhere.

One pathway opened up before me as work on the book progressed: a vision of and commitment to a sustainable theology which expresses and explores the interconnectedness of Spirit and all created beings. This theology arises through the power-from-within creation and emerges in the interaction between all beings. It comes to consciousness within human communities. It is nourished for me by the companionship of faith and the friendship of those who would not call themselves theologians, or even believers, yet whose lives are clearly guided by the desire to dwell unconditionally in the truth. Together we may find a deeper awareness of the mystery of our sustenance through the earth's fertility, a mystery re-presented to us by the imperatives of ecological community.

> Look. The tree of our hands is for all.
> It is converting the wounds which were cut
>   in its trunk
> the soil works
> and among the branches heady sweet blossoms
> of haste

Aimé Césaire

Appendix: Genesis 1–3

This new English version of the Hebrew text of Genesis 1–3 is included by kind permission of the translator, Mary Phil Korsak, exegete and ex-lecturer at the Brussels Institut Supérieur de Traducteurs et Interprètes. She lays emphasis on what the text says, as compared to what it "means". No attempt has been made to adapt the original text with a view to feminist interpretation. The line-by-line pattern reflects the order of meaning and the rhythms of the Hebrew text when recited.

AT THE START GOD CREATED . . .

CHAPTER 1

1   At the start God created the skies and the earth

2   – the earth was tohu-bohu
    darkness on the face of the deep
    and God's breath
    hovering on the face of the waters –

3   God said
    Let light be
    Light was

4   God saw the light How good!
    God separated the light from the darkness

5   God called to the light "Day"
    To the darkness he called "Night"
    It was evening, it was morning
    One day

6   God said
    Let a vault be in the middle of the waters
    it shall separate waters from waters

7   God made the vault
    It separated the waters under the vault
    from the waters above the vault
    It was so

8   God called to the vault "Skies"
    It was evening, it was morning
    A second day

9 God said
Let the waters under the skies be massed to one place
Let the dry be seen
It was so

10 God called to the dry "Earth"
To the massing of the waters he called "Seas"
God saw How good!

11 God said
Let the earth grow grass
plants seeding seed
fruit-tree making fruit of its kind
with its seed in it on the earth
It was so

12 The earth brought forth grass
plants seeding seed of their kind
and tree making fruit with its seed in it of its kind
God saw How good!

13 It was evening, it was morning
A third day

14 God said
Let lights be in the vault of the skies
to separate the day from the night
They shall be signs for set times, for days and years

15 They shall be lights in the vault of the skies
to light upon the earth
It was so

16 God made the two great lights
the great light for ruling the day
the small light for ruling the night
and the stars

17 God gave them to the vault of the skies
to light upon the earth

18 to rule the day and the night
and to separate the light from the darkness
God saw How good!

19 It was evening, it was morning
A fourth day

20 God said
Let the waters swarm with a swarm of living souls
and let fowl fly above the earth
upon the face of the vault of the skies

21 God created the great monsters
    all living souls that creep
    with which the waters swarm of their kind
    and every winged fowl of its kind
    God saw How good!
22 God blessed them, saying
    Be fruitful, increase, fill the waters in the seas
    Let the fowl increase on the earth
23 It was evening, it was morning
    A fifth day

24 God said
    Let the earth bring forth living souls of their kind
    cattle, creeper and beast of the earth of its kind
    It was so
25 God made the beast of the earth of its kind
    the cattle of their kind
    and every creeper of the ground of its kind
    God saw How good!

26 God said
    We will make a groundling [Adam]
    in our image, after our likeness
    Let them dominate the fish of the sea
    the fowl of the skies, the cattle, all the earth
    every creeper that creeps on the earth
27 God created the groundling in his image
    in the image of God created it
    male and female created them
28 God blessed them God said to them
    Be fruitful, increase, fill the earth, subject it
    govern the fish of the sea, the fowl of the skies
    every beast that creeps on the earth
29 God said, Here I give you
    all plants seeding seed upon the face of all the earth
    and every tree with tree-fruit in it seeding seed
    For you it shall be, for eating
30 and for every beast of the earth
    for every fowl of the skies
    for all that creeps on the earth with living soul in it
    all green of plants shall be for eating
    It was so
31 God saw all he had made Here! it was very good

It was evening, it was morning
The sixth day

CHAPTER 2

1   They were finished, the skies, the earth
    and all their company
2   God had finished on the seventh day
    his work that he had done
    He ceased on the seventh day
    from all his work that he had done
3   God blessed the seventh day, he made it holy
    for on it he ceased from all his work
    that God had created and done

4   These are the birthings of the skies and the earth
    at their creation

    On the day YHWH[1] God made earth and skies
5   no shrub of the field was yet in the earth
    no plant of the field had yet sprouted
    for YHWH God had not made it rain on the earth
    and there was no groundling to serve the ground
6   But a flow went up from the earth
    and gave drink to all the face of the ground
7   YHWH God formed the groundling, soil of the ground
    He blew into its nostrils the blast of life
    and the groundling became a living soul

8   YHWH God planted a garden in Eden in the east
    There he set the groundling he had formed
9   YHWH God made sprout from the ground
    all trees attractive to see and good for eating
    the tree of life in the middle of the garden
    and the tree of the knowing of good and bad
10 A river goes out in Eden to give drink to the garden
    From there it divides and becomes four heads
11 The name of the first is Pishon
    It winds through all the land of Havilah
    where there is gold
12 The gold of that land is good
    Bdellium is there and Onyx[2] stone
13 The name of the second river is Gihon

It winds through all the land of Cush
14   The name of the third river is Tigris
It goes east of Asshur
The fourth river is Euphrates

15   YHWH God took the groundling
and set it to rest in the garden of Eden
to serve it and keep it
16   YHWH God commanded the groundling, saying
Of every tree of the garden eat! you shall eat
17   but of the tree of the knowing of good and bad
you shall not eat
for on the day you eat of it
die! you shall die

18   YHWH God said
It is not good for the groundling to be alone
I will make it a help to confront it
19   YHWH God formed out of the ground
all beasts of the field, all fowl of the skies
and brought them to the groundling
to see what it would call them
Everything the groundling called
"living soul" was its name
20   The groundling called names for all the cattle
for all fowl of the skies, for all beasts of the field
But for a groundling he found no help to confront it

21   YHWH God made a swoon fall upon the groundling
it slept
He took one of its sides
and closed up the flesh in its place
22   YHWH God built the side
he had taken from the groundling into woman
He brought her to the groundling
23   The groundling said
This one this time
is bone from my bones
flesh from my flesh
This one shall be called wo-man
for from man
was taken this one

24   So a man will leave his father and his mother

he will cling to his wo-man
and they will become one flesh

25 The two of them were naked
the groundling and his woman
they were not ashamed

CHAPTER 3

1 The serpent was the most cunning
of all the beasts of the field
that YHWH God had made
It said to the woman, So God said
You shall not eat of any tree of the garden...

2 The woman said to the serpent
We will eat the fruit of the trees of the garden

3 but of the fruit of the tree
in the middle of the garden, God said
You shall not eat of it, you shall not touch it
lest you die

4 The serpent said to the woman
Die! you shall not die

5 No, God knows that the day you eat of it
you eyes will be opened
and you will be as God knowing good and bad

6 The woman saw that the tree was good for eating
yes, an allurement to the eyes
and that the tree was attractive to get insight from
She took of its fruit and ate
She also gave to her man with her and he ate

7 The eyes of the two of them were opened
they knew that they were naked
They sewed fig leaves together
and made themselves loinclothes

8 They heard the voice of YHWH God
walking in the garden in the breeze of the day
The groundling and his woman hid from YHWH God
in the middle of the tree of the garden

9 YHWH God called to the groundling and said to him
Where are you?

10 He said, I heard your voice in the garden

and I was afraid for I was naked
and I hid

11　He said, Who told you that you were naked?
Did you eat of the tree
I commanded you not to eat of?

12　The groundling said
The woman you gave to be with me,
she, she gave me of the tree and I ate

13　YHWH God said to the woman
What have you done?
The woman said
The serpent enticed me and I ate

14　YHWH God said to the serpent
　　　Because you have done this
　　　you are the most cursed of all the cattle
　　　of all the beasts of the field
　　　You shall go on your stomach
　　　and you shall eat soil
　　　all the days of your life

15　I will put enmity between you and the woman
　　　between your seed and her seed
　　　It, it shall strike at your head
　　　and you, you shall strike at its heel

16　To the woman he said
　　　Increase! I will increase your pains when you
　　　conceive
　　　In pain you shall birth[3] sons
　　　For your man your longing
　　　he, he shall rule you

17　To the groundling he said
Because you heard your woman's voice
and ate of the tree
about which I commanded you, saying
You shall not eat of it!
　　　cursed shall be the ground because of you
　　　With pains you shall eat of it
　　　all the days of your life

18　　Thorn and thistle it shall sprout for you
　　　you shall eat the plants of the field

19　　With the sweat of your face you shall eat bread

till you return to the ground
for from it you were taken
for soil you are and to the soil you shall return

20 The groundling called his woman's name Eve [Life]
for she is the mother of all the living

21 YHWH God made for the groundling and his woman
robes of skins and clothed them

22 YHWH God said
Here, the groundling has become as one of us
knowing good and bad
Now, let it not put out its hand
to take from the tree of life also
and eat and live for ever!

23 YHWH God sent it away from the garden of Eden
to serve the ground from which it was taken

24 He cast out the groundling
and made dwell east of the garden of Eden
the Cherubim and the scorching, turning sword
to keep the road to the tree of life

NOTES

1. YHWH: the personal name of the God of the Hebrews is not
   pronounced. Read Adonai, or Yahweh, or the Lord.
2. Onyx: meaning of Hebrew uncertain
3. Birth: A single Hebrew verb, neologism "to birth", covers
   both parental roles "to beget" and "to bear".

Notes

Introduction

1. James Lovelock, *The Ages of Gaia: A Biography of our Living Earth* (London, 1989), p. 178. See also *From One Earth to One World: An Overview by the World Commission on Environment and Development* (Taken from the Brundtland Report, Oxford 1987), p. 21. "Over the course of this century, the relationship between the human world and the planet that sustains it has undergone a profound change. When the century began, neither human numbers nor technology had the power radically to alter planetary systems. As the century closes, not only do vastly increased human numbers and their activities have that power, but major, unintended changes are occurring in the atmosphere, in the soils, in waters, among plants and animals, and in the relationships among all of these. The rate of change is outstripping the ability of scientific disciplines and our current capabilities to assess and advise. It is frustrating the attempts of political and economic institutions, which evolved in a different, more fragmented world, to adapt and cope."

2. *Spiritus sanctus vivificans vita/movens omnia/et radix est in omni creatura/ ac omnia de inmunditia abluit/ et sic est fulgens ac laudabilis vita/suscitans et resuscitans omnia.* See Barbara Newman, trans. and ed., *St. Hildegard of Bingen: Symphonia; A Critical Edition of the Symphonia armonie celestium revelationum* (Cornell, 1988), pp. 140–1.

Chapter 1: Ecological Foundations

1. See *From One Earth to One World* (Oxford, 1987), p. 19.

2. See Radha Bhatt in *Healing the Wounds: The Promise of Ecofeminism* (Philadelphia, 1989), pp. 168–73; also Vandana Shiva, *Staying Alive* (London, 1989), p. 1. Her book is a clear and expert exposition of what she calls "maldevelopment" and its links with Western theories of progress.

3. See Morris Berman, *The Reenchantment of the World* (Cornell, 1981), p. 115. For the impact of this on European thought, see p. 41: "The lives of Newton and Galileo stretch across the whole of the seventeenth century, for the former was born in the same year that the latter died, 1642, and together they embrace a revolution in human consciousness. By the time of Newton's death in 1727, the educated European had a conception of the cosmos, and of the nature of 'right thinking', which was entirely different from that of his counterpart of a century before. He now regarded the earth as revolving around the sun, not the reverse; believed that all phenomena were constituted of atoms, or corpuscles,

in motion and susceptible to mathematical description; and saw the solar system as a vast machine, held together by the forces of gravity. He had a precise notion of experiment (or at least paid lip service to it), and a new notion of what constituted acceptable evidence and proper explanation. He lived in a predictable, comprehensible, yet (in his own mind) very exciting sort of world. For in terms of material control, the world was beginning to exhibit an infinite horizon and endless opportunities." See also Carolyn Merchant, *The Death of Nature; Women, Ecology and the Scientific Revolution* (New York, 1982), pp. 275f: "The world in which we live today was bequeathed to us by Isaac Newton and Gottfried Wilhelm von Leibniz . . . The legacy left by Newton was the brilliant synthesis of Galilean terrestrial mechanics and Copernican-Keplerian astronomy; that of Leibniz was dynamics – the foundation for the general law of the conservation of energy. Both contributions are fundamental in generality; they describe and extend over the entire universe. Classical physics and its philosophy structure our consciousness to believe in a world composed of atomic parts, of inert bodies moving with uniform velocity unless forced by another body to deviate from their straight line paths, of objects seen by reflected light of varying frequencies, and of matter in motion responsible for all the rich variations in colors, sounds, smells, tastes and touches we cherish in human beings . . . Newton's *Philosophiae Naturalis Principia Mathematica*, 1687, epitomized the dead world resulting from mechanism. Throughout the complex evolution of his thought, Newton clung tenaciously to the distinguishing feature of mechanism – the dualism between the passivity of matter and the externality of force and activity."

4. For an impressive discussion of technology, see Ursula Franklin, *The Real World of Technology* (Toronto, 1990). The effects of the technological mindset on education were argued by Gregory Bateson before the Regents of the University of California in 1978. He was filling out remarks he had made at a meeting of the Committee on Educational Policy. The presuppositions upon which teaching is based are *obsolete*, he said, and enumerated them as follows:

a. the Cartesian dualism separating "mind" and "matter";

b. the strange physicalism of the metaphors which we use to describe and explain mental phenomena – "power", "tension", "energy", "social forces", etc.;

c. Our anti-aesthetic assumption, borrowed from the emphasis which Bacon, Locke and Newton long ago gave to the physical sciences, viz. that all phenomena (including the mental) can and shall be studied and *evaluated* in quantitative terms.

The view of the world – the latent and partly *unconscious* epistemology – which such ideas together generate is out of date in three different ways:

a. Pragmatically, it is clear that these premises and their corollaries lead to greed, monstrous over-growth, war, tyranny, and pollution. In this sense, *our* premises are daily demonstrated false, and the students are half aware of this.

b. *Intellectually*, the premises are obsolete in that systems theory, cybernetics, holistic medicine, ecology, and gestalt psychology offer demonstrably better ways of understanding the world of biology and behaviour.

c. As a base for *religion*, such premises as I have mentioned became *clearly intolerable and therefore obsolete* about 100 years ago. In the aftermath of Darwinian evolution, this was stated rather clearly by such thinkers as Samuel Butler and Prince Kropotkin. But already in the eighteenth century, William Blake saw that the philosophy of Locke and Newton could generate only "dark Satanic mills". cf. Bateson, *Mind and Nature* (London, 1980), pp. 231f.

5. James Lovelock, *The Ages of Gaia* (Oxford, 1988), p. 30. See also John Polkinghorne in *Science and the Theology of Creation* (Bossey, 1988), pp. 26f.

6. See the report in "The New Road"; *The Bulletin of the WWF Network on Conservation and Religion*, Issue No. 10. (1989), p. 3. The problems are excellently described by Wendell Berry: "Our dilemma in agriculture now is that the industrial methods that have so spectacularly solved some of the problems of food production have been accompanied by 'side effects' so damaging as to threaten the survival of farming . . . Pen feeding of cattle in large numbers involves, first, a manure-removal problem, which becomes at some point a health problem for the animals themselves, for the local watershed, and for the adjoining ecosystems and human communities. If the manure is disposed of without returning it to the soil that produced the food, a serious problem of soil fertility is involved. But we know too that large concentrations of animals in feed lots in one place tend to be associated with, and to promote, large cash-grain monocultures in other places. These monocultures tend to be accompanied by a whole set of specifically agricultural problems: soil erosion, soil compaction, epidemic infestations of pests, weeds and disease. But they are also accompanied by a whole set of agricultural-economic problems (dependence on purchased technology; dependence on purchased fuels, fertilisers, and poisons; dependence on credit) – and by a set of community problems, beginning with depopulation and the removal of sources, services and markets to more and more distant towns." Wendell Berry, *The Gift of Good Land* (San Francisco, 1981), pp. 134f.

7. See Bruntland Report, *From One Earth to One World* (Oxford, 1987), p. 14.

8. See Berry, *The Gift of Good Land*, pp. 136f.

9. For a discussion of a systems theory of ecology see Gregory Bateson, *Steps to an Ecology of Mind* (New York, 1972), especially pp. 437f. For a working out of it as a scientific system, see Lovelock, *The Ages of Gaia*.

10. For a similar conclusion in the field of biology, see Lovelock: "This gift, this ability to see the Earth from afar, was so revealing that it forced the novel top-down approach to planetary biology. The conventional

wisdom of biology on Earth had always been forced to take a bottom-up approach by the sheer size of the Earth when compared with us or any living thing we knew. The two approaches are complementary. In the understanding of a microbe, an animal, or a plant, the top-down physiological view of life as a whole system harmoniously merges with the bottom-up view originating with molecular biology: that life is an assembly made from a vast set of ultramicroscopic parts." *The Ages of Gaia*, p. 29.

11. John Lane, *The Living Tree* (Devon, 1988), p. 30.

12. Ibid., p. 63.

13. Ibid., p. 64.

14. Berman, *The Reenchantment of the World*, pp. 16-40.

15. See *From One Earth to One World* p. 19.

16. See Murray Bookchin *The Ecology of Freedom: the Emergence and Dissolution of Hierarchy* (California, 1982), pp. 4, 107–12.

17. See Konrad Raiser, *Ökumene im Übergang: Paradigmwechsel in der ökumenische Bewegung* (Munich, 1989), pp. 53f. for a very good discussion of the constellation of meanings attached to the word "paradigm" and their significance for theology. See also Thomas S. Kuhn, *The Structure of Scientific Revolutions* (Chicago, 1970), esp. pp. 10, 43. He defines a paradigm as an achievement that shares these two characteristics: to attract an enduring group of adherents away from competing modes of scientific activity and, simultaneously, to be sufficiently open-ended to leave all sorts of problems for the redefined group of practitioners to resolve. It provides a model from which spring coherent traditions of scientific research. Close investigation of a given speciality at a given time discloses a set of recurrent and quasi-standard illustrations of various theories in their conceptual, observational and instrumental applications. These are the community's paradigms, revealed in its textbooks, lectures and laboratory exercises. By studying them and by practising with them, the members of the corresponding community learn their trade. See also Bill Devall, *Simple in Means, Rich in Ends: Practising Deep Ecology* (London, 1990), p. 36.

18. See Devall, *Simple in Means, Rich in Ends*, p. 36.

19. See Alan Watts, *Nature, Man and Woman* (London, 1976), pp. 51–5, for a very good discussion of the problems of translating perceptions of Nature into words.

20. This is what Bateson calls the "cybernetics of self", which is shorthand for a systemic view of the world – the total information-processing, trial-and-error completing unit. In principle, if you want to explain or understand or recover anything in human behaviour, you must always deal with total circuits, completed circuits. This is basic to cybernetic thought. In delineating any system, you must draw the line in such a way that you do not cut any pathways which interact with

and affect the primary system. If you do, you block off any possibility of transforming it for good or ill. *Steps to an Ecology of Mind*, pp. 459f.

21. See Watts, *Nature, Man and Woman*, p. 15.

22. Ibid., p. 434.

Chapter 2: Ecology and Feminism

1. See Juan Luis Segundo, *An Evolutionary Approach to Jesus of Nazareth* (London, 1989), p.80. Writing of the similarity between the ideal expression of human rights in the U.N. Declaration of Human Rights and the Christian ideal of love, he says: "Do they not imply that the ideal society should integrate into its circuit *all* the circuits represented by individuals, in *all their richness and risk* as circuits? Thus the female would cease to be integrated in the usual way: as a circuit limited to labours of her sex, as merely housewife or homemaker or housekeeper. Her creative liberty would be respected in every domain, and she would be integrated into the circuit of global society." See also the definitions given by Bill Devall in *Simple in Means, Rich in Ends* (London, 1990), pp. 24-5.

2. Nature needs to be defined in this relationship. In this book, I give "Nature" a capital letter where it refers to the material world, that part of it which predated the human species, a vast infrastructure of organisms tightly coupled with their environments to create a living planet. See Salvatore Cucchiari, "The Origins of Gender Hierarchy", in *Sexual Meanings: The Cultural Construction of Gender and Sexuality*, ed. Ortner and Whitehead (Cambridge, 1981), p. 43. See Carolyn Merchant, *The Death of Nature: Women, Ecology and the Scientific Revolution* (New York, 1982), p. xix: "*Nature* in ancient and early modern times had a number of interrelated meanings. With respect to individuals, it referred to the properties, inherent characters and vital powers of persons, animals or things. With respect to the material world, it referred to a dynamic creative and regulatory principle that caused phenomena and their change and development. A distinction was commonly made between *natura naturans*, or Nature creating, and *natura naturata*, the natural creation. Nature was contrasted with *techne*, (art) and artificially created things. It was personified as a female-being, e.g. Mother Nature. The course of Nature and the laws of Nature were the actualization of her force. The state of Nature was the state of mankind prior to social organization and prior to the state of grace. In both Western and non-Western cultures, Nature was traditionally feminine. In Latin and the romance languages of mediaeval and early modern Europe, Nature was a feminine noun, and hence personified as female. The Greek word *physis* was also feminine."

For an exposition of the ecofeminist position, see Ynestra King, *The Ecofeminist Imperative*, and Stephanie Leland, *Feminism and Ecology: Theoretical Connections*, in L. Caldecott and S. Leland, eds., *Reclaim the Earth* (London, 1983), pp. 9-19; 67-72. See also Ursula Franklin, *The Real World of Technology* (Toronto, 1990), p. 87.

3. This is not the usual perception of ecology. The ecological movement which arose in the developed countries in the 1950s addressed itself primarily to the question of the exploitation of natural resources caused by policies of over-consumption. Ecologists denounced the political ideologies used to justify these policies. As that seemed to have little effect, some of them, as did my friend Adrian Farey, concentrated on living 'sustainably' or 'self-sufficiently'. A change occurred in public consciousness of the issues they had been raising when various ecological disasters became more visible and struck closer to the homes of the affluent consumers of the "First" world. In *The Eco Wars: A Layman's Guide to the Ecology Movement* (London, 1989), David Day gives an account of the ecological activism which has come about in response to these disasters. He also constructs a notional pyramid from the coffins of those now killed in what he calls "the ecology wars" in just one year. At the peak are the most conspicuous casualties: the scores of conservationists murdered outright for their stand against the destruction of the environment and species. Next come the coffins of the hundreds of tribal people massacred for their lands. Beneath these are the coffins of those drowned in the many floods which directly result from the ruthless cutting-down of mountain forests. Then come the tens of thousands of coffins of those who die through chemical poisoning, toxic waste pollution, atomic radiation and industrial fires and explosions. Below those are the coffins of those who die in droughts and famines brought on by farming and grazing methods which result in soil erosion and desertification. The base of the pyramid is built of over twenty-five million coffins for those people who are killed through drinking and using polluted water. But the primary casualties, he says, are the plant and animal species that are threatened with extinction. If these were also taken into account, the colossal human pyramid would only be the tiny tip of another staggeringly huge pyramid representing the total biomass destroyed each year.

Any of these deaths and their circumstances is now likely to be brought to our attention by the media. The usual response is horror and a desire to do something. A lot is being done, as Day himself chronicles. But there are two major omissions. The first one is the necessary absence of the poor nations, who see and experience such ecological activism and conservation policies as the selfish concern of the affluent nations, worried to preserve their own living space and styles. The poor nations are forced to live with an ever smaller share of natural resources in absolute or relative terms. Their understandable reaction to this is one of desperation. They suffer the full impact of any cataclysm. In the shantytowns around cities such as Mexico City, floods and drought, heat and cold, pollution and epidemics will all have their greatest impact on the poor. For them, ecological activism as understood in the rich nations is another luxury they cannot afford.

The second omission from the usual ecological programme is the essentially new way of thinking about life which Albert Einstein called for after unleashing the power of the atom. This is the type of ecology outlined here. It does not exclude activism, indeed it requires it, but it primarily seeks to lay bare the presuppositions on which we act.

4. Nelle Morton defines patriarchy comprehensively as a way of structuring reality in terms of good/evil, redemption/guilt, authority/ obedience, reward/punishment, power/powerless, haves/have-nots, master/slave. The first in each opposite was assigned to the patriarchal father, or the patriarch's Father God, frequently indistinguishable from one another, the second to women as "the other" and in time to all "others" who could be exploited. The father did the naming, the controlling, the ordering, the forgiving, the giving, considering himself capable of making the best decisions for all. Patriarchy polarized human beings by gender and endowed each gender with certain roles and properties so that neither could experience full humanness. It evoked cosmic myths to support the structures, and maintained them by assuming the right of ordering by divine right, and, by the same, demanded obedient response. See *The Journey is Home* (Boston, 1985), pp. 75f. See also Rita Gross, "Androcentrism and Androgyny in the Methodology of History of Religions", in Rita Gross ed., *Beyond Androcentrism: New Essays on Women and Religion* (Montana, 1977), pp. 9f.

5. In *The Spiritual Dimension of Green Politics* (Santa Fé, 1986), Charlene Spretnak points to the suffering this can cause men. Because woman is regarded as the denigrated "Other", men are pressured to react and continually prove themselves unlike the stereotype of the female. The process begins with beating the tenderness and empathy out of small boys and directing their natural human curiosity and joy into arrogant attitudes and destructive paths. This dynamic results in what men themselves have called "the male machine", which has skewed much of our behavioural and cognitive science (p. 61). The classic instance of it is the function of military combat as an initiation into true manhood and full citizenship. Even away from military combat, the constellation of martial metaphors used for work turns it into a competitive "battle" for markets and products. Goals, objectives, forces and targets are "aimed at" by those "deployed" in the "field". David Day's book, *The Eco Wars*, (mentioned in note 3) does the same for the environmental movement. The other day, I heard a man urging us to action on behalf of the rainforests with the words: "The cold war is over. The environmental war has begun!" This is not to deny "feminine" characteristics to men – but it is a fact that tender and emotional reactions are not encouraged in their upbringing, to say the least. For a succinct account of the three elements of patriarchy mentioned here, see also Rosemary Radford Ruether, "Woman, Body and Nature: Sexism and the Theology of Creation", in *Sexism and God-talk* (Boston, 1983), pp. 72f.

6. The dualism on which this distinction rests is traced by Murray Bookchin to the foundation of the Athenian city-state, in which home, or *oikos*, and the *agora*, the marketplace or civic centre, were counterposed to each other. The *agora* was seen as 'the realm of freedom' and the *oikos* as 'the realm of necessity'. These classifications will be

discussed in more detail in the following chapter. See Murray Bookchin, *The Ecology of Freedom* (California, 1982), p. 107.

7. A brilliant account of this split in our culture and its consequences is found in Dorothy Dinnerstein, *The Rocking of the Cradle and the Ruling of the World* (London, 1987). Our view of men is conditioned by present child-care arrangements, she says, where women are the ones who first care for our physical selves when we are babies, and who first fail us in our hopes for never-ending physical satisfaction. We thus come to hold women responsible for bodily sickness, and ultimately, for death. (This bears on the way in which women have been held responsible for them theologically through a particular interpretation of the Genesis narrative). Dinnerstein suggests that because they have minimal contact with our infant selves, men always seem to represent cleanliness, antiseptic order and even immortality. (Think of how relationships between male doctors and female nurses in hospitals are set in the same mould.) According to Dinnerstein, we want man to control woman and Nature so that our infant experience of being vulnerable to the bodily suffering identified with women will not be repeated. We thus tend to place men in exclusive command of our adult public lives – our laws, government, and military activities – with the hope that they will save us from our own mortality. Women are relegated to the private sphere of domesticity. Dinnerstein believes that if we could involve men in infant care to the same extent as women, we would no longer identify ills of the flesh exclusively with females. Then we could involve both sexes in the business of running the world. The present segregation of the sexes and the values each represents cuts men off from our bodily disappointments, and at the same time, from responsibility for basic processes of life. Their public culture gets caught up with machines and emphasizes non-living things.

This rather detailed analysis of Dinnerstein is based on that of Naomi Goldenberg in her discussion of the relationship between Christianity and witches. See *Changing of the Gods* (Boston, 1979), pp. 106f. It is important here for opening up key points in relationships between men and women, crucial for common cultural attitudes to Nature, to be discussed later in this book. Such are attitudes to work and to death, and the dichotomy between the domestic private sphere appointed to women and the cultural public one assumed by men.

See also Shulamith Firestone, *The Dialectic of Sex* (London, 1979), p. 53, in which she quotes the influential psychologist Eric Fromm who speaks of "Mother" as the home we come from, Nature, soil, the ocean: father does not represent any such natural home. He has little connection with the child in its early years, and his importance for the child cannot be compared with that of the mother. He does not represent the natural world, but the other pole of human existence: the world of thought, of man-made things, of law and order, of discipline, of travel and adventure. Father is the one who teaches the child and shows him the road into the world.

8. See the discussion of the poetic power needed to express ecological

insights in Bill Devall, *Simple in Means, Rich in Ends* (London, 1990), pp. 73-80.

9. See Rita Gross, "Female God Language in a Jewish Context", in *Womanspirit Rising* (San Francisco, 1989), eds. Carol Christ and Judith Plaskow, p. 167.

10. Brian Wren, *What Language Shall I Borrow?* (London, 1989), p. 1. See Mary Daly, *Beyond God the Father* (London, 1986), pp. 8f. Women's creativity is emerging today as a way of speaking about themselves, the world and God. "Words which, materially speaking, are identified with the old become new in a semantic context that arises from qualitatively new experience". See also Carol Christ, *Diving Deep and Surfacing* (Boston, 1980), p. xviii. See also Goldenberg, *Changing the Gods* (London, 1979), p. 118.

11. Stephanie Coontz and Peta Henderson, eds., *Women's Work, Men's Property* (London, 1986), pp. 35f.

12. Ibid. pp. 192-206. See especially Carolyn Merchant, *The Death of Nature: Women, Ecology and the Scientific Revolution*, pp. 10-28, for an extended treatment of this philosophical framework and its continuance in Renaissance Neoplatonism. For further implications of the Apollo myth see Mary Daly, *Gyn/Ecology* (London, 1979), pp. 59-64. For the connection with the non-human world, see Rosemary Radford Ruether, in *Sexism and God-talk* (New York, 1974), pp. 78f. For the dualistic basis of the inferiorization see again Murray Bookchin, *The Ecology of Freedom*, pp. 106-12. For the role of classification in Athenian society and its relationship to the Pandora myth, see Eve Cantarella, *Dangling Virgins: Myth, Ritual, and the Place of Women in Ancient Greece*, in Susan Suleman, ed., *The Female Body in Western Culture* (Massachusetts, 1985), pp. 57-67.

13. See Anne Michelle Tapp: "An Ideology of Expendability: Virgin Daughter Sacrifice", in Mieke Bal, ed., *Anti-Covenant: Counter-Reading Women's Lives in the Hebrew Bible* (Sheffield, 1989), p. 159. Contrast this with the narrative in Genesis 22, in which Abraham's son is saved.

14. Carol Delaney; "The Legacy of Abraham", in *Beyond Androcentrism: New Essays on Women and Religion*, pp. 228f. The echoes of this in traditional Christian teaching on Mary's role in the Incarnation and in the exposition of the relationship between Father and Son in John 17 will be noted in Chapter 6.

15. Gregory Bateson, *Steps to an Ecology of Mind* (New York, 1972), pp. 499f. See also Umberto Eco, *The Open Work* (Harvard, 1989), pp. 72f. for a similar notion under the heading of "acquired experience". Time and again, he says, we end up relying on our experience as the formative agent of perception. We relate to a stimulus pattern with a complex, probability-like integration of our past experience with such patterns. In the context of a philosophy of aesthetics, he argues that we respond to works of art with this integration as "openness of the first degree", but it needs to be supplemented with the apprehension of the continuously open process that allows one to discover ever-changing

profiles and possibilities in a single form. He calls this "openness of the second degree". This takes us back to the kind of openness argued for in the ecological paradigm, and its relevance for redressing the kind of habit and image formation being discussed in this chapter. It also reminds us of Bateson's arguments against the anti-aesthetic thrust of scientific consciousness and its quantitative methodology. See note 3 to chapter 1.

16. Page duBois, *Sowing the Body* (Chicago, 1988), pp. 39-43. See also the discussion of "seed" in Mary Condren, *The Serpent and the Goddess* (San Francisco, 1989), p. 202.

17. Ibid., p. 68.

18. Ibid. p. 69.

19. Bateson, *Steps to an Ecology of Mind*, p. 462

20. Fritjof Capra, *Uncommon Wisdom* (London, 1988), pp. 225f.

21. Bateson, *Steps to an Ecology of Mind*, p. 462. Ursula Franklin's approach to technology is more creative. She sees no reason why our technologies could not be more participatory and less expert-driven. See *The Real World of Technology*, p. 115.

22. An American woman, Andrée Collard, sums up "the state of the art" in her country as follows: "I see team upon team of eugenicists converging on laboratory animals and electronic machinery like vultures on a carcass exposed in the desert. I see billions of government monies taken from people around the world, earmarked for military, space and domestic research, being spent on perfecting a total man-machine 'partnership'. I read everywhere that all this is happening for our safety, our wellbeing, our convenience (robots to vacuum our carpets and clean our toilets, for instance), our mental and physical health, our craving for adventure. I see that people are standing in line for organ transplants, the new reproductive technologies, biofeedback, robots, computers, video games, all of which are but a short step away from the chimera, subhuman, parahuman, cyborg. And as we wait in those lines, we would do well to contemplate the fact that we are not just what we eat but also what we connect with." Andrée Collard, *Rape of the Wild* (London, 1988), p. 126.

23. Ibid., p. 116. See also Paul Shepard quoted in Murray Bookchin, *The Ecology of Freedom*, p. 279.

24. Ibid., p. 108.

25. Ibid., p. 108. See also, *A New Form of Infanticide*, by Manushi Collective, in Caldecott and Leland, *Reclaim the Earth*, pp. 179f.

26. The theologian Nelle Morton remarks that in 1875 when the union of the male and female gametes was observed for the first time, the final blow should have been dealt to the male's illusion that he was the sole parent. However, the image has been so deeply internalized by a patriarchal culture that to this day it has not been shattered. Morton,

The Journey, pp. 34f. Thus a myth out of an ancient culture continues to organize us, fix our relationships, determine our actions, and inform our communication to this day. See also Collard, *Rape of the Wild*, p. 130. See also Adrienne Rich, *Of Woman Born* (London, 1977), for the history of male domination of women's birthing processes down to the present.

27. Collard, *Rape of the Wild*, p. 108.

28. Eugene Bianchi and Rosemary Radford Reuther, *Machismo to Mutuality: Essays on Sexism and Woman-Man Liberation* (New York, 1976), pp. 87-8.

Susan Griffin, in *Made From This Earth* (London, 1982), pp. 111f., writing of the chauvinist and pornographic mind that is so much part of our culture, says that as we explore its images, we find that the bodies of women are mastered, bound, silenced, beaten, and even murdered. They themselves are reduced to a mere thing, to an entirely material object without a soul. This projection of woman as an object to be used and abused affects us all, willingly or not, since it pervades our popular culture and especially the tabloid press. The other (woman or Nature) is presented as a body without a spirit: passive and docile.

In conjunction with the influence of "the male machine" and the cultivation of psychic celibacy, a model is produced of the "civilized" man which may at first seem a caricature, but is therefore all the more frightening for being recognizable. Ursula K. Leguin draws it as follows in "Women/Wilderness", in Judith Plant, ed., *Healing The Wounds* (Philadelphia, 1989), p. 45:

"Civilized Man says: I am Self, I am Master, all the rest is Other - outside, below, underneath, subservient. I own, I use, I explore, I exploit, I control. What I do is what matters. What I want is what matter is for. I am that I am, and the rest is women and the wilderness, to be used as I see fit."

This myth of male superiority depends on what the psychologist James Hillman calls the fantasy of female inferiority. This runs with undeviating fidelity from antiquity to psychoanalysis. Misogyny would seem inseparable from analysis, he says, which in turn is but a late manifestation of the Western, Protestant, scientific, Apollonic ego. This structure of consciousness has never known what to do with the dark, material, and passionate part of itself, except to cast it off and call it Eve. What we have come to mean by the word "conscious" is "light", this light is inconceivable for this consciousness without a distaff side of something else opposed to it that is inferior and which has been called - in Jewish, Greek and Christian contexts - female. He goes on to say that the *locus classicus* in our culture for male primacy and the secondary, derivative nature of women is the Adam and Eve story in the Genesis creation myth (Gen. 2). The psychological history of the male/female relationship in our ci civilisation, he says, may be seen as a series of footnotes to this tale. See *The Myth of Analysis* (New York, 1972), pp. 8, 217, 246. The same is true of our religious history, as we shall see.

29. See the discussion "From Nature-As-Mother to Nature-As-Wife", in Elizabeth Dodson Gray, *Green Paradise Lost* (Massachusetts, 1979), pp. 27-42. She concludes: "[Men] have by their technologies worked steadily and for generations to transform a psychologically intolerable dependence upon a seemingly powerful and capricious 'Mother Nature' into a soothing and acceptable dependence upon a subservient and non-threatening 'wife'. This 'need to be above' and to dominate permeates male attitudes to Nature. It is as though men did not like *any* feelings of depending upon 'Mother Nature'. Nature must be below, just as Wife must be below, for to be a man *a man must be in control!*" See also Vandana Shiva, *Staying Alive* (London, 1989), pp. 15, 219. She quotes Evelyn Keller: "Science has been produced by a particular subset of the human race, that is, almost entirely by white, middle class males. For the founding fathers of modern science, the reliance on the language of gender was explicit; they sought a philosophy that deserved to be called 'masculine', that could be distinguished from its ineffective predecessors by its 'virile' powers, its capacity to bind Nature to man's service and make her his slave." She goes on to say later: "The domination of Nature by Western industrial culture and the domination of women by Western industrial man is part of the same process of devaluation and destruction that has been characterized in masculinist history as 'the enlightenment'."

Chapter 3: Ecofeminism and Dualism

1. This takes us back to the distinction made in the preceding chapter between *oikos*, the domestic realm of necessity, and *agora*, the public realm of freedom. See Murray Bookchin, *The Ecology of Freedom* (California, 1982) p.107. See also Ynestra King, "The Ecology of Feminism", in *Healing the Wounds* (Philadelphia, 1989), p. 22. For a similar analysis of the Nature/history split, see Beverley Harrison in Carol Robb, ed., *Making the Connections* (Boston, 1985), p. 230. This split was the basis of the anthropologists' argument in *Women's Work: Men's Property* discussed in the previous chapter. For a view of "civilization" as struggling for freedom from Nature, see Gerda Lerner, *The Creation of Patriarchy* (Oxford, 1986), p. 52, and the reference in Starhawk, *Truth or Dare* (San Francisco, 1987), p. 33. See also Shulamith Firestone, *The Dialectic of Sex* (London, 1979), pp. 53f.

2. See Lerner, *The Creation of Patriarchy* (Oxford, 1986), pp. 238f. for these definitions and their importance. See also S. Ortner and H. Whitehead, eds., *Sexual Meanings: The Cultural Construction of Gender and Sexuality* (Cambridge, 1981), for an anthropological treatment of these concepts. See Dale Spender, *Invisible Women: The Schooling Scandal* (London, 1982), for the history of this particular form of discrimination against women and its effects. See also Dale Spender, *Man Made Language* (London, 1985); in particular its revised introduction on the perpetuation of patriarchy.

3. See Bookchin, *The Ecology of Freedom*, p. 109.

4. See Susan Griffin, *Made From This Earth* (London, 1982), pp. 163f.

5. Quoted in Bill Devall, *Simple in Means, Rich in Ends* (London, 1990), p. 29.

6. Ibid.

7. Dorothy Dinnerstein, *The Rocking of the Cradle and the Ruling of the World* (London, 1987), p. 9.

8. For well-researched accounts of the links between these forces, the degradation of Third World lands and the problems of overpopulation, see Vandana Shiva, *Staying Alive* (London, 1989); Tissa Balasuriya, *Planetary Theology* (London, 1984); Sean McDonagh, *To Care for the Earth* (London, 1986); and *The Greening of the Church* (London, 1990); Enrique Dussel, *Ethics and Community* (Tunbridge Wells and Maryknoll, 1990).

9. See in particular the two authoritative accounts of unpaid household labour as a social justice and economic issue in "A Woman's Work Is Never Done", by Barbara Hilkert Andolsen, and "Women in the Cutback Economy", by Nancy Bancroft, both in Andolsen, Gudorf and Pellauer, eds., *Women's Consciousness: Women's Conscience* (New York, 1987), pp. 3-31. See also Fritjof Capra, *Uncommon Wisdom* (London, 1987), p. 260. See also Rosemary Radford Ruether, *Sexism and God-Talk* (Boston, 1983), p. 262. See also Ivan Illich, *Gender* (London, 1983), for an encyclopaedic discussion of work and what he calls "economic sex". This book includes comprehensive bibliographies on related subjects. See also Shiela Rothwell, *Time for Women: New Patterns of Work*, and Lin Simonon, *Personal, Political and Planetary Play*, both in L. Caldecott and S. Leland, eds., *Reclaim the Earth*, (London, 1983), pp. 189-202. See also Janet Finch and Dulcie Groves, eds., *A Labour of Love: Women, Work and Caring* (London, 1983), especially the first three chapters.

10. Simone Weil, eds. D. T. McFarland and W. Van Ness, *Formative Writings: 1929-1941* (London, 1987), pp. 152f., 193.

11. Dorothee Soelle, *To Work and To Love* (Philadelphia, 1984), p. 77. This whole book is important for re-thinking attitudes to work. See also John Lane, *The Living Tree: Art and the Sacred* (Devon, 1988), p. 74, on living our lives as works of art. See also E. F. Schumacher, *Good Work* (London, 1979), with his suggestions for education, pp. 112-20.

12. See the magnificent reflection by Primo Levi on Nature's work in recycling the basic building block of the world, the carbon atom, in *The Periodic Table* (London, 1985), pp. 224-33.

13. Soelle, *To Work and to Love*, p. 144.

14. See Alan Watts, *Nature, Man and Woman* (London, 1976), p. 121.

15. James Lovelock, *Gaia: A New Look at Life on Earth* (London, 1982), and *The Ages of Gaia* (London, 1989).

16. See James Robertson, in *New Economics*, the newsletter of the New Economics Foundation, 12 (Winter 1989), p. 12. Robertson is a founder member of the Foundation. See also his *Future Wealth: A New Economics*

for the Twenty-First Century (London, 1989), where he describes an economy for the sane, humane, ecological future, as opposed to the Hyper-Expansionist future. See also Hazel Henderson in *Uncommon Wisdom* (London, 1987), p. 234.

17. For an account of surveys done at Yale on the attitudes of American citizens toward wildlife in an attempt to assess them in cost-benefit analyses, see Devall, *Simple in Means, Rich in Ends*, pp. 31f.

18. Andrew Brennan, *Thinking About Nature: An Investigation of Nature, Value and Ecology* (London, 1988), p. 173. See also the whole discussion of the philosophy of Arne Naess in Devall, *Simple in Means, Rich in Ends*, pp. 29-37.

19. James Rachels, *Created From Animals: The Moral Implications of Darwinism* (Oxford, 1990), pp. 173f.

20. Quoted in Devall, *Simple in Means, Rich in Ends*, p. 29.

21. Joseph Shepherd, *A Leaf of Honey and the Proverbs of the Rainforest* (London, 1988).

22. Ursula King: "The Great Indian Goddess. The Significance of Female Symbolism for the Divine and its Relationship to the Image and Status of Indian Women." Talk given at Third International Conference of European Society of Women for Theological Research, Arnoldshain, September 1989.

23. Shiva, *Staying Alive*, pp. 55-80 and p. 208. For a short analysis of the interrelationship between ecofeminism, these movements and the global degradation of women in the cycle of poverty, see McDonagh, *The Greening of the Church*, pp. 154f.

24. Ron Birch, "Only God Can Make A Tree", in *Resurgence* 140 (May/June 1990), p. 26.

25. Carolyn Merchant, *The Death of Nature; Women, Ecology and the Scientific Revolution* (New York, 1982), pp. 2, 30f.

26. See Bookchin, *The Ecology of Freedom*, pp. 109f.

27. A. Friedberg, ed., *Corpus Iuris Canonici* (Leipzig, 1879-81), Vol. I, Pt. II. C. 33. q. 5, c. 12, 13, 17, 18. See also Susan Griffin, *Woman and Nature* (London, 1984), p. 11. "And it is said that all sin originated in the flesh of the body of a woman and lives in her body." Anyone who would like to think that these Decrees are merely interesting historical documents should read the research by Ida Raming: *Der Ausschluss der Frau vom priesterlichen Amt* (Cologne, 1973), which is an investigation into the use of Canon 968 of the *Corpus* in present discrimination against women in the Catholic Church.

Chapter 4: Apocalypse Now

1. See Joseph Blenkinsopp, *Prophecy and Canon* (Indiana, 1977), pp. 112f, esp. p. 115.

2. This was corroborated at the 1988 Conference of the Schumacher

Society. One of the speakers, the poet Robert Bly, asked the audience of eight hundred how many of them believed in the consciousness of animals. Nearly every hand went up. Then he asked how many believed in the consciousness of plant life. About half the hands went up. In response to his final question about the consciousness of stones, hills and rivers, less than a quarter were prepared to acknowledge its possibility.

For a good process theological treatment of the question of the consciousness of the earth, see Jay McDaniel, *Earth, Sky, Gods and Mortals* (Connecticut, 1989), pp. 86-106. Basing his arguments on Whiteheadian theories of evolution and physics, he says that we can perceive the mountain and rock as something more than inert stuff. We can perceive it as an expression of living energy or vibrant matter, as a primitive form of aliveness. From the point of view of an ecological Christianity, he says, to see physical matter as alive is to see it as God sees it. God sees and appreciates things as they are.

Carolyn Merchant gives an account of some revolutionary social consequences of treating the non-human world as self-active, an idea which underlay some of the preaching of radical sects and their history of dissent. See *The Death of Nature* (New York, 1982), p. 121f.

3. Paul Hanson, ed., *Visionaries and Their Apocalypses* (London, 1983), p. 1.

4. Quoted in Christopher Rowland, *The Open Heaven* (London, 1982), p. 27. He points out elsewhere that today peasants in Latin America find in the stark dualism of the *Apocalypse* and the conflict between good and evil a graphic portrayal of their own struggles, as they seek to subsist amidst the violence and destruction of counter-insurgency campaigns in El Salvador, of Contra terrorist raids in Nicaragua or in the face of the powerful land-owning forces who seek to drive peasants off their land in remote areas of Brazil. See Rowland, *Radical Christianity* (Oxford, 1988), p. 67.

5. See *From One Earth to One World* (Oxford, 1987), p. 3. See also A. Peacocke, *Creation and the World of Science* (Oxford, 1979), pp. 265f., for what he calls "prognoses", such as the 1972 report sponsored by the Club of Rome, which predicted collapse of the economic and industrial systems of developed countries by about the year 2100.

6. Rowland, *Open Heaven*, p. 11.

7. See John Stott, *Why care for the Planet?*, Tear Times, 50, Autumn 1990.

8. See typically the discussion in Jürgen Moltmann, *Theology of Hope* (London, 1967), p. 63: "Whereas in Augustinian mysticism. . . . the correlation of knowledge of God and self-knowledge could be taken as immediate and unmediated, for the Reformers, and still for Pascal, both are mediated by the knowledge of Christ: the crucified Christ is the mirror of God and the mirror of ourself. Nevertheless, in the Reformers too, as already in Augustine, this concentration of theology upon the knowledge of God and of self leaves no room over for any consideration

of God's world. On the contrary, this threatens to be banished from theology. Descartes then drops all proofs of God from the world . . . What theology says, thinks and proclaims about the action of God has been directed ever more strongly to that subjectivity of man which was given a free rein precisely by the secularization of the world effected by the Enlightenment."

In a discussion of revelation and knowledge of God, Moltmann states categorically: "The presupposition for the knowledge of God is the revealing of God by God", and goes on to say that he reveals himself in his name, i.e. as Yahweh, the God revealed in the Bible, and that this name is one of promise, which promise is "one side of the covenant in which God's association with the people of his choice is grounded". This God "who reveals himself in Jesus must be thought of as the God of the Old Testament". Op. cit. pp. 114-43.

See also the discussion by Rahner of Original Sin in the light of God's self-communication. He says: "God's self-communication in grace comes to man not from 'Adam', not from the beginning of the human race, but from the goal of this history, from the God-Man Jesus Christ." Of the nature of this self-communication, he says that it is "supernatural existential", that is, that such an existential does not become merited and in this sense "natural" by the fact that it is present in all men. See *Foundations of Christian Faith* (New York, 1978), pp. 114f. In *Geist in Welt* (Munich, 1964), his anthropology of man as the self-questioning being brings us back to the Cartesian notion of the self mentioned by Moltmann, in which the individual human consciousness, acted directly upon by God in Jesus Christ, is the primary place of encounter with God.

9. See accounts of the power of this kind of presentation in Fundamentalist circles, where those who are "saved" from hell are given a sense of personal worthlessness and self-hatred, as well as dislike of "outsiders" (the damned), reinforced by frequent assertions of mankind's essentially evil nature. See Rod L. Evans and Irwin M. Berent, *Fundamentalism* (Illinois, 1988), pp. 7-10. The devaluation of human natural capacity to know God lies behind this idea of separating the "saved" from all other forms of life. This attitude will be discussed at some length in Chapter 6.

10. See Rowland, *Radical Christianity*, pp. 150f.

11. Tissa Balasuriya, *Planetary Theology* (London, 1984), p. 5.

12. Christianity from its inception has integrated Hellenism into its expression of the divine mystery, beginning with the New Testament documents themselves. The sub-apostolic writers continued the process, and it is a Christian cliché to say, with the author of the Epistle to Diognetus, that: "Christians are in the world what the soul is in the body . . . The soul inhabits the body, but does not belong to the body: Christians inhabit the world, but 'do not belong to the world'. The soul is invisible and is kept in custody in the visible body."

See Henry Bettenson, trans. and ed., *The Early Christian Fathers*

(London, 1956), p. 75. He gives Plato's *Phaedo* as reference for this notion of the imprisoned soul.

Paul Ricoeur, discussing the endemic role of Hellenism in Christianity as a linguistic phenomenon, writes that the Christian church was unable to elaborate a theological discourse without the help of Greek conceptuality. Christianity borrowed from Hellenism its forms of argumentation, and even its fundamental semantics. Such words as sin, grace, redemption, atonement, eternal life, etc., received their chief meaning through the mediation of philosophical concepts available at the time and above all under the influence of some prominent problematics in the cultural world of the day; the concern for eternity in Neo-Platonic spirituality, for example. Paul Ricoeur, "Biblical Hermeneutics", in *Semeia* 4 (1975), ed. J. D. Crossan, p. 129.

See also Rosemary Radford Ruether: "For Plato, the authentic soul is incarnated as a male, and only when it succumbs to the body is it reincarnated in the body of a female and then into the body of some beast resembling the evil character into which it has fallen. The salvation of the liberated consciousness repudiates heterosexual for masculine love and mounts to heaven in flight from the body and the visible world. The intellect is seen as an alien, lonely species that originates in a purely spiritual realm beyond time, space and matter, and has been dropped, either as into a testing place or, through some fault, into this lower material world . . . The body drags the soul down, obscuring the clarity of its knowledge, debasing its moral integrity. Liberation is a flight from the earth to a changeless, infinite world beyond. Again we see the emergence of the liberated consciousness in a way that alienates it from Nature in a body-fleeing, world-negating spirituality. Christianity brought together both of these myths – the myth of world cataclysm and the myth of the flight of the soul to heaven . . . The dominant spirituality of the Fathers of the Church finally accepted the anti-body, antifeminine view of late antique religious culture . . . Christianity did not originate this view . . . [It] took over this alienated world view of late classical civilisation." "Motherearth and the Megamachine", in Carol Christ and Judith Plaskow, eds., *Womanspirit Rising: A Feminist Reader in Religion* (San Francisco, 1979), p. 48.

13. Douglas Hall, *Reintegrating God's Creation* (Geneva, 1987), p. 6.

14. See Matthew Fox, *Western Spirituality: Historical Roots, Ecumenical Routes* (New Mexico, 1981), p. 16.

See also Balasuriya, *Planetary Theology*, pp. 194, 205. "A renewed, planetary concept of mission and evangelism has to give priority to the fostering of relationships of solidarity among persons and peoples based on the biblical values of the rule of righteousness, the kingdom of God. The churches must be directly and primarily concerned with just relationships among peoples and in regard to Nature. A new ecclesiology or self-understanding of the churches is implied by such an orientation."

15. Grace Jantzen, *Julian of Norwich* (New Jersey, 1988), pp. 132f.

16. Alexander Carmichael, *Carmina Gadelica*, Vol. III (Edinburg and London, 1976), p. 25.

For a short account of Celtic spirituality and its potential for Christianity today, see Sean Mcdonagh, *The Greening of the Church* (London, 1990), pp. 168f.

Chapter 5: The Traditional Christian Paradigm: Hierarchy

1. See Anne Lonergan and Caroline Richards, eds., *Thomas Berry and the New Cosmology* (Connecticut, 1987), pp. 15-38. See Tissa Balasuriya, *Planetary Theology* (London, 1984), pp. 121-8. It is worth giving such exhaustive lists at this point since they include most of the issues addressed in this book, and elsewhere by such theologians as Elizabeth Dodson Gray, Rosemary Radford Ruether, Sean McDonagh, Matthew Fox, John Cobb, Jay MacDaniel et. al. Dodson-Gray and Ruether name hierarchical structures of reality and authority as mechanisms for maintaining the orientations deplored by them all. It is also worth giving these lists since I have been accused of describing a form of Christianity which is either a caricature, outdated or no longer exists. Would that the accusation were correct.

2. See Naomi Goldenberg, *Changing of the Gods* (Boston, 1979), pp. 47f. For literary and related theories of myth, see Northrop Frye, *The Great Code* (London, 1982). See also the whole discussion of myth (a story about the Gods) and Aristotelian *muthos* (plot) in Paul Ricoeur, *Time and Narrative*, Vols. I, II and III (Chicago, 1983, 1985, 1988). In the sense of spanning time from the beginning (Genesis) to the end (Apocalypse) of the world, he says, the Bible is the grandiose plot (*muthos*) of the history of the world, and each literary plot is a sort of miniature version of the great plot that joins Apocalypse and Genesis (Vol. II. p. 23). For a discussion of the subversion of myth by paradox and parable *within the Bible itself*, see my thesis *The Cross and the Rose: Lutheran Paradox and Hegelian Dialectic in the Theology of Jürgen Moltmann* (London University, 1987).

For a treatment of myth as the processes of the spirit and the operations of the pre-rational powers and structures in human life that have played an essential part in the symbolics of early Christianity, see Amos Wilder "Myth and Dream in Christian Scripture", in Joseph Campbell, ed., *Myths, Dreams and Religions* (Dallas, 1988), pp. 68-90.

See also Campbell's own contribution to this volume, "Mythological Themes in Creative Literature and Art", pp. 136-75, for a treatment of the four functions of mythology. For the way in which hierarchies function as structures of estrangement, in which "function follows form", see Starhawk, *Dreaming the Dark* (Boston, 1982), p. 114.

For an anthropological definition of ideology functioning in an allied way, see Stanley Brandes, "Male Sexual Identity in an Andalusian Town", in Ortner and Whitehead, eds., *Sexual Meanings: The Cultural Construction of Gender and Sexuality* (Cambridge, 1981), p. 217.

3. Pseudo-Dionysius, *Mystical Theology and the Celestial Hierarchies*

(Surrey, 1965), p. 29. See also Andrew Louth, *Denys the Areopagite* (London 1989), pp. 38f. For who he was, see pp. 1f.

4. Representations of the Trinity in art, such as Masaccio's magisterial work, depict this as the Father (a bearded venerable male) seated or standing over a cross on which the Son is suspended, with the Spirit represented by a dove hovering between them.

5. See Louth, *Denys the Areopagite*, pp. 12f.

6. Ibid. pp. 54f.

7. Walter Abbott, S.J., ed., *The Documents of Vatican II* (London-Dublin, 1966), pp. 37-56.

8. E. Colledge O.S.A. and J. Walsh S.J., trs., *Julian of Norwich: Showings* (New York, 1978), p. 184. See Pseudo-Dionysius: "For each of those who is allotted a place in the Divine Order finds his perfection in being uplifted, according to his capacity, towards the Divine Likeness . . . I hold, therefore, that those who are being purified ought to be wholly perfected and free from all taint of unlikeness; those who are illuminated should be filled full with divine light, ascending to the contemplative state and power with the most pure eyes of the mind; those who are being initiated, holding themselves as apart from all imperfection, should become participators in the Divine Wisdom which they have contemplated". *Mystical Theology*, p. 30.

9. See Elizabeth Dodson Gray, *Patriarchy as a Conceptual Trap* (Massachusetts, 1982), p. 86: "It took Christians a long time to deal with Darwin and the evolutionary picture of our place in Nature. But we did, and I found it fascinating that, a century after Darwin, J. Bronowski could entitle his TV series and book *The Ascent of Man*. He could do this because the mental picture you and I have of evolution is still the biblical pyramid or hierarchy of being and value – with God now absent from the top. The beginning of everything comes now not from God as spirit creating everything from above. Instead it all started out in the primeval soup, and species emerge and evolve *upward* from below. We visualize the complex species on top, and the simple species underneath. That complexity should be more valued than simplicity is an interesting assumption. And, of course, we again are on the top and most valued!"

For another version of endemic Western hierarchies see Gregory Bateson: "A part of the story of our loss of the sense of unity has been elegantly told in Lovejoy's *Great Chain Of Being*, which traces the story from classical Greek philosophy to Kant and the beginnings of German idealism in the eighteenth [century]. This is the story of the idea that the world is/was timelessly created upon *deductive logic*. The idea is clear in the epigraph from *The City of God*. Supreme Mind, or Logos, is at the head of the deductive chain. Below that are the angels, then people, then apes, and so on down to the plants and stones. All is in deductive order and tied into that order by a premise which prefigures our second law of thermodynamics. The premise asserts that the 'more perfect' can never be generated by the 'less perfect'.

In the history of biology, it was Lamarck who inverted the great chain of being. By insisting that mind is immanent in living creatures and could determine their transformations, he escaped from the negative directional premise that the perfect must always precede the imperfect. He then proposed a theory of 'transformism' (evolution) which started from infusoria (protozoa) and marched upward to man and woman. The Lamarckian biosphere was still a *chain*. The unity of epistemology was retained in spite of a shift in emphasis from transcendent Logos to immanent mind." Gregory Bateson, *Mind and Nature* (London, 1985), pp. 28f.

10. In *The Honest To God Debate* (London, 1963), p. 269.

11. See Nelle Morton, *The Journey Is Home* (Boston, 1985), p. 56. See also Starhawk, *Dreaming the Dark*, p. 100, for the way in which hierarchical groups function.

12. See again Pseudo-Dionysius, note 2 above, on "dissimilarity" and "unlikeness".

13. Reported in *The Tablet* (6 January 1990), p. 29. See again the argument about man's inability to know God from the world in Chapter Four, note 8. Rahner is quite explicit about the correlation between Adam and Jesus Christ, hence his category of "super"natural existential.

14. Balasuriya, *Planetary Theology*, p. 122.

15. Aimé Césaire, *Return to my Native Land*, trs. John Berger and Anna Bostock (Middlesex, 1969), p. 50. See *A South African Comment on the European Ecumenical Assembly* (Basle, May 1989), from the Belydende Kring, an association of ministers in the "daughter-churches" of the Dutch Reformed Church in South Africa, p.o. Box 69, Plumstead, 7600, South Africa.

16. See Virginia Mollenkott, *Godding* (New York, 1987), p. 56. See also Susan Griffin, *Woman and Nature* (London, 1978), p. 8. Bringing together theological devaluation of blacks, women and Nature on the hierarchical spectrum is not intended to take away from the problems dividing black womanists and white feminists. See Susan Thistlethwaite in *Sex, Race and God* (London, 1990).

17. See Beverley Harrison, *Making the Connections* (Boston, 1985), pp. 34f.

18. See Page duBois, *Sowing the Body* (Chicago, 1988), pp. 184f. Heading a chapter entitled "The Defective Female Body", she quotes Aristotle: "the female is as it were a deformed male and the menstrual discharge is semen, though in an impure condition; i.e., it lacks one constituent, the principle of soul". See also Rosemary Radford Ruether, *Sexism and Godtalk* (Boston, 1983), pp. 95f. See also Harrison, *Making the Connections*, p. 32. Even if such statements are no longer proclaimed as doctrine, they cast long shadows today in the myriad ways in which women are still degraded in Christian hierarchies.

For conclusions on the deficiency of females as a psychological norm see Carol Gilligan, *In a Different Voice* (Harvard, 1982), pp. 6f.

19. See Anne Primavesi and Jennifer Henderson, *Our God Has No Favourites* (Tunbridge Wells and San Jose, Ca., 1989), for an extensive treatment of this theme. The tension between these two perceptions of Jesus will be explored later in this book.

20. See Bill Devall, *Simple in Means, Rich in Ends* (London, 1990), p. 56.

21. See the far-ranging discussion of the Christian origins of this in the aptly named *Dirt, Greed and Sex: Sexual Ethics in the New Testament and Their Implications for Today*, by L. William Countryman (London, 1989). For a contrary view within Christianity see Julian of Norwich, in *Julian Of Norwich: Showings*, p. 186.

22. See the discussion of this absolute transcendence in Grace Jantzen, *God's World, God's Body* (Philadelphia, 1984), pp. 101f.

23. See again Ruether, *Sexism*, Ch. 4, n. 9.

24. See Matilda Gage, *Woman, Church and State* (Massachusetts, 1980), p. 210. See also Dodson Gray, *Patriarchy as a Conceptual Trap*, p. 74.

25. See Harrison, *Making the Connections*, p. 216.

26. See René Descartes, *Discourse on Method* (London, 1912), p. 222. For a comment on these philosophical principles, see Jacques Maritain, *The Dream of Descartes* (London, 1946). For its psychological effects, see James Hillman, *Re-Visioning Psychology* (New York, 1975), pp. 1f.

27. T. Corbishley S.J., tr., *The Spiritual Exercises Of St Ignatius* (London, 1963), p. 22, n. 23; p. 80., n. 235.

28. See *Letter to the Friends of the Conference of European Churches* (December 1989), P.O. Box 2100, 150 Route de Ferney, Ch-1211 Geneva 2.

29. See J. A. Lyons, *The Cosmic Christ in Origen and Teilhard de Chardin* (Oxford, 1982), pp. 38, 59f.

30. Albert Schweitzer, *My Life and Thought: An Autobiography* (London, 1933), pp. 185f, 277.

31. Jay MacDaniel, *Earth, Sky, Gods and Mortals* (Connecticut, 1989), p. 51. See also John Cobb on Hartshorne's "Beyond Humanism". It is a sustained attack against all the ways in which human beings have set themselves up as the ultimate and inclusive reality. Against this he argues that animals also feel, and that as we descend [sic] the scale of organisms we find simpler and simpler feelings but never cross the line to units that do not feel at all. Similarly, when we ascend [sic] the scale we can go beyond ourselves to the universe as a whole, which is also a unit of feeling incomparably superior to us. Entities such as stones and plants, which do not themselves possess feelings, are made up of molecules and cells, which do. That most such feelings are not conscious in any ordinary sense of "conscious" is no argument against this position. J. Cobb, *Process Theology as Political Theology* (Manchester, 1982), p. 34. See also Arthur Peacocke, *Creation and the World of Science* (Oxford, 1979), pp. 140f., in which he describes this as the most systematic

attempt to date to understand God's action in the world in relation to the scientific picture of that world.

Chapter 6: Fundamental Christian Questions

1. See Juan Luis Segundo, *An Evolutionary Approach to Jesus of Nazareth* (London, 1988), pp. 65, 85.

2. See Andrew Louth, *Denys the Areopagite* (London, 1988), p. 58.

3. See, under the heading "Aquinas on the Atonement", ed. Henry Bettenson, *Documents of the Christian Church* (Oxford, 1963), pp. 145-7. One of the basic texts on this doctrine, Vincent Taylor's, *The Atonement in New Testament Teaching* (London, 1940), concentrates on the common faith of the first Christian communities in relation to the suffering and death of Jesus. This is the only data taken into account. Taylor states that Jesus undoubtedly [sic] believed that his sufferings were not due to chance or human violence alone, but were events lying deep in the Providence of God. "His death would fulfil the end determined in the divine counsels, and in this purpose His will and that of the Father were at one."

4. Gabriel Daly, *The Tablet*, 27 Jan. 1990, p. 112.

5. Such a stock answer is readily learnt at an impressionable age, and is then made acceptable through sermons and rituals which sum up the Christian experience in these terms. This is true even when the people who repeat them are very good at exercising their critical faculties in every other aspect of their lives. What Bateson calls Gresham's Law of simplification takes over, that "oversimplified ideas will always displace the sophisticated": Gregory Bateson, *Mind and Nature* (London, 1979), p. 14. In religious education this is partly the case because practically all formal teaching in this subject is imparted at pre-adult level, and is very often a memory exercise, a matter of teaching "truths" by rote. The fact that these "truths" are couched for the most part in an abstruse language about expiation for sin, redemption of slaves, fall from grace and salvation, penalty and satisfaction which have little to do with experience makes the pupils even readier to give stock answers to stock questions. See the fine discussion of these problems in "School, Society and Catechetics" by Didier Piveteau in Dermot Lane, ed., *Religious Education and the Future* (Dublin, 1986).

6. Jay McDaniel, *Earth, Sky, Gods and Mortals* (Connecticut, 1989), pp. 137f.

7. What is being said here harks back to the previous chapter's discussion, and in particular to the references in note 2. In this context, what would be called the myth of original sin functions in the following ways: by reconciling consciousness with the preconditions of its own existence; by validating and maintaining some specific social order, authorizing its moral code as a construct beyond criticism or human emendation; by shaping individuals to the aims and ideals of their various social groups, bearing them on from birth to death through the

course of a human life. See ed. Joseph Campbell, *Myths, Dreams and Religion* (Dallas, 1988), pp. 138f.

8. See Arthur Peacocke, *Creation and the World of Science* (Oxford, 1979), p. 91.

9. Dietrich Bonhoeffer, *Letters and Papers from Prison*, ed. E. Bethge, tr. R. Fuller (London, 1956), p. 140.

10. See José Comblin, *The Holy Spirit and Liberation* (Tunbridge Wells and Maryknoll, N.Y., 1989), p. 14.

11. Thomas Szasz quoted in Mary Daly, *Beyond God the Father* (London, 1986), p. 76.

12. James Barr, *Fundamentalism* (London, 1977), p. 27.

13. *The Church Times*, 2 November 1990, p. 11.

14. See the Chalcedonian definition: "Therefore, following the holy Fathers, we all with one accord teach men to acknowledge one and the same Son, our Lord Jesus Christ, at once complete in Godhead and complete in manhood, truly God and truly man, consisting also of a reasonable soul and body; of one substance with the Father as regards his godhead, and at the same time of one substance with us as regards his manhood." Bettenson, *Documents of the Christian Church*, p. 51.

15. Barr, *Fundamentalism*, p. 169. See again Nelle Morton's analysis of doing away with the devalued humanity of Jesus, chapter 5, note 7.

16. See Segundo, *An Evolutionary Approach* , p. 84.

17. This argument has been around a long time. It is to be found in the second century document *De Resurrectione* in which the author, PseudoJustin Martyr, says that just as certain matters are settled by the senses and there is no possibility of appealing to higher authority, other matters must be settled by the Christian message. He defends this view by appealing to Christ. He is personally the guarantor of the truth of Christian faith, since he is the Son of God from heaven. See Gunnar af Hällström, *Carnis Resurrectio* (Helsinki, 1988), p. 17.

18. Barr, *Fundamentalism*, p. 171.

19. See the discussion of Jesus' human fallibility and its denial in Rod. L. Evans & Irwin M. Berent, *Fundamentalism: Hazards and Heartbreaks* (Illinois, 1988), chs. 6 and 7. See also Segundo, *An Evolutionary Approach*, pp. 88-91.

20. Peacocke, *Creation and the World of Science*, p. 241.

21. Hal Lindsey, *The Late Great Planet Earth* (London, 1970), p. 111. See the essay on this by Gore Vidal: "Armageddon?" in *Armageddon?* (London, 1987).

22. See Jonathan Schell, *The Fate of the Earth* (London, 1982), pp. 108f.

23. For an extensive treatment of this relationship and its implications, see the discussion of Christian "security" in Anne Primavesi & Jennifer

Henderson, *Our God Has No Favourites* (Tunbridge Wells and San Jose, Ca, 1989), esp. chs. 4 and 5. See also Sallie McFague, *Models of God* (London, 1987), p. 55.

24. This shattering is what Alan Watts refers to as "the first principle of the spiritual life". A careful study of comparative religion and spiritual philosophy reveals that abandonment of belief, of any clinging to a future life for one's own, and of any attempt to escape from finitude and mortality, is a regular and normal stage in the way of the spirit. *The Wisdom of Insecurity* (London, 1974), p. 24.

This creation of insecurity is the function of paradox and parable within the context of a myth which creates security. Myths are agents of stability, parables agents of change. Myth reconciles the individual to existence (see Campbell note 7 above), and parable challenges that by making us aware of the fact that *we made up* the reconciliation. Jesus' teaching in parables performed this function. See Dominic Crossan, *The Dark Interval* (Illinois, 1975), p. 57.

25. See Amos Wilder, "Myth and Dream in Christian Scripture", in Campbell, *Myths, Dreams and Religion*, pp. 85f.

26. See John Robinson, *The Honest to God Debate* (London, 1963), p. 271.

Chapter 7: Ecofeminism and Christian Imagery

1. See Ursula King: *Women and Spirituality: Voices of Protest and Promise* (Basingstoke, 1989), pp. 20, 35. Judith Plaskow first raised the great "What if?" question in relation to women and Judaism. She tackled the question: what if the subordination of women is not simply a matter of Jewish interpretation of surrounding cultural and social attitudes, but is in part created and sustained by Torah itself? The implications of the Jewish feminist answer, she says, demand a new understanding of Torah, God and Israel: an understanding of Torah that begins with an acknowledgment of the profound injustice of Torah itself. See Nelle Morton, *The Journey is Home* (Boston, 1985), p. 222.

2. For a similar exercise based on women's experience of male divinity faculties, see Morton, *The Journey is Home*, pp. 44f. For a condensed treatment of women's experiences of exclusion, loss of identity, frustration and the pain of not being heard, see J. Crawford and M. Kinnamon, eds., *In God's Image: Reflections on Identity, Human Wholeness and the Authority of Scripture* (Geneva, 1983). See also Bärbel von Wartenberg-Potter, *We Will Not Hang Our Harps on the Willows* (Geneva, 1987). See especially Susan Dunfee, *Beyond Servanthood: Christianity and the Liberation of Women* (Langham, 1989), p. 81. All the women's theological works cited, whether on spirituality, language or Biblical imagery, contain similar experiences and analyses of oppression by Christian patriarchal practices. See also Brian Wren, *What Language Shall I Borrow?* (London, 1989), for a profoundly sympathetic male understanding of Christian women's oppression by sexist language.

3. Carol Christ, *Diving Deep and Surfacing* (Boston, 1980), p. 117.

4. John A. T. Robinson, and ed. David Edwards, *The Honest To God Debate* (London, 1963), pp. 256f.

5. The book *In God's Image*, already mentioned, is a collection of reports on the Study of the Community of Women and Men in the Church funded since 1975 by the World Council of Churches and continuing with much valuable work. See again Wren, *What Language Shall I Borrow?*

6. Carolyn Merchant, *The Death of Nature* (New York, 1982), pp. 132, 143f.

7. R. C. Zaehner, *Mysticism Sacred and Profane* (Oxford, 1975), p. 33.

8. See again the quote from Rosemary Radford Ruether in chapter 4, note 12.

9. Christ, *Diving Deep*, p. 17.

10. James Hillman, *Re-Visioning Psychology* (New York, 1975), p. 5.

11. Simone Weil, *Waiting On God* (London, 1959), pp. 40, 41, 47. See again ch. 6, note 21, for Amos Wilder on the universalism of Jesus.

12. Martin Buber, *I-Thou* (Edinburgh, 1970), p. 156. See also p. 157.

13. Juan Luis Segundo, *An Evolutionary Approach to Jesus of Nazareth* (London, 1988), pp. 39f.

14. See Charlene Spretnak, *The Spiritual Dimension of Green Politics* (Santa Fe, 1986), p. 52; *To Work and To Love: a Theology of Creation* (Philadelphia, 1984), p. 50.

15. "*Praemisit tibi naturam magistram, summissurus et prophetiam, quo facilius credas prophetiae discipulus ante naturae*". *De Resurrectione*, 12.8, cited in Gunnar af Hällström, *Carnis Resurrectio* (Helsinki, 1988), p. 77. For Hooker, see Merchant, *The Death of Nature*, p. 7.

16. Anne Bancroft, *Weavers of Wisdom* (London, 1989), p. 46.

17. See the development of these arguments in Anne Primavesi & Jennifer Henderson, *Our God Has No Favourites* (Tunbridge Wells and San Jose, Ca., 1989).

18. See Gregory Bateson: *Mind and Nature* (London, 1980), p. 13.

19. Quoted in Elizabeth Dodson Gray, *Green Paradise Lost* (Massachusetts, 1984), pp. 141f. For Stone's reflections on the evaluative frameworks and principles such cases establish, see *Earth and Other Ethics: The Case for Moral Pluralism* (New York, 1987), pp. 92ff. See also Bill Devall, *Simple in Means, Rich in Ends* (London, 1990), p. 29 See also the discussion of the moral issues behind such thinking by James Rachels in *Created from Animals: the Moral implications of Darwinism* (Oxford, 1990).

20. Dodson-Gray, ibid.

Chapter 8: Metaphor and Context

1. Aimé Césaire, trans., John Berger and Anna Bostock, *Return to my Native Land* (London, 1969), p. 49.

2. See Gregory Bateson, *Mind and Nature* (London, 1979), p. 110. See Paul Ricoeur, *The Rule of Metaphor* (London, 1986), and also "Biblical Hermeneutics", in *Semeia* 4 (1975), pp. 88 and 143. See also Naomi Goldenberg, *Changing the Gods* (Boston, 1979), p. 62.

3. Donal A. McIlraith, *The Reciprocal Love between Christ and the Church in the Apocalypse* (Rome, 1989), pp. 170, 196f.

4. See Alan Watts "Western Mythology: Its Dissolution and Transformation", in Joseph Campbell, ed., *Myths, Dreams and Religion* (Dallas, 1979), p. 22: "But somehow more in line with twentieth-century science would be an *organic* image of the world, the world as a body, as a vast pattern of intelligent energy that has a new relationship to us. We are not in it as subjects of a king, or as victims of a blind process. we are not *in* it at all. We *are* it!" James Lovelock's Gaia theory presents this image scientifically and coherently.

5. R. C. Zaehner, *Mysticism, Sacred and Profane* (Oxford, 1973), pp. 201f.

6. See Mircea Eliade, *From Primitives to Zen* (London, 1967), pp. 87f.

7. Rita Gross, "Female God Language in a Jewish Context", *Womanspirit Rising* (New York, 1979), p. 171.

8. Douglas Hall, "The Integrity of Creation: Biblical and Theological Background of the Term", *Reintegrating God's Creation* (Geneva, 1987), p. 34.

9. See Nelle Morton, *The Journey is Home* (Boston, 1985), p. 224.

10. Anne Bancroft, ed., *Weavers of Wisdom* (London, 1989), p. 14.

11. Hall, *Reintegrating God's Creation*, p. 25.

Chapter 9: Ecofeminism and Canon

1. This is usually known as the Vincentian canon, formulated by Vincent of Lérins. See Henry Bettenson, ed., *The Documents of the Christian Church* (Oxford, 1963), p. 82.

2. Walter Abbott, ed., *Documents of Vatican II* (London and Dublin, 1966), pp. 112f. On the implications of this for the relationship between Scripture and Tradition, see Gabriel Moran, *Theology of Revelation* (London, 1967).

3. Karl Barth, *The Doctrine of the Word of God* (Edinburgh, 1936), p. 113. For a discussion of the formation of the Hebrew canon, see Joseph Blenkinsopp, *Prophecy and Canon* (Notre Dame, 1977).

4. Brian Wren, *What Language Shall I Borrow?* (London, 1989), p. 6.

5. Carol Meyers, *Discovering Eve; Ancient Israelite Women in Context* (London, 1988), p. 12.

6. Wayne Meeks, *The First Urban Christians: The Social World of the Apostle Paul* (Yale, 1983), p. 9.

7. See Andrew Louth, *Denys the Areopagite* (London, 1989), pp. 10–11.

8. See Mary Douglas, *Purity and Danger* (London, 1966), pp. 41-57. See also the interesting discussion on the cultural basis of purity codes in L. W. Countryman, *Dirt, Greed and Sex* (London, 1989), p. 12. See also the distinctions he makes between the Israelite notion of the family and its subversion in the teachings of Jesus, pp. 168f.

9. Meyers, *Discovering Eve*, p. 18.

10. See Rosemary Radford Ruether, *Women-Church: Theology and Practice* (San Francisco, 1985), p. 12.

11. Ibid., pp. 78f. See suggestions for baptismal ceremonies, pp. 183f., and other liturgies celebrating the life cycle of living beings. See also Huub Oosterhuis, *Prayers, Peoms and Songs* (London, 1971), pp. 123f. for an imaginative baptismal liturgy.

12. See Elaine Pagels, *Adam, Eve, and the Serpent* (London, 1990). She brings out the implications for nature of Augustine's doctrine of the fall of Adam in his debate with Julian of Eclanum, and goes into some of the reasons why Augustine's negative assessment was adopted as official orthodox teaching from then on.

13. See Susan Thistlethwaite, *Sex, Race and God* (London, 1990), p. 85, for an interesting and challenging expansion of this notion in terms of differences between black and white women.

14. Arthur Peacocke, *Creation and the World of Science* (Oxford, 1979), p. 279.

15. See R. C. Zaehner, *Mysticism Sacred and Profane* (London, 1957), p. 33. Defining strictly religious mysticism, he says it means a total and absolute detachment from Nature, from *"all that is not God"*.

16. See the discussion of the historic basis for these claims formulated by Irenaeus in Pagels, *The Gnostic Gospels* (New York, 1979), pp. 23f.

17. José Comblin, *The Holy Spirit and Liberation* (Tunbridge Wells and Maryknoll, N.Y., 1989), p. xiv.

18. Ibid., pp. 25f.

19. Blenkinsopp, *Prophecy and Canon*, p. 152.

Chapter 10: Hierarchical and Ecological Power

1. See the disscussion of *credo* in Wilfred Cantwell Smith, *Faith and Belief* (Princeton, 1979), pp. 69-104.

2. See Michel Foucault, *The Use of Pleasure; The History of Sexuality*, Vol. 2 (London, 1987), p. 25. See also Beverley Harrison, *Making the Connections* (Boston, 1985), p. 35. See also the anthology Andolsen, Gudorf, Pellauer, eds., *Women's Consciousness, Women's Conscience* (New York, 1987), especially June O'Connor, "On Doing Religious Ethics", pp. 265f.

3. Carol Meyers, *Discovering Eve; Ancient Israelite Women in Context* (Oxford, 1988), p. 61.

4. Mary Condren, *The Serpent and the Goddess* (New York, 1989), p. 202.

5. From an article in the *Observer* (15 July 1990), p. 45.

6. The subject of holiness and pollution covers a vast field, and the comment made here is meant to direct attention to the way in which the acceptance of classifications on such a basis acts as legitimation for the exercise of power over sub-classes, consciously or not. For a wider discussion of a few of the religious and cultural issues involved, see the discussion by Mary Douglas in *Purity and Danger* (London, 1989), pp. 41-57.

7. Meyers, *Discovering Eve*, pp. 80f.

8. There is no question here of trying to postulate either the priority of one text over the other or to argue for different authors or stages of editing. R. N. Whybray has successfully shown that the Documentary hypothesis is just that, a hypothesis. See *The Making of the Pentateuch* (Sheffield, 1987). See especially Mieke Bal, "Sexuality, Sin and Sorrow" in S. R. Suleman, ed., *The Female Body in Western Culture* (Massachusetts, 1985), pp. 317-38, for a detailed literary analysis of the narrative.

9. Phyllis Trible, *God and the Rhetoric of Sexuality* (Philadelphia, 1987), pp. 79f.

10. Meyers, *Discovering Eve*, p. 81.

11. Peter Brown, *The Body and Society* (London, 1990), pp. 193f., 350f.

12. Ibid., pp. 398-447.

13. See Susan Brownmiller's study *Against our Will: Men, Women and Rape* (London, 1975).

14. Montague Summers, tr., *Malleus Maleficarum* (London, 1928), pt. 2, sec. 6. See Carolyn Merchant, *The Death of Nature* (New York, 1980), pp. 132–42; See also Starhawk, *Dreaming the Dark* (Boston, 1982), p. 189. "The persecution of Witches was linked to three interwoven processes: the expropriation of land and natural resources; the expropriation of knowledge; and the war against the consciousness of immanence, which was embodied in women, sexuality and magic." See also Condren, *The Serpent and the Goddess*, pp. 166f.

15. Condren, *The Serpent and the Goddess*, p. 173.

16. Brown, *The Body and Society*, pp. 422, 427.

17. Condren, *The Serpent and the Goddess*, p. 173.

18. For a discussion of these types of power see Starhawk, *Truth or Dare* (San Francisco, 1990), pp. 8-26, and *Dreaming the Dark*, pp. 3f., 94. See also Bill Devall, *Simple in Means, Rich in Ends* (London, 1990), p. 123.

Chapter 11: Uncommon Perceptions of Genesis

1. See Maurice Wiles, *The Christian Fathers* (London, 1977), p. 18.

2. Carol Meyers, *Discovering Eve* (Oxford, 1988), pp. 77, 87.

3. Gottfried Quell, *Sin, Bible Key Words* (London, 1951), p. 15. The story of the "fall", he says, affords a vista of man's life as a whole. He does not agree with the suggestion of another scholar that the creation of woman may have been the result of sin, i.e. an act of divine anger [*sic*], and rebukes yet another scholar for saying that this is fairly certain. This footnote skirmish is useful here for showing the general tenor of male scholarly interpretation of Genesis, especially when Quell states that the aetiological interpretation of the myth of the fall "undoubtedly justifies our basing upon it a theory of 'original sin' in the sense of man's universal sinfulness".

4. Ibid., p. 23. Compare this with Meyers, *Discovering Eve*, pp. 87f.

5. See Meyers, *Discovering Eve*, pp. 50f.

6. This point was made by Elizabeth Cady Stanton. See Celia Kitzinger "Why Men Hate Women", in *New Internationalist*, October 1990, p. 14.

7. The effects of this assumption on the Christian doctrine of resurrection are powerfully argued in Jacques Pohier's book, *God – in Fragments*, (London, 1985). The whole book is a commentary from a different perspective on issues raised throughout this one, and I am grateful to Professor Rowan Williams for drawing my attention to this, even though too late for me to do more than refer to it.

8. See Elaine Pagels, *Adam, Eve and the Serpent* (London, 1990), pp. 130– 50, for a full and fascinating discussion of the issues raised in their debate and summarized here.

9. Phyllis Trible, *God and the Rhetoric of Sexuality* (Philadelphia, 1978), p. 139.

10. Pagels, *Adam, Eve and the Serpent*, p. xix. See also James Hillman, *The Myth of Analysis* (New York, 1978), p. 218. See also Rosemary Radford Reuther, *Womanguides* (Boston, 1985), pp. 81–102.

11. Wiles, *The Christian Fathers*, p. 29.

12. See Athalya Brenner, *The Israelite Woman* (Sheffield, 1985), pp. 122- 31. See also Juan Luis Segundo, *The Humanist Christology of Paul* (London, 1986), p. 176.

13. For a related discussion of structural sin, see Segundo, *The Humanist Christology of Paul*, pp. 174f. See also Virginia Mollenkott, *Godding* (New York, 1987), p. 41.

14. Judith Plaskow in a lecture at the European Society of Women in Theological Research, Arnoldshein, 1989, pp. 16f. See also Virginia Mollenkott's questioning along the same lines of the God revealed in the Job narrative, *Godding*, p. 29. This type of questioning is what I understand Pohier to mean by "the decomposition of God".

15. See Juan Luis Segundo, *An Evolutionary Approach to Jesus of Nazareth* (London, 1988), pp. 84f.

16. Meyers, *Discovering Eve*, pp. 82–5.

17. Ibid., p. 90. See also Francis Landy, *Paradoxes of Paradise: Identity and Difference in the Song of Songs* (Sheffield, 1983), p. 226. On the Genesis narrative, he says that the repetition and variation amplify the statement with purely emotive effect. The duplication of language suggests a surcharge of meaning contained within the metrical structure.

18. Ibid., pp. 50–63.

Chapter 12: The Spirit of Genesis

1. See Virginia Mollenkott, *Godding* (New York, 1987), p. 103. She quotes the Hebrew scholar David Freedman who translates *ezer neged* as "a power equal to man", since in the Hebrew scriptures the word *ezer* always refers to help coming from a position of power. See also Phyllis Trible, *God and the Rhetoric of Sexuality* (Philadelphia, 1987), p. 90. She says that the word here specifies identity, mutuality and equality.

2. Quoted in Carol Christ and Judith Plaskow, eds., *Womanspirit Rising* (San Francisco, 1979), p. 190. This attitude to death is not meant in any way to detract from the horror and unacceptability of the deaths resulting from exploitation, starvation and disease recounted in ecological apocalyptic documents; nor of violent deaths resulting from power struggles; nor is it intended to endorse the premise advanced by some today that famine in Africa or the AIDS epidemic is acceptable or desirable as a way of dealing with overpopulation. The death envisaged here is that which normally follows a life lived to maturity. The fact that people like Hannah Senesh chose, in the face of the Holocaust, to resist unto death the slaughter of her people, underlines the instinctive human reaction to murder and mass murder, whether in Auschwitz, El Salvador or Kurdistan.

3. See Virginia Mollenkott, *Godding: Human Responsibility and the Bible* (New York, 1987), p.5. An off-the-cuff reply by the scientist J. B. S. Haldane makes the same point. Asked what he would conclude as to the nature of the Creator on the basis of his lifetime study of the Creation, he replied: "An inordinate fondness for beetles!" Out of the various forms of life that inhabit the earth, there are well over a million species of insect, and of these, one third are beetles.

4. Julian of Norwich, *Showings* (New York, 1978), pp. 267–8.

5. Ibid., pp. 270–1.

6. Ibid., pp. 274–5.

7. Peter Brown, *The Body and Society* (London, 1990), p. 352–3.

8. See Francis Landy, *Paradoxes of Paradise* (Sheffield, 1983) pp. 260–1.

9. See Juan Luis Segundo, *An Evolutionary Approach to Jesus of Nazareth* (New York, 1988), pp. 85-91 for a lengthy discussion of the issues raised here. See also Anne Primavesi and Jennifer Henderson, *Our God Has no Favourites* (Tunbridge Wells and San Jose, Ca., 1989), for a similar exposition of the connection between Jesus' table companionship and his death.

10. See Rosemary Radford Ruether, *Sexism and God-Talk* (Boston, 1983), pp. 246-9, for an interesting discussion of the effects of such doctrines on canonized teaching about women's bodies.

11. For a full discussion of these themes, see Primavesi & Henderson, *Our God Has No Favourites*, especially Chapters 2 and 3.

12. See Segundo, *Faith and Ideologies* (New York, 1984), p. 44. He writes that when Jesus declared all foods clean (Mark 7:19), the statement no longer scandalizes us. Its anti-religious import was lost once people began to worship Jesus himself as God and so ceased to see anything abnormal in his utterance. For here he is making clean foods that Yahweh had declared unclean according to the traditions of the Bible. We have lost sight of the radical thrust of Jesus's argument. The basic criterion of Christian morality is to be found in what the heart bids a person do in the face of the needs of our fellow human beings.

13. Segundo, *An Evolutionary Approach to Jesus of Nazareth*, p. 87.

14. See James Dunn, *Jesus and the Spirit* (London, 1975), pp. 48f.

15. See José Comblin, *The Holy Spirit and Liberation* (Tunbridge Wells and Maryknoll, N.Y., 1989), pp. xii, xiv.

16. See Mollenkott: The traditional Christian interpretation tends to spotlight Jesus as a one-time-only phenomenon, someone out of the past who will rescue us single-handed and who thus relieves us of our contemporary responsibility to struggle to bring forth justice in our world. *Godding*, p. 7.

17. Starhawk, *Dreaming the Dark* (London, 1990), pp. 94–5.

18. See Comblin, *The Holy Spirit and Liberation* for a detailed account of the effects of the Spirit's power on the communities of Latin America, pp. 20–42.

19. See Nelle Morton, *The Journey is Home* (Boston, 1985), p. 99.

Select Bibliography

Andolsen B., C. Gudorf and M. Pellauer, eds. *Women's Consciousness: Women's Conscience*. San Francisco: Harper & Row, 1987.

Bal, M., ed. *Anti-Covenant: Counter-Reading Women's Lives in the Hebrew Bible*. Sheffield: Almond Press, 1989.

Bancroft, A., *Weavers of Wisdom*. London: Arkana, 1989.

Bateson, G., *Mind and Nature*. London: Wildwood House, 1979; London: Fontana, 1985.

Bateson, G., *Steps to an Ecology of Mind*. New York: Random House, 1972.

Berry, W., *The Gift of Good Land*. San Francisco: North Point Press, 1981.

Bookchin, M., *The Ecology of Freedom*. Palo Alto: Cheshire Books, 1982.

Brennan, A., *Thinking About Nature: An Investigation of Nature, Value and Ecology*. London: Routledge, 1988.

Brown, P., *The Body and Society*. New York: Columbia University Press; London: Faber and Faber, 1990.

Brundtland, G., Chairman *Our Common Future: The World Commission on Environment and Development*. Oxford: OUP, 1987.

Buber, M., W. Kaufmann, tr. and ed. *I and Thou*. Edinburgh: T & T Clark, 1970.

Caldecott, L. and S. Leland, eds. *Reclaim the Earth*. London: Women's Press, 1985.

Christ, C., *Diving Deep and Surfacing*, 2nd. ed. Boston: Beacon Press, 1980.

Christ, C., and J. Plaskow, eds. *Womanspirit Rising: A Feminist Reader in Religion*. San Francisco: Harper & Row, 1979.

Cobb, J., *Process Theology as Political Theology*. Manchester: Manchester University Press; Philadelphia: The Westminster Press, 1982.

Collard, A. with J. Contrucci, *Rape of the Wild*. London: The Women's Press, 1988.

Comblin, J., *The Holy Spirit and Liberation*. Tunbridge Wells: Burns & Oates; Maryknoll, N.Y.: Orbis Books, 1989.

Condren, M., *The Serpent and the Goddess*. San Francisco: Harper & Row, 1989.

Coontz C., and P. Henderson, eds. *Women's Work, Men's Property*. London: Verso, 1986.

Daly, M., *Beyond God the Father*. Boston: Beacon Press, 1973; London: Women's Press, 1986.

Daly, M., *Gyn/Ecology*. Boston: Beacon Press, 1978; London: The Women's Press, 1979.

Devall, B., *Simple in Means, Rich in Ends*. London: Green Print, 1990.

Dinnerstein, D., *The Rocking of the Cradle and the Ruling of the World*. London: The Women's Press, 1987.

Dodson Gray, E., *Green Paradise Lost*. Wellesley, Mass.: Roundtable Press, 1984.

Dodson Gray, E., *Patriarchy as a Conceptual Trap*. Wellesley, Mass.: Roundtable Press, 1982.

Dodson Gray, E., ed. *Sacred Dimensions of Women's Experience*. Wellesley, Mass.: Roundtable Press, 1988.

Douglas, M., *Purity and Danger*. London and New York: Ark Paperbacks, 1989.

duBois, P., *Sowing the Body*. Chicago: University of Chicago Press, 1988.

Finch J. and D. Groves, *A Labour of Love: Women, Work and Caring*. London: Routledge and Kegan Paul, 1983.

Fox, M., *Original Blessing*. New Mexico: Bear & Company, 1983.

Foucault, M., *The Use of Pleasure: The History of Sexuality*, Vol. 2. London: Penguin Books, 1987.

Franklin, U., *The Real World of Technology*. Toronto: CBC Enterprises, 1990.

Frye, N., *The Great Code*. London: Routledge and Kegan Paul, 1982.

Gilligan, C., *In a Different Voice*. Cambridge, Mass.: Harvard University Press, 1982.

Goldenberg, N., *Changing of the Gods*. Boston: Beacon Press, 1979.

Goodison, L., *Moving Heaven and Earth: Sexuality, Spirituality and Social Change*. London: The Women's Press, 1990.

Grey, M., *Redeeming the Dream: Feminism, Redemption and Christian Tradition*. London: SPCK, 1989.

Griffin, S., *Made From This Earth*. London: The Women's Press, 1982.

Griffin, S., *Woman and Nature*. New York: Harper & Row, 1978; London: The Women's Press, 1984.

Gross, R., ed. *Beyond Androcentrism: New Essays on Women and Religion*. Montana: Scholar's Press, 1977.

Hanson, P., ed. *Visionaries and Their Apocalypses*. London: SPCK, 1983.

Harrison, B., C. Robb, ed. *Making the Connections*. Boston: Beacon Press, 1985.

Haughton, R., *The Re-Creation of Eve*. Illinois: Templegate Publishing, 1985.

Hillman, J., *The Myth of Analysis*. New York: Harper Torch Books, 1978.

Hillman, J., *Re-Visioning Psychology*. New York: Harper & Row, Perennial Library, 1975.

Illich, I., *Gender*. London and New York: Marion Boyars, 1983.

Jantzen, G., *God's World, God's Body*. Philadelphia: The Westminster Press, 1984.

Jantzen, G., *Julian of Norwich*. Mahwah, N.J.: Paulist Press, 1988.

King, U., *Women and Spirituality: Voices of Protest and Promise*. Basingstoke: Macmillan Education, 1989.

Lerner, G., *The Creation of Patriarchy*. Oxford: OUP, 1986.

Lonergan, A., and C. Richards, eds. *Thomas Berry and the New Cosmology*. Mystic, Conn.: Twenty Third Publications, 1987.

Louth, A., *Denys the Areopagite*. London: Geoffrey Chapman; Wilton, Conn.: Morehouse-Barlow, 1989.

Lovelock, J., *The Ages of Gaia: A Biography of our Living Earth*. Oxford: OUP, 1989.

Lovelock, J., *Gaia: A New Look at Life on Earth*. Oxford: OUP, 1982.

Lyons, J. A., *The Cosmic Christ in Origen and Teilhard de Chardin*. Oxford: OUP, 1982.

McDaniel, J., *Earth, Sky, Gods and Mortals*. Mystic, Conn.: Twenty Third Publications, 1989.

McDonagh, S., *To Care for the Earth*. London: Geoffrey Chapman, 1986.

McDonagh, S., *The Greening of the Church*. London: Geoffrey Chapman; Maryknoll, N.Y.: Orbis Books, 1990.

McFague, S., *Metaphorical Theology*. London: SCM Press, 1983.

McFague, S., *Models of God*. London: SCM Press, 1987.

Merchant, C., *The Death of Nature; Women, Ecology and the Scientific Revolution*. New York: Harper & Row, Perennial Library, 1982.

Meyers, C., *Discovering Eve; Ancient Israelite Women in Context*. Oxford: OUP, 1988.

Mollenkott, V., *Godding: Human Responsibility and the Bible*. New York: Crossroad, 1987.

Mollenkott, V., *The Divine Feminine: The Biblical Imagery of God as Female*. New York: Crossroad, 1987.

Morton, N., *The Journey is Home*. Boston: Beacon Press, 1985.

Newman, B., ed. *Saint Hildegard of Bingen: Symphonia*. Ithaca and London: Cornell University Press, 1988.

Ortner, S., and H. Whitehead, eds., *Sexual Meanings: The Cultural Construction of Gender and Sexuality*. Cambridge: Cambridge University Press, 1981.

Pagels, E., *The Gnostic Gospels*. New York: Random House, 1979.

Pagels, E., *Adam, Eve, and the Serpent*. London: Penguin Books, 1990.

Plant, J., ed., *Healing the Wounds: The Promise of Ecofeminism*. Philadelphia: New Society Publishers, 1989.

Pohier, J., *God in Fragments*. London: SCM Press, 1987.

Primavesi A., and J. Henderson, *Our God Has No Favourites*. Tunbridge Wells: Burns & Oates; San Jose, Ca.: Resource Publications, 1989.

Rich, A., *Of Woman Born*. London: Virago, 1977.

Ricoeur, P., *The Rule of Metaphor*. London: Routledge & Kegan Paul, 1986.

Rowland, C., *The Open Heaven*. London: SPCK, 1982.

Ruether, R., *Sexism and God-talk: Towards a Feminist Theology*. Boston: Beacon Press, 1983.

Ruether, R., *Womanguides: Readings Towards a Feminist Theology*. Boston: Beacon Press, 1985.

Ruether, R., *Women-Church: Theology and Practice*. San Francisco: Harper & Row, 1988.

Seed, J., et al., *Thinking Like a Mountain: Towards a Council of All Beings*. Philadelphia: New Society Publishers, 1988.

Segundo, J., *Faith and Ideologies*. Maryknoll, N.Y.: Orbis Books; Melbourne: Dove Communications; London: Sheed & Ward, 1984.

Segundo, J., *The Historical Jesus of the Synoptics*. Maryknoll, N.Y.: Orbis Books; Melbourne: Dove Communications; London: Sheed & Ward, 1985.

Segundo, J., *The Humanist Christology of Paul*. Maryknoll, N.Y.: Orbis Books; London: Sheed & Ward, 1986.

Segundo, J., *An Evolutionary Approach to Jesus of Nazareth*. Maryknoll, N.Y.: Orbis Books; London: Sheed & Ward, 1988, 1989.

Shiva, V., *Staying Alive*. London: Zed Books, 1989.

Soelle, D. with S. Cloyes, *To Work and To Love: a Theology of Creation*. Philadelphia: Fortress Press, 1984.

Spretnak, C., ed. *The Politics of Women's Spirituality*. New York: Anchor Books, 1982.

Starhawk, *Dreaming the Dark*. London: Mandala, Unwin Paperbacks, 1982.

Starhawk, *Truth or Dare*. San Francisco: Harper & Row, 1990.

Stone, C., *Earth and Other Ethics*. New York: Harper & Row, 1987.

Swimme, B., *The Universe is a Green Dragon*. Santa Fé: Bear & Company, 1984.

Trible, P., *God and the Rhetoric of Sexuality*. Philadelphia: Fortress Press, 1978.

Wren, B., *What Language Shall I Borrow?* London: SCM Press, 1989.

Index